WOMEN
TECHNOLOGY
& POWER

WOMEN TECHNOLOGY & POWER

TEN STARS AND THE HISTORY THEY MADE

MARGUERITE ZIENTARA

amacom

American Management Association

This book is available at a special
discount when ordered in bulk quantities.
For information, contact Special Sales Department,
AMACOM, a division of American Management Association,
135 West 50th Street, New York, NY 10020.

Library of Congress Cataloging-in-Publication Data

Zientara, Marguerite.
Women, technology & power.

Bibliography: p.
Includes index.
1. Women executives--United States--Case studies.
2. Women in business--United States--Case studies.
3. Success in business--United States--Case studies.
4. Computer industry--United States--Case studies.
I. Title. II. Title: Women, technology, and power.
HD6054.4.U6Z54 1987 658.4'09'088042 85-47670
ISBN 0-8144-5820-3

Printing number

10 9 8 7 6 5 4 3 2 1

To my parents,
ANNE
and
WALTER
ZIENTARA

Preface and Acknowledgments

Only rarely does a Golden Age occur, creating seemingly endless excitement, glamour, and rewards for those involved. In 1975 the personal computer was born and within five years the industry had created its own Golden Age, offering the participants a steady stream of breakthrough technologies and financial triumphs. With record-breaking successes rushing one after the other, it's no wonder that thousands of entrepreneurs sought to get in on the action.

As it happened, most of them were men, just as every high-tech industry in existence today is overwhelmingly dominated by men. That does not mean, however, that sexism is rampant in the microcomputer industry. Quite the contrary is true, both men and women say.

The micro industry is blind to sex but wide-eyed at innovation, guts, and smarts, they insist. Historically and typically, women have simply spurned the technical world—usually out of fear, inexperience, or disinterest. Very few women have given computer technology a second thought, much less invested their careers in it.

This book will introduce ten outstanding women who took more than a second glance at the world of chips and integrated circuits, and who have made major contributions affecting the entire industry—as well as the lives of those with an affection for the personal computer.

The nation's business schools are producing more female graduates than a decade ago, and increasing numbers of women are now choosing to study electronics. Both factors will undoubtedly change the high-tech climate of the future. But the ten people discussed in these pages were among the first, male or female, to brave the uncharted territory that became the dazzling and complex story of personal computers.

A host of questions arises as to how these ten women got where they are today. Whatever possessed them to enter the world of technology in the first place? What made them excel where many were mediocre? What drove them on when the outlook was bleak? What effect has business had on family and family on business? And where do they go from here? The answers to such questions weave a compelling tale of inspiration, courage, and reward in the chronicles of ten of the most fascinating people in American business today.

In preparing to write this book, I first visited each of the ten women in their own business settings: in California, New York, Texas, and Florida. I wanted to observe them in action, if possible, to see exactly what their days were like. In some cases it wasn't possible for them to give me a full day, but they all took time out from their extraordinarily busy schedules to meet with me and at least be interviewed face-to-face.

The meetings were followed by many, many telephone interviews in which I asked more questions, clarified the information I already had, and brought myself (again and again) up to date. Remaining current, in fact, turned out to be the hardest part of this project.

During the course of writing this book, between late 1984 and early 1987, the personal computer industry went through convulsive changes, requiring a constant rethinking and reworking of its history as well as of these women's stories. In 1985, especially, major changes occurred in several of their lives and in the industry at large. By 1987, things seem to have settled down and leveled out somewhat, so there is a welcome sense of closure to their stories.

I want to extend my deepest thanks to the ten women about whom I've written this book—for their willingness to participate, their openness and honesty in discussing their business experiences (good and bad), and especially the considerable time they've given me in preparing to write it. I also want to thank their colleagues and, in some cases, family members who gave me valuable insights into their personalities and experiences. I hope these ten women recognize themselves perfectly in these pages.

My sincere thanks must also go to CW Communications, Inc. (now IDG Communications, Inc.), publisher of *InfoWorld* newspaper (which, when I worked there, was a magazine), for which I wrote a cover story in May 1984 on "The Five Most Powerful Women" in the personal computer industry. If it hadn't been for that assignment, I would never have had the opportunity to write this book.

Besides my fateful authorship of an interesting story, I must further thank *InfoWorld* for granting me a leave of absence to work on the book. It was only when I realized I couldn't finish the project by the time the leave expired that I left my position as senior writer at *InfoWorld.*

Naturally, any errors or omissions in this book are my responsibility alone, but there are two people whose help was immeasurable in telling the stories within. For explaining and clarifying the complexities of the business world and the stock market, my heartfelt thanks go to Robert A. Mamis of *Inc.* magazine. For his insights into the personal computer industry and particularly his remarkable memory for the details of company histories, I want to thank David Needle, editor of *Computer Currents* magazine. I also deeply appreciate the patience and support of my editor at AMACOM, Ron Mallis. Many thanks also go to Janet Frick for her excellent copy editing.

Finally, I must thank my family and friends for their continual support while I worked on this book. Special thanks go to Dave Bouffard, whose encouragement was invaluable to me.

Marguerite Zientara
Boston, 1987

Contents

Janelle Bedke,
Co-founder,
Software Publishing Corp.

Photo by Ann Yow

Esther Dyson,
Owner,
Edventure Holdings, Inc.,
Publisher, RELease *1.0 newsletter*

Lore Harp,
Co-founder,
Vector Graphic, Inc.

Portia Isaacson,
Founder,
Future Computing, Inc.

Lorraine Mecca,
Founder,
Micro D, Inc.

Jacqueline Morby,
General Partner,
TA Associates

Therese Myers,
Co-founder,
Quarterdeck Office Systems

Ann Piestrup,
Founder,
The Learning Company

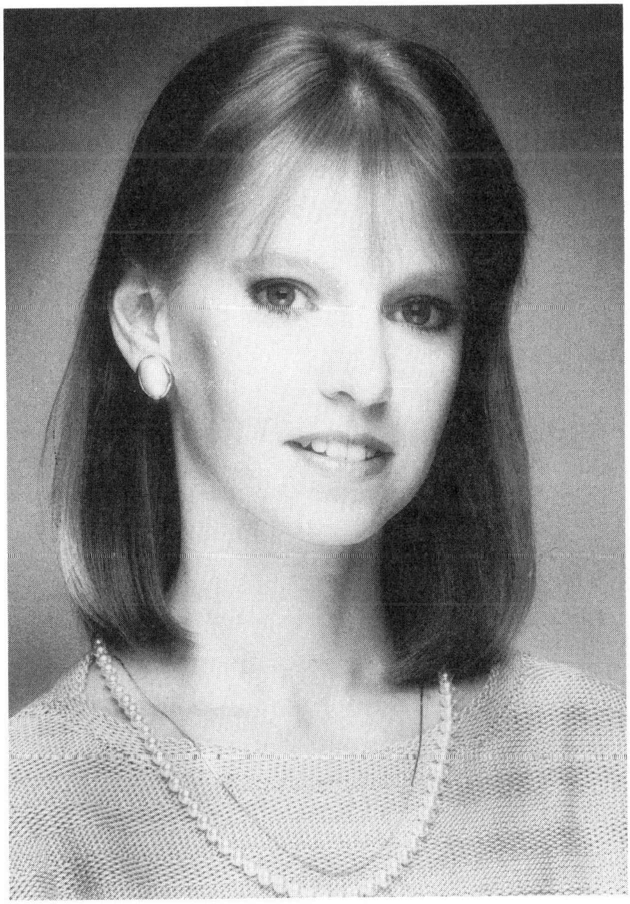

Ann Winblad,
Co-founder,
Open Systems, Inc.

Joyce Wrenn,
former Director of Software Publishing,
Entry Systems Division, IBM Corp.

Prologue: Ten Women with Power

Power. The very word does something to people—especially those without any. It goes hand-in-hand with money, prestige, and freedom, and therefore carries with it the promise of all the things millions of people strive for every working day.

The ten women described in this book made their mark in one of the most exciting, fast-moving, and unpredictable industries ever to emerge. The microcomputer burst onto the scene in the mid-1970s, and the popular culture hasn't been the same since.

At the beginning, very few people had any inkling of how significant the personal computer was to become. Even the main players were astounded to discover just how many like-minded people were out there, from Maine to California, secretly yearning for computers of their own. For some time, the phenomenon was more like an underground movement than a rising star.

The industry got off to a scraggly start—in tinkerers' garages, in tiny and far-flung grass-roots computer clubs, and in the minds of people who found it fun to flip innumerable switches just to hear a machine play "A Bicycle Built for Two."

At first there weren't even any software programs available for people who bought a personal computer, so there was actually very little anyone could *do* with one. Understandably, for years many people regarded the whole phenomenon as a passing fad.

Not everyone was so blind, of course. Along with several thousand men who saw the commercial potential of the tiny micro and rushed to start businesses around it were a handful of women who did the same.

Historically, most women have avoided the technical world. But a few who dared and persevered in this industry have reaped great rewards: Several are multimillionaires; all are highly respected within the industry.

The ten women in this book represent virtually all aspects of the personal computer business: venture capital, hardware and software product development, product distribution, and industry analysis. Through their personal stories, *Women, Technology, and Power* explains the history and the inner workings of an industry that has just entered its second decade.

What They've Done

Although of course no one person can take full credit for creating an entire industry, **Portia Isaacson** has very possibly done more than any other single person to help shape the microcomputer business.

Isaacson was a true pioneer of personal computing, having opened one of the first microcomputer stores in the nation with her then-husband in 1976—only one year after the microcomputer had become a reality. She was one of the very first to see the enormous potential of the tiny machine, and she put herself on the line early by speaking out on its behalf, though often to deaf ears. "I remember listening to her speak in those days, and she would talk about things I'd never even thought about," recalls one industry veteran.

"I became well known because I was really evangelistic about personal computers being the most important technology the computer industry's ever brought to mankind," Isaacson says, "and possibly the most important technology that's been brought to mankind from any source."

She rather quickly became *the* expert on personal computers. "I experienced everything about the industry as it grew," Isaacson explains. "I lived through all its mistakes and I learned more about it than anybody else."

Isaacson also founded the first, and at one time the largest, microcomputer-related market research firm in the country: Future Computing, Inc., in Dallas. Future Computing—which was sold to McGraw-Hill in 1984—was for years the only source for hard statistics about industry sales.

Besides sales figures, Future Computing furnished analyses and projections concerning personal computer markets through its many reports, newsletters, and seminars. Future Computing seminars presented as speakers all the major figures of the industry, including the rest of the women in this book.

Future Computing's major clients were hardware and software vendors and distributors, who used the company's information services to develop marketing strategies and products. The company grew phenomenally fast, along with the micro industry itself, and Isaacson's reputation spread like wildfire.

Constantly quoted and called upon by the press to predict the future of various markets, Isaacson quickly realized the true impact of her opinions. "Frankly, it was more fun when my comments didn't make a stock price go up or down," she said while still at the helm.

Isaacson isn't the only industry guru in this group. When **Esther Dyson** talks, people listen. The youngest of the ten people in this book, Dyson has become one of the most frequently quoted observers of the micro industry, both in the computer trade press and the general press. She is quoted regularly in *The Wall Street Journal, The New York Times, Business Week, Fortune,* and countless trade publications.

Dyson—who entered the PC industry several years after Isaacson—is the owner and president of EDventure Holdings, Inc., in New York, publisher of an influential newsletter in which she discusses the hottest technical topics of the day. She too is regarded as a "kingmaker," but she is an analyst of a completely different sort than Portia Isaacson.

Dyson specializes in scoping out the present, rather than predicting the future. She's a grass-roots type of researcher, with an endless itinerary of visits to computer companies large and small to find out firsthand exactly what is happening in the industry.

In her elegant Park Avenue offices, Dyson has a staff of just two, with whose assistance she publishes *RELease 1.0,* a witty and revealing newsletter that attempts to explain the significance of what goes on in the industry. Written entirely by Dyson, *RELease 1.0* comes out about 15 times a year and costs $495 to its 1,000 or so subscribers, most of whom are in upper-management positions and a fifth of whom are in the investment community.

The peripatetic Dyson spends almost as much time working in California's Silicon Valley as she does in New York, basing her operations there out of Rickey's Hyatt Hotel in Palo Alto. Dyson regularly logs 250,000 or so airline miles a year keeping up with the industry.

Besides writing her newsletter, Dyson hosts a yearly three-day conference, the Personal Computer Forum. The "must-see" event attracts several hundred of the top names in the industry at $1,000 a head. The list of attendees invariably reads like a "Who's Who in Personal Computing." In 1984, for example, the speakers included three of the subjects of this book—Lorraine Mecca, Ann Winblad, and Joyce Wrenn.

Dyson also writes articles for various trade publications and does what she calls "very little" consulting. Although she actually discourages consulting jobs, the clients she accepts pay $2,500 a day for her expertise.

Dyson's approach is to get a close and early eye on new developments. "If Esther doesn't know about a new and interesting product, then someone is keeping a damned good secret," says one industry figure. It's no wonder she finds herself unendingly wined and dined by those who seek a kind mention in her newsletter.

For sheer power, **Joyce Wrenn** may be considered the most influential person in this lineup, simply from having operated within IBM. As the director of software publishing from 1982 to 1985 for IBM's Entry Systems Division in Boca Raton, Florida, Wrenn could essentially accept or reject software developed for IBM's Personal Computer, known as the PC—which became the de facto industry standard while Wrenn was in Boca.

The choices she and her staff made had enormous implications for the people and companies involved. To be selected by IBM to supply anything for the PC is to be touched by a golden hand, especially for a small company. Besides the prestige gained, it's not unusual for a third-party (outside) supplier to double its production output in a year, just from having landed one IBM contract.

Wrenn, acutely aware of the power of IBM, felt "highly responsible" for her decisions. Too much cannot be said about what it means simply *to be IBM.* In a sense, IBM *is* the personal computer industry. As in other markets this industry giant has entered relatively late, IBM managed to corner a majority share of the market by 1983, only two years after entering the arena.

Even though its share has since eroded somewhat, the industry still very much revolves around Big Blue (IBM's nickname, from the color of its large mainframe computers). IBM is a very old, very established, and very rich company that can draw on a stupefying arsenal of resources to fight any war it cares to wage.

Unlike the countless tiny ragtag start-up companies that characterized the early days of the micro industry, IBM can easily be compared with an entire government, with hundreds of offices, thousands of employees, and billions of dollars at its disposal. Even though the group that cranks out IBM's PC products is relatively small, it benefits greatly from the rich and complex backdrop that is IBM.

In fact, the IBM PC became the most popular product IBM ever offered, in terms of units sold. For the two and a half years that Wrenn headed Entry Systems software, she had the entire industry tracking her group's decisions regarding appropriate software for the IBM PC.

One company that has directly profited from Wrenn's choices is Software Publishing Corp. (SPC), whose pfs: series of software is sold under the IBM label as the IBM Assistant Series.

SPC was one of the first companies whose product IBM chose to endorse, call its own, and distribute through its own extensive channels. The reward to SPC for the IBM nod has been approximately 10 percent of its annual revenues and the chance to bask in the reflected glory of the acknowledged industry leader.

Janelle Bedke is one of three cofounders of Software Publishing Corp. in Mountain View, California. The company was the first to create easy-to-use business software for executives lacking the time and desire to spend hours, or even days, learning how to make a computer do something useful.

Software Publishing's pfs: line of business software is consistently on the software Top Ten sales charts and invariably gets excellent reviews. The software may be simple to use, but it is not simplistic, as evidenced by executives who praise its utility over its ease of use.

While SPC cofounder and company president Fred Gibbons has largely assumed the role of company spokesman, Bedke is deeply involved in the day-to-day operations of the company, especially in the all-important area of research and development.

It was Bedke who quit her high-paying job at Hewlett-Packard to start SPC, working alone and unpaid in her home for the first year, after which her two cofounders quit their HP jobs and joined her. Bedke has helped foster a strong team spirit among her employees, resulting in a strength of unity that is not lost even on the casual observer visiting Mountain View. Such a collective single-mindedness toward company goals would be the envy of many a torn and tattered company in this volatile industry.

Another company that has benefited from an IBM contract is The Learning Company, of Menlo Park, California, which is widely recognized for its innovation in the area of educational software. Started by **Ann Piestrup** in 1979 with little more than a dream, the company has built its reputation on consistently high-quality educational software products that stretch and please the imaginations of both children and adults.

From a humble but encouraging start, the firm moved quickly to distinguish itself as a leader in learning software for the home and for schools. Piestrup's mission was no less ambitious than to change the way children learn, and she saw the computer as the perfect tool to effect that change.

By designing award-winning educational software packages for her company, she has reached a wide audience for her ideas about learning, as well as making the company a success in the process.

In 1983, IBM tapped The Learning Company to convert all its software packages for IBM's personal computers, an event that gave welcome credibility to the very small, privately held company.

"IBM had the world to choose from, and it chose our software to endorse," Piestrup says.

But the IBM pendulum swings both ways, and the sweep of its arc has cast a long shadow across the paths of many gifted innovators. One such survivor of adverse circumstance is **Therese Myers,** cofounder and president of Quarterdeck Office Systems, of Santa Monica, California. Quarterdeck's first and extremely creative product presaged a similar product from IBM.

The story of Quarterdeck Office Systems is the flip side of the story of IBM, as many small companies in this business have discovered. It is the saga of a small rival's struggle against a force of great magnitude and competitive resources. But while many companies have crumbled under the weight of IBM, Quarterdeck forges ahead.

Quarterdeck's story started out on a high note. In its first full year, 1982, Quarterdeck was able to attract $6.4 million in venture capital—helped by the fact that high-tech investments were then flowing like a mountain stream in springtime—and the firm suddenly became "something to watch." In an era of software excitement, Quarterdeck was one of the flashiest spectacles around.

The cause of such a stir was an idea for integrating software, which was diametrically opposed to the industry fad at the time of integrat*ed* software (which crammed as many functions as possible into one software package).

Quarterdeck had a working prototype called Desq, which would allow a user to combine up to nine application software packages *of his or her choice* from different vendors and switch back and forth among them easily. The idea was unique, brilliant, and obviously worth a lot of cash.

But life can be dangerous for a small company with a single product. Once IBM gets that gleam in its eye, it can call on its army of development and marketing personnel to bring a product to fruition quickly and lay it out gloriously before the public.

After the enormously hard work of actually developing Desq, Quarterdeck was in for a real shock. Just three months after Desq finally came out, the news that every small computer company dreads was winging its way from the Florida coast to the Pacific shore.

IBM had done it. The giant had set its sights on the integrating software market and had jumped right in with the announcement of a product remarkably like Desq. "It just proves Desq was a brilliant idea," Myers said then, unconsoled by the thought.

Myers knows all about the power of IBM, having had the misfortune to design and introduce a product similar to one that IBM had decided would be its own "strategic software product." When IBM preannounced its Topview software in August 1984, Quarterdeck could only sit and wait for it to come out, so that people could compare the two.

Myers's only consolation was her deep belief that Desq was a superior product. She believed that, but how could she convince everyone else? Even with superiority, a rival often loses out to IBM simply because of IBM's proven stability in an unstable world.

Besides IBM, Quarterdeck faced other formidable competition, like giant Microsoft Corp., developer of the IBM PC's operating-system software. Microsoft also developed an integrating software product of its own.

But Quarterdeck has indeed survived. Desq and its follow-up product, Desqview, received excellent reviews, which is more than IBM can say about Topview. By making smart and solid marketing agreements, by getting good press, and by sticking it out when the going got very rough, Quarterdeck surprised many observers who wrongly sensed a sinking ship.

The battle isn't quite over for this company, but you won't see Terry Myers waving a white flag anytime soon. In an industry where any software company has only a 50-50 chance of surviving beyond its fifth year, Quarterdeck has already beaten the odds.

Lore Harp's high-tech story is simultaneously one of the most spectacular and one of the most dismal in the industry. Harp got into the microcompputer business early, back when most people thought of a chip mainly as something to eat. In spite of her meager technical knowledge at the time, Harp started a memory-board mail-order business, Vector Graphic, Inc., from her home in Westlake Village, California, in 1976 with her best friend, Carole Ely.

What started as a wild and woolly neighborhood adventure quickly evolved into a company that Wall Street found very attractive. Harp and Ely, relying mainly on instinct, managed to reorder the priorities in an industry still filled with computer "nerds." In place of supplier indifference, they substituted excellent service and support. In place of drab packaging, they introduced style. Instead of keeping a low profile, they advertised heavily and attended all the trade shows. They ended up with high visibility, lots of good press, a reputation for quality—and plenty of money.

After five years of skyrocketing growth, Vector went public in 1981. The company seemed to be Wall Street's dream come true. Unfortunately, its fortunes changed dramatically after IBM came onto the scene, and Vector failed to keep up with what was to become the industry standard.

The 500-employee company died an agonizing death over a period of years, finally succumbing in 1987. But Lore Harp, a true pioneer of the micro industry, went on to start and manage a venture capital fund, followed by another noncomputer business.

Jacqueline Morby started out in venture capital in the early days and helped shape the personal computer industry by pouring $8 million into four then-fledgling micro software companies for her Boston employer, TA Associates, one of the oldest and largest venture firms in the country.

It's not *how much* she invested that sets her apart, however, but rather *when* she invested it. Morby was one of the first to discern the lucrative potential of micro software in the late 1970s, and she helped blaze the investment trail. In spite of some doubt and controversy within her own company, she recommended—and TA made—four highly promising investments in software companies.

Morby, who reentered the business world after 15 years as a homemaker, had immediately gotten onto a fast track, both within her company and out in the world at large. Her controversial risk taking paid off big, for the software industry and for her personally. Only four years after joining TA Associates, she was made a general partner in 1982.

Money isn't the only factor in the success of a computer company, of course. A vendor has to have good distribution channels for its products, to get them out on the computer-store shelves and in the buying public's eye. Many a good product has failed simply because it didn't find its way onto enough store shelves.

As the founder and former CEO of Micro D, Inc.—one of the largest distributors of micro software and peripherals, and the only one to have gone public—**Lorraine Mecca** helped supply an essential link in the industry's chain of supply.

Small hardware and software developers frequently distribute a product on their own through independent agreements with perhaps several hundred individual retail stores, but having a distributor increases exponentially the number of consumers who will see and possibly buy a product. Most key companies in the personal computer industry, unless they're large enough and rich enough to have their own distribution system, have agreements with several distributors. The distributor picks products that look like good sellers to funnel from vendors to thousands of retail outlets all over the country.

The network is designed to be mutually beneficial, especially when the product is a hit: The vendors get their goods out there for a large audience to see, and the distributors get a percentage of every product sold by the dealers.

Mecca started Micro D in 1979 with one other person. From sales of $3.6 million in its first year, Micro D grew extraordinarily fast, to tally $114 million by 1984.

In a stroke of luck and genius, Micro D went public at the optimum moment, in July 1983, precisely at the height of the romance between investors and high tech. Mecca became an overnight multimillionaire just before investors started tightening their grip on the high-tech purse strings.

Mecca joins Lore Harp as two of the handful of women who have founded and taken public their own companies. Fewer than 15 women in the United States run public companies at all, and most of them inherited the businesses from their fathers or husbands. Lorraine Mecca was also the first woman to grace the cover of *Nation's Business,* in June 1984.

Another case of dynamic growth from a humble beginning is the story of **Ann Winblad,** who is well known for two major things: first, cofounding and running a successful software company and, second, selling it for $15.5 million in cash seven years later, in 1983. Her share: $3.8 million.

That turn of events gave Winblad luxuries beyond what money can buy—namely, power and freedom. A year after selling Open Systems, Inc., to Uccel Corp., Winblad left the company, sold her house in Minneapolis, and settled just north of Silicon Valley, in San Francisco. At 34, she could afford to stand back from the industry, observe it in its larger sense, and pluck the juiciest plums from a cornucopia of possibilities.

Her business experience, like those of Bedke, Harp, Isaacson, Mecca, and Piestrup, was of fast growth from a shoestring beginning. Open Systems was started in 1976 with just $500 from the personal savings of Winblad and Tim Dickinson, one of its four cofounders.

Open Systems was something of an anomaly right from the start simply from being located half a continent away from Silicon Valley, in wintry Minnesota. Its Minneapolis orientation, while removing it from the excitement of the California club, gave the firm a seriousness of purpose that Winblad feels was integral to its success. "If it's 20 below outside," she says, "you don't have a strong urge to leave the office until your work is done." The Midwest work ethic and a relatively conservative approach to business combined to make Open Systems the third-largest publisher of micro accounting software by 1983.

On Being Powerful

"Powerful people are big and have hairy hands. I'm not one of them," says Lorraine Mecca. "I don't think of myself as a powermonger or someone who's out there wielding power."

Mecca's reluctance to apply the word "powerful" to herself is shared by most of the other nine women here, even though others describe them as powerful figures. Mecca prefers to call her former position "influential" and, as the other nine would agree, "It's also quite a responsibility."

As happens to many ambitious people, occasionally a less flattering word is used to describe someone: "ruthless," for example. "I am very focused," Mecca said while at Micro D. "Ruthless tends to mean you hurt people along the way. I don't think I do that. But if I get a contract, that means someone else doesn't. I'm not consciously ruthless. I have a very high ethical and moral code. I like 'predatory' better—it's a little more calculated. That means I'll plan, engineer, and execute it."

Mecca wasn't always predatory, either. "Starting out," she explains, "it was very hard to put myself first, in terms of who was to make how much money. It was hard to say, 'Look, sorry, I've got to have it on terms, and that's the best price you get, regardless of how nice you are and how much you want to succeed.' It was hard to be selfish. I had to learn how. I'm still learning, but you're always taught to be nice and share. Business is not like that at all. It's one of the more difficult things, for sure."

Lore Harp, nicknamed "The Ice Maiden" by the press, has a reputation for being very tough. And she offers no apologies for it. "If making decisions that are necessary for the longevity of the company and really for the betterment of everybody involved is ruthless, then by all means, let me be ruthless," Harp says. "But I don't pussyfoot around and I stand up for what I believe.

"Ruthless in terms of business negotiations, yes, maybe I have been," she admits. "But it was basically for the good of the company. It's a dog-eat-dog business and world out there. You don't really accomplish that by being shoved around."

In 1982 in the *Harvard Business Review,* Harp described an exchange with the underwriters before Vector Graphic went public. "I was very firm in negotiating the stock price with the underwriters. I stood my ground and said, 'You have five more minutes. We must have a deal at the end of that time or else we're going to walk.' When they looked shocked, I said, 'Okay, that's 30 seconds.' "

Does Harp see herself as powerful? "I don't think one ever looks at oneself as powerful. One is. Personally I feel I'm not. It surprises me that people perceive me that way. If powerful means the ability to make decisions and get things done and to activate people to do things, then yes, but not to use or abuse people. Power is a funny term. It scares me a bit."

Janelle Bedke is also a bit uneasy with the word. "I like to guide people, to lead a cooperative team," she says. " 'Power' suggests an autocratic, sole ruler, and we don't have that here. I just enjoy taking responsibility, showing leadership, and making decisions."

Bedke describes herself as "very goal-oriented. I set goals and achieve them, and at the same time I care a lot about people. It's not worth any goal to step on people to get there. You don't have to succeed by tearing something down or attacking it head-on. You can bypass it instead."

Software Publishing cofounder Fred Gibbons calls Bedke "the engine of the organization. She makes it run. If she has to climb a mountain, she'll do it. We agree on something and she makes it happen from beginning to end. Once we agree on the principles of the strategy and to some degree the specifics, like we're going to acquire Harvard Software in Boston, she says, 'Okay, I'll go do it.' "

Bedke's influence also extends beyond the bounds of Software Publishing. The December 1985 issue of *Esquire* magazine listed her in its "1985 *Esquire* Register—America's New Leadership Class—Men and Women Under Forty Who Are Changing the Nation." The roster included such luminaries as actress Jessica Lange, rock star Cyndi Lauper, and Boston Celtic Larry Bird. Joining Bedke in the "Business & Industry" category was Esther Dyson.

"I know I'm considered a powerful person," Dyson says. "I don't take myself very seriously but I do take the newsletter seriously. If people pay attention to what you say, *you'd* better pay attention to what you say, too."

At the same time, Dyson is realistic about the extent of her influence. "I'm not trying to be famous worldwide," she says. "What I really want is the couple of thousand people whose opinion I respect to respect me, rather than *The Today Show* or something. I'm writing for a rather small audience, which is fine by me—they're the best people around."

Part of Dyson's power comes from her easy access to the VIPs of the industry. "Probably no one in the business knows as many people and companies as I do," she says. "If I want to find out what's going on, I can actually talk to the people involved. I'm privy to secrets and I really know what's going on."

Does Dyson have the clout to actually make or break a company? "I guess I do to some extent," she says. "With small companies, I can make people pay attention to something that no one's heard of." But it's not the clout she cares about. "What drives me is intellectual curiosity," Dyson says, "and I like to make things clear. I like to make people understand and think clearly and know how things work.

"From my perspective, I have the best job in the world," she believes. "I wouldn't want Ronald Reagan's job or [Apple Computer Chairman] John Sculley's job or anybody's job because I'm right at the center of the most exciting industry around."

Dyson has also put into practice a tenet long held by Portia Isaacson. "I like to be the best," Dyson says. "I've found something only I do, so it's easy to be a success."

Isaacson calls that "unique value," and she developed it for herself early on. "By giving great value in our society, you get great rewards back," Isaacson says. "In hindsight, I spent my life building unique value. That is, if you have anyone who competes with you in skills or in products, then that limits the value of what you offer, because someone else offers it too."

When Isaacson realized in college that physics was the most difficult of the sciences, she decided, "I will be a physicist." She reasoned that if she became something that few people were, she'd easily be able to get a job and make a living.

Although she went on to become possibly the most influential voice in the personal computer industry, Isaacson has reservations about how to describe herself. "The word 'powerful' turns me off a little bit, but if you'll allow me to think of it in a positive way, the answer has to be yes [I am powerful]. We use the word 'influence' most often."

Like others, Isaacson feels keenly the responsibility that goes along with power. "In our own company we discuss a lot what influence means and how we should manage it," she said at Future Computing. "We think there's an ethic regarding influence. I had influence before I started Future Computing, which is one of our biggest assets. I was at least famous. People would listen to what I had to say."

Now she's so famous that in early 1986 Isaacson and ex-husband Egil Juliussen, with whom she ran Future Computing, were filmed for the television show *Lifestyles of the Rich and Famous.* Did she ever expect to be rich and famous? "No," she says. "In fact, I have a theory that you don't get it by planning the end result that way.

"The way I think you should approach life is not what you can get from it—not by saying, 'I want to be a millionaire by the time I'm 30'—but by asking, 'What can I give to it?' That is, 'What unique value can I give the world?' "

Ann Piestrup agrees. "You don't become successful by having that as your goal," she says. "To do a particular thing must be your goal. The reason I feel so powerful is that I was so determined about all this. Nothing would stop me. It wasn't out of a desire for power in the sense of ruling other people or grabbing great gobs of money, but to make this dream happen."

Piestrup never particularly wanted to be the head of a company, just as she never particularly wanted to be rich, famous, or powerful, or to have a book written about her. All those things are mere by-products of her lifelong goal: to make the world better by changing the way children learn.

And that she has done. As one educator put it, "The Learning Company was the turning point in educational software. They moved away from strictly computer-assisted instruction and dared to be original. Their color and graphics are superb and yet the programs have stayed educationally sound." Said one computer expert on first seeing The Learning Company's software, "You've reached the absolute basics of thought."

Besides her accomplishments, Piestrup has yet another sort of power, she feels. "I can get to the movers and shakers in the industry. I'm seen as credible by the government and by business. I'm an influence maker."

Piestrup is among the top ten experts in both education and computing in the country, but most of her fame is from her work in computer software. Do educators talk about Piestrup's theories of learning? "I'm known by the people in my field, but certainly I wouldn't be in people's [education] textbooks, because I'm not Skinner or Piaget," Piestrup explains. "But I might be in the future, because I'm starting to be asked to write textbook chapters about my theories."

Besides having influenced two fields of endeavor (education and software), Piestrup has a lot of personal power. "Several people I worked with just dropped away because they couldn't stand the intensity of it and the fact that whatever I was interested in had to be the focus," Piestrup admits. "I have a deep conviction in myself. I feel that's one reason I have power, because people sense that in me."

At the same time, Piestrup is not personally aggressive. "I kind of sneak up on people," she says. "They don't realize how powerful I am. I'm soft-spoken and nice, but really determined. They don't know how determined I am."

Jacqueline Morby has had similar feelings. "People misjudge me," she says. "They wonder, 'Is she tough enough?' They don't understand there's a difference. You don't have to act and look tough to be tough. Your mannerisms can be friendly and nice, but underneath is a determination to achieve what you want to achieve. It's easier with friendliness and niceness instead of confrontation."

What Morby may not realize is how others see her. "She has a powerful presence," says one industry observer. "When she walks into a room, you know she's there." Morby, though, has amazed herself. "It surprised me that I was as aggressive and competitive as I am," she says. "I really want to have the best investments and do the best. I need to compete."

In addition to her inner resources, Morby also has the strength of her well-funded company, TA Associates, behind her. "We're dealing with people's dreams," she says. "And those dreams can come true because we're able to say, 'We think you've got something here and we think you can do it,' and give them the pure start-up money to start a company.

"On the other hand," she notes, "people come in and for reasons completely extraneous to them we cannot finance them. Maybe we've just decided that we're not going to do a certain type of product, or we've already invested in their type of company. It's no reflection on the company at all, but we have to say, 'We're sorry, because of our portfolio we can't look at it.'

" 'Power' is not the right word, but I guess a venture capitalist does feel a sense of responsibility to all these dreams," Morby says. "We get hundreds of business plans, but I don't think power is what we think about. Our business is to get a good return on our investment dollars."

In the actual negotiations with companies that want venture capital, Morby is tough. "You can't go in like a gambler," she says. "You decide ahead what you'll pay and stick to it. It's hard when you like the company and the people. On the other hand, if people are extremely difficult, why lose sleep? Why work with them?"

Also with the power to "make" a small company by giving its software the nod, and even with the enormous power of the IBM name behind her, Joyce Wrenn never perceived herself in terms of her own influence, but rather in terms of her ability to get the job done. "I guess I don't really think so much about power as such," Wrenn said while at IBM. At the same time, Wrenn and other IBMers are highly sensitive to IBM's formidable impact on the rest of the computer industry.

Therese Myers, at the other end of the spectrum in terms of size, does not in any way see herself as powerful. "No, we're a small company," she says. "Our work was done as a team effort. None of us could have done it without the others. I couldn't have done it without Gary [cofounder Gary Pope]."

Power, however, resides not necessarily in numbers, but sometimes in attitude. Myers and Pope had to have the daring to compete, as well as a strong survival instinct and the mettle for sticking it out through the hard times. For Quarterdeck, with a dozen or so employees, to compete against Microsoft with its hundreds and IBM with its thousands takes, quite simply, guts.

Myers won't take the credit, but she is undoubtedly a large part of the company's success. "Terry Myers is a great manager," says a Quarterdeck publicist. "She's rarely wrong. She has the thoroughness of the small-business mentality but the strategic capability of a corporate executive."

Ann Winblad understands that her personal wealth gives her a certain aura of power in others' eyes—but not in her own. "A sense of contribution is a great sense of power to me," she says. "At Open Systems, I wanted to do a good job and know every day I was doing exactly what I wanted to do. I didn't expect that people would make me a multimillionaire."

Still, she knows her own considerable strengths. "I'm a very opinionated person, I'm a very strong leader, I'm a very strong advocate of ideas I believe in," she says, "and I'm very, very goal-oriented. One of the reasons our company worked is that all the people who worked for us knew exactly in which direction we were marching. And it was very easy with a small company, with all the soldiers basically fighting the same wars."

Nevertheless, as she discovered, running a company can be very draining. "Some people get a sense of power as a leader of people, like a general in the army," she notes. "I never enjoyed that feeling.

"I had it with my own company, but it's a tremendous responsibility and a tremendous diversion. As a leader, you're a counselor, psychiatrist, visionary. You must be very unselfish to be a leader of people. You must be willing to give up some of your own free thinking to get them through the next phase of the company."

Although some element of power comes from the risk taking that all of these women have done, they typically don't look at a risk as potential disaster. "Every time you go forward," says Winblad, "there's no risk because you know the way back."

On Being Female

"Women at all levels generally set their goals too low," says Portia Isaacson. "You'd be surprised how many women there are with master's degrees who are secretaries," Ann Piestrup agrees. "The world is full of them." And Lorraine Mecca believes, "It's not beyond the capabilities of most women to start and manage a company."

"But how many women would think of leaving Intel or Texas Instruments and going after venture capital to start their own company?" asks Isaacson. "It's a very important point that very few women set their goals on doing that. What can change that situation are things like this book, that show women how they can break out of the mold and be a success."

In many cases, what holds women back is simply a traditional outlook, says Esther Dyson. "There are lots and lots of reasons," she says. "You can go back to the social upbringing of women not to be aggressive. People don't mind dealing with women as peers in other businesses. The real problem is with men reporting to women—both on the men's side and to some extent on the women's side.

"Personally," she admits, "I'm not a very good boss. I'm really not a manager. I like to think that's because of something to do with my socialization as a female. God knows there are a lot more women [at the top] than blacks, unfortunately," she notes. "It's the same thing. Equal opportunity is great, but people start businesses with their friends—not with sex and race characteristics. So I think that's part of it."

While Dyson laments the paucity of women executives in the micro world, she feels that the situation is improving. "This business is better than most," she says. "It is changing and it is getting better but it's very, very slow—because, you see, people still have this image of what a vice president or a president looks like. Women have to be brought up differently and men have to be brought up differently. Time has to pass."

Joyce Wrenn has seen the number of women in high tech grow very slowly over the last 25 years or so. "When I got into this business in 1959, there were some women in the business, but very few," she recalls. Although it has admittedly been a slow process, a lot has changed since then. "I think men are seeing more and more women who are competent in their positions, and it's a matter of the entire culture and the comfort level," Wrenn says. "I think they're just becoming more comfortable with working with women as their peers and their superiors."

These ten successful women are unanimous in their belief that the micro industry welcomes women much more warmly than many other industries do. "This industry is unique," says Ann Winblad. "It's one of the few industries created out of thin air. You're judged totally on competence, you can't bluff your way. That puts women on an equal basis. Here you can be a smart mutt with no pedigree and jump right in."

"There are more women in power in the micro industry than anywhere else, certainly compared with the *Fortune* 1,000 companies," says Jacqueline Morby. "There are women heading companies and many vice presidents of marketing."

But there are still many more men. Again, time may cure the imbalance. "Women have been going to business school in respectable numbers only for the last ten years, so they haven't had time to rise within companies," Morby says. "In another ten years, we'll begin to see lots more."

Lorraine Mecca experienced directly the dearth of female executives. "None of our vice presidents were women because we could not find women with five years' business experience in large companies," she explains.

For women who started their own companies, there have been other difficulties. "I still remember walking into my bank, six months pregnant, asking them how much money they could lend me without getting approval from their head office," Mecca recalls. "Before I chose a bank, I wanted to make sure I got one with some lending authority. They didn't want to tell me! I think being female had more to do with it than the pregnancy."

Once Mecca had made her company a success, she faced some minor but recurring stumbling blocks as a woman. "I have to be real careful not to give men the wrong signals, if you know what I mean," she said while at Micro D. "I go to lunches all the time, and avoid dinners, because dinner gives an evening indication, where lunch gives a business indication.

"Often with, say, Oriental firms, I would introduce myself, pour tea, and leave because that's a situation where I would inhibit the flow of business rather than helping it."

Janelle Bedke has met with occasional resistance from men, but she shrugs it off. There have been instances when people have asked to speak to her boss. "There will be people who don't take you seriously at first blush," she says. "My attitude is, don't back down; it's their problem, not mine.

"What sex you are is irrelevant in a business world, and to dwell on something that's irrelevant is a waste of time," she believes. "I never expected anything from anybody. Like anyone, I believed I should work, do a good job, and be recognized. At Hewlett-Packard, that did happen. Why are women bitter, I ask myself? It's not been my experience. I've been recognized, encouraged to advance, and I've never bumped into walls."

"I've never had problems being female," Jacqueline Morby claims. "And it's getting less unusual now, but when I started here [at TA Associates], you didn't find *any* women in venture capital.

"In the beginning, when I was first calling on companies, I worried they might look at me as a woman and not want to deal with me," she admits. "But they were always interested in my background, how I got into the business. It was more of a curiosity than anything else."

That scarcity of women worked to Morby's advantage in some cases. Entrepreneurs unaccustomed to dealing with women in business were often surprised into letting down their guard. "I sometimes find out incredible things that the entrepreneur really shouldn't tell me," Morby told *Business Week* magazine in 1981, "and then I don't invest in the company."

Ironically, the major drawback to being a rare woman in venture capital came from women themselves. "I became real well known," Morby says. "Then all the women in the country thought they could call and get advice—*free* help and advice. They wanted to know how I did it at my age.

"If someone calls about the industry or about TA, I'll talk to them," she says. "If women's magazines call, I don't return the calls. I'm interested in women doing well, but I have to be practical about it."

Women don't get any special treatment from Lore Harp either, who has little patience for self-described feminists who complain about a lack of opportunity. "I feel that most women gain acceptance from peers, male or female, by proving integrity and intelligence—not by talking about job discrimination and all sorts of other complaints," she says. "I just don't have time for that."

In fact, Harp declines invitations to speak before feminist groups. "If women want to get off their duffs, they've got to get off them on their own and not suddenly start leaning on strong women when before they were leaning on strong men," she told the *Harvard Business Review* in 1982. "To succeed you have to do it for yourself and not because somebody else is telling you to. We come into the world alone and the decisions we make, we make ourselves."

Indeed, Harp found that being female worked to her advantage in the business world, especially in terms of negotiating. "I think the situation is changing and it has changed," she says. "But you have to remember this was around 1976, when there were still relatively few women in this industry.

"And ... how can I say this gently? ... a lot of men you were dealing with wanted to take a sort of protective role and help you out, so because you couldn't fight that, really, you were taking advantage of it," she says. "I don't think it holds true now as much as it did then."

At the same time, Harp is proud to have accomplished what she knows few women have. "I'm not a feminist, not now, never have been and probably never will be," she says, "but I'm sure that deep down there's a little of 'I'm a woman and I've done it.' "

Janelle Bedke also has some reservations about the feminist attitude. "I'm not a women's libber," she says. "I don't like that philosophy because it's sexist either way. I have my own attitude. Many women's libbers have a chip on their shoulder and cause their own problems. I've never felt discriminated against. I've worked hard and been recognized for it."

When Bedke is asked to join societies of women engineers and other women's groups, she declines. "I don't believe in sexist organizations one way or the other." Was it advantageous for Bedke to be a woman in a man's domain? "I don't think so," she says. "I didn't think of myself as different. I was the only woman in most of my classes, out of hundreds of students. At HP I was the only woman. It didn't bother me."

Ann Winblad, on the other hand, thinks being female "definitely" helped her succeed. "Being small and blonde was not a drawback," she assures. "I don't know what happens when you get to be an older woman. We'll see."

Winblad, too, eschews women's groups. "They try to make things women's issues. I don't think there are women's issues. Maybe it's just my own experience, but I believe women need to be mainstreamed or they don't understand what other people are doing."

She also has little sympathy for jealous wives. "Wives complain that their husbands are out carousing," Winblad says. "They're probably not. They're probably very tired. You work long hours in a competitive business. Cocktail parties sound like frivolity but it's so integral. I did it. It's not all fun. Wives don't understand that. They want to have their cake and eat it too."

Portia Isaacson also feels that being a woman was a plus, but in a different way from most. "In front of an audience, I get by with things a normal person wouldn't, in a way a three-piece-suited guy wouldn't," Isaacson says, "because they have no set of expectations, because I'm not out of any mold. In fact, at that point, being female becomes very much an advantage, except for the occasional guy who's threatened by it. But they're very rare nowadays."

She understands, though, that her dynamism can backfire. When Isaacson speaks in public, she holds her audience in the palm of her hand through a combination of dramatics, startling opinions, and sheer personal magnetism. "I'm reasonably entertaining," she says, "and 90 percent of the audience winds up liking me, but the rest are thinking, 'My God, what a brassy, ballsy, yucky lady!' "

Whatever their personal styles, whether they took advantage of their femininity or not, these ten women had the gumption to enter an obviously male-dominated industry and compete with the best of them.

Piestrup speaks for all ten women here when she says, "My message to other women is not to see themselves as limited. I'm not mathematically inclined, but I started my own company. First, think about what you want to do, and then go after it."

I

The Stirrings of Ambition

Those who have it don't know exactly how they got it, but it is without doubt the keystone of anyone's success: an unwavering certainty that he or she will make it. That faith in oneself allows a person to take risks, even fail, because winners see failure not as a humiliation but as an opportunity to learn.

Portia Isaacson has thought a lot about "the difference between those who talk about entrepreneurialism and those who do it." She believes that risk taking is a learned skill that begins in childhood. "I was constantly coming up with some meager little scheme to do something—like not eating and saving my lunch money for three months to buy something," Isaacson says.

"That means you learn risk taking in small steps when you're young, and then that means you've failed many times. And you learn, 'Oh, you don't die when you do that.' So you get over the fear of failure, which is *the* thing that keeps would-be entrepreneurs from really doing it."

These ten women share basic characteristics of determination, a deep belief in themselves, high energy levels, a willingness to work very hard and to take risks, a competitive spirit, insight, and intelligence. Although they grew up in different eras with totally different influences and lived vastly different lives, they all ended up in the same industry within a few years of one another. Their immediate motivations for going into business are surprising, diverse, and fascinating.

Lorraine Mecca: Seizing Control

Only *The National Enquirer* could tell the story so pointedly. The headline wails, "Owner of $100 Million Computer Firm Says: I Had to Cry to Get a Raise—So I Made ME a Boss." The owner in question is Lorraine Mecca, immortalized for the supermarket checkout crowd on September 4, 1984. There she sits, forever smiling cheerfully into the *Enquirer*'s camera while shuffling papers in her briefcase.

The headline and story are absolutely true, and the incident they describe was a turning point in Mecca's life. "I always knew I was capable of a lot," Mecca says, "but no one else seemed to think so." If it took a flood of tears for her to get a raise, she reasoned, then she would just as soon be on the other side of the desk.

The crying incident took place in 1977, not long after Mecca had entered the business world. After a short stint as a junior high school teacher, Mecca took an entry-level job with Connector Distribution Corp., a Los Angeles firm that distributes electronic components.

She loved the adult business environment after two and a half years of being "locked in a room with 40 kids who didn't want to be there," as she describes teaching. Before long, Connector Distribution promoted her to operations coordinator, a position that taught her the intricacies of the distribution business.

Unfortunately, although she performed her job very well, management didn't want to give her a raise. Determined to get her due, Mecca used the only weapon she felt she had left: that tearful scene in her boss's office.

Mecca's instincts served her well; she got a raise. But she could no longer deny to what extent she was subject to the wills of others. The most important people in her life were running circles around her. At work, she faced her unappreciative boss. At home, her husband of seven years had decided he didn't want to start the family she longed for, after all. Her position was emphatically not one of power.

Mecca was deeply distressed, especially since she was used to calling the shots. A charmer from the start, Lorraine had been a favorite both at home and at school. "I should have had 20 [children] if they were all like her," her mother laughs. As it was, Ruth and Leonard Mecca only had eight. Lorraine was the second.

Lorraine was a good student, a creative child poet, and a fine natural athlete. Early in life she discovered a secret to success that has stayed with her. "I use visualization," she says, "just picturing a situation in my mind and dreaming about it and thinking about it so much, that when it actually comes to it, I feel like I've done it before and that's how it should be."

The visualizing process takes place many times every day. "I'm a good daydreamer," she says. "The first time I ever did that and realized it absolutely worked, I was about seven. I really wanted to ice-skate. I saw myself doing it so many times that when I finally got skates for Christmas, I knew how to do it."

During her senior year in high school, when she attended a coeducational public school for the first time, Lorraine discovered the true extent of her personal power. "I had dates all the time," she says. "That year, I dated 85 fellows and went steady three times. Once I had three dates in one day."

So complex was her social calendar that she certainly could have made good use of a personal computer to keep track of it, if only such a thing had existed at the time. Technology being what it was in the sixties, however, she had to rely on a bulging appointment book, which she kept next to the family telephone. "It was a lot of fun," she says.

Armed with such proof of her own irresistibility, she later fearlessly engineered a romance with a fellow student at Lynchburg College in Virginia. By frequently planting herself in his path, and by carrying math books that she hoped would pique his scientific mind, Mecca succeeded beautifully in attracting his attention. A year later they were married.

So far, so good. But she could not dictate her husband's goals in life. When it became clear after seven years that he was not interested in starting the family she so badly wanted, she knew she would have to move on. Several attempts at leaving were so painful, however, that each time she went back. Ultimately, however, she had to face the fact that the situation was untenable; if she wanted children, it would have to be with someone else. She left for good and filed for divorce.

After separating from her husband in 1977, Mecca started seeing Connector Distribution coworker Geza Csige, with whom she shared an office. "Geza had been madly in love with me for two years," Mecca says. "I wanted a situation where I'd be in control and I figured that was it." It was a calculated move whose emotional richness took her completely by surprise.

Csige met her foremost criteria in a man: scientific "with big brains." Furthermore, Csige was not afraid of parenthood or unwilling to assume it. Separated from his mother early in life, he had come with his father to the United States in 1959 as a refugee from the Hungarian revolution. Six years later his father died, leaving Geza completely on his own at 18. His mother was unable to track Geza down until he was grown, but she finally did in 1973 with the help of the Red Cross.

With his uncertain past, Csige was just as enthusiastic as Mecca about the idea of having a family. Mecca was hooked. It wasn't long before the two decided to get married. By the time her divorce became final, their wedding plans had long been set. "I was only unmarried for six days," Mecca smiles. And with good reason. Csige would prove to be, on many levels, the best thing that ever happened to her.

On the professional front, he was the agent by which she discovered the personal computer. Csige is a scientist at heart who, in his spare time and with a partner, in 1977 opened one of the first microcomputer stores in southern California. By the time he and Mecca were about to be married, in 1978, he had quit his Connector Distribution job to run his two computer stores full-time. Mecca, meanwhile, was still immune to the charms of technology.

"When I went to computer shows with Geza before we were married," she explains, "the one thing I absolutely didn't want to do was get involved in the computer industry. The people who were there were just such tweaks that that wasn't my idea of the people I wanted to surround myself with. So I was there socially, but I tried not to get involved in any of the bits-and-bytes conversation."

Her sudden awakening took place about a month before their wedding. Having quit her job at Connector Distribution and enrolled in the business program at El Camino College, Mecca was doing a work-study project that called for her to produce a weekly fashion show for the Marriott Inn in Marina Del Rey.

Among other things, the project called for her to write the script for the show—a task she found tedious on a typewriter. When Csige lent her his Radio Shack TRS-80 word processor, the quality of her prose took a quantum leap. "It made writing creative and my shows got much better," she says. "I thought nothing of rewriting and, by the end, the shows had gone from 6 minutes to 20 minutes long."

Of course, Mecca didn't want to selfishly hoard the secret of word processing. She would share her discovery with the world. If someone nontechnical like Mecca, who previously had no interest in computers, could suddenly and completely be convinced of their usefulness, there had to be thousands of others out there just like her, she reasoned. And therein must lay enormous commercial potential.

At the same time, Csige and other computer-store owners were having problems stocking their computer stores with essential computer peripherals such as monitors, printers, and modems. Something clicked. Mecca saw a perfect opportunity to help her husband and at the same time possibly turn a profit. Discerning the unmet need for good distribution channels for micro products, she decided to apply her experience in the electronics distribution world to micro peripherals.

She wasted no time. Less than a year after making her decision, she and her cousin Perry "Mitch" Mitchell launched Micro D, in July 1979. Six months pregnant with her first child, Mecca incorporated using $25,000 from the sale of the house from her first marriage. In its first year, Micro D would have sales of $3.6 million—and that was just the beginning.

Lore Harp: Bored in Suburbia

It's just possible that Lore Harp's good business instincts were inherited, or at least learned. Lore Lange Hegermann was born in Bottrop, West Germany, on March 3, 1944, the older of two children. Her father and grandfather owned several businesses and, although Harp* had no conscious desire to enter business when she grew up, she used to like playing with the accoutrements of commerce.

"There were a tremendous number of banking and business forms around," she recalls. "I always enjoyed putting them together and making little merchandising decisions. I remember that vividly."

But she minimizes the significance of such childish dabbling. "Yesterday's gone," she says. "Yes, you build on experiences, but I'm not so sure that going back to the womb necessarily has the answer." With the endless variables and circumstances in a human life, she says, "It could have been the moon and the stars for all I know."

Still, the facts are not so mysterious. Harp has always been competitive, which almost by definition implies ambition. In her youth she ran track for Northern Westphalia against other states in Germany in the 100-meter sprint and the long jump. Very often she won. She also assumed leadership roles in school, including class president. She was never by any means content to remain in the background.

"I guess I've been somewhat headstrong and determined all my life," she says, "but I don't know where that came from. I think sometimes the combination of everything in your life is such that you do things you hadn't really contemplated doing. As things develop you meet the challenges and stand up to them, and if people respond to what you're doing, then it feeds on itself."

In conversation, Harp exudes a self-confidence and straightforward belief in herself that apparently are the core of her personality. Her considrable inner strength is unmistakable. One can hardly imagine her hesitating over any decision for very long.

By the time Geza Csige had turned Lorraine Mecca's life around, Harp had already been indirectly influenced by him. Some

* To avoid confusion, women are referred to in this chapter by the same last names used throughout the book, even though several had different names before they became well known.

of Csige's earlier scientific dabbling on the side was in company with Bob Harp, a senior staff scientist at Hughes Aircraft. The two of them engineered a few memory boards basically for the fun of it. Their marketing plans remained vague and the boards lay dormant, forsaken in favor of newer projects.

Bob Harp's love of electronics not only amused him in his spare time, but earned him a generous salary at Hughes that allowed his family to lead a very pleasant suburban California existence. For several years, his wife's days were filled with tennis, volunteer work, and caring for her husband and two young daughters—a version of the American Dream that would have made many women perfectly happy.

But eventually Lore Harp's dreams began to settle on quite a different sort of happiness. At 32, she felt that time was passing through her hands with nothing to show for it. She remembers thinking, "My God, suddenly I'll be 40, the children will be gone, and where am I going to be?" Furthermore, she was miserable as a housewife. "I cannot stand staying at home," she says. "It drives me insane."

The volunteer work that many young mothers enjoy struck her as a meaningless waste of time, along with the majority of her suburban neighbors' other activities. "I was considered strange because I wouldn't go to the bridge club or have my nails done," she recalls.

Although her dissatisfaction undoubtedly puzzled some, it was almost inevitable that she would grow tired of a quiet and predictable life. Harp is an explorer at heart, a fact she had demonstrated very dramatically a decade earlier.

The year before she was to start college in her native Germany, Harp came alone to the United States to visit family friends in Santa Cruz, on California's coast. She stayed the planned six months and then simply informed her family in Germany that she wasn't ready to go back home.

"I just wanted to see what else there was," she explains. The year was 1964 and there was plenty to see a few miles north in San Francisco, which was blossoming as the peace, love, and drug mecca of America. The drug culture was not what interested Harp, however. "I was just very curious about life and people," she says. "Everyone I had met in the United States was white, Republican, and wealthy. So many other things were going on that I wanted to experience."

Going back to Germany was not one of them. She shocked her parents by selling her return-trip ticket and moving to San Francisco. They responded by cutting off her allowance. Harp's parents hoped they could starve her out and get her to come back to Germany that way. But she stayed.

In San Francisco, her experiences were emphatically not "white, Republican, and wealthy." With only a visitor's visa, she couldn't enroll as a student and she couldn't officially work. "So I did little things like baby-sitting and odd jobs," she recalls. And she made just enough to get by.

"At one point I was down to $20, but I just would not call my parents and ask them for money," she says. Her independent and willful nature had come to the fore. At the same time, she had the luxury of knowing that if things got really bad, her parents would gladly pay her way home.

Harp is quick to point out that she was not running away from her life in Germany or from anything else; she simply was running *toward* the rest of the world. "I had a very normal childhood, in what you would call 'a very nice family,' " she says. Her grandfather was a successful politician during the Weimar Republic and her father's twin sister was an attorney. Harp respected them both enormously and especially admired her aunt's spontaneity and varied interests.

Living close to the edge, Lore never did break down and ask her parents for a lift back home. She eked it out on her own, and just as she began toying with the idea of taking up where she'd left off back in Germany, she met Bob Harp, who was then working toward his Ph.D. in electrical engineering at Stanford University. They were married a year later, in 1967, and moved to Los Angeles. Lore was then eligible to enroll at California State University, where she studied anthropology.

Then came motherhood. Two daughters two years apart served to interrupt her education, but certainly not her ambition. When her children were three and five, she enrolled in law school, but soon felt overwhelmed by the demands that placed on her. "I just could not do the massive amount of reading," she says. "My husband was not the kind of person who would take over half the chores while I studied, even though he was otherwise very supportive."

After eight months, she left law school, planning to finish up later. With her days suddenly looking very empty, Harp took up tennis with all the zeal she had hoped to apply to the study of law. "I actually became quite good at it, but just playing tennis all the time was not quite what I had in mind either," she says. "I had a lot of pent-up energy that needed to have some positive release, and I guess I had a greater mental need."

She intensified her search for something to lend deeper meaning to her life. Harp and her friend Carole Ely, a former bond trader, began knocking around ideas for starting a business. They considered opening a travel agency, but in the end it seemed impractically complex.

She needed something manageable but interesting, that wouldn't take much money to start up and could be orchestrated from her living room if necessary. She began to think about her husband's memory boards.

Even with no technical background, she could easily understand the concepts behind the boards, which were quite a bit like Tinkertoys: just plug the right chip into the right socket and there's your product. The dormant boards beckoned. "Why don't I see what I can do with them?" she suggested to Bob.

Ely was game. "When I asked Carole if she'd be interested in joining a little start-up company that markets memory boards, she said, 'Sure. . . . What's a memory board?' " Harp laughs. And that would have been the reaction of most people back in 1976. The two suburban housewives got in at the very beginning, when the computer hobbyist industry was still sucking its thumb.

Once the idea took form, these two women moved like lightning. Within 48 hours, they were at the Southern California Computer Society's show, surveying the market. What they saw floored them. Here were hordes of "techies" who Harp thought were "the weirdest people I'd ever met," peeling off $800, $900, $1,000 in cash on the spot for a few memory boards. The nerds suddenly began to look very attractive.

Although she had arrived a bit later than the technological innovators, Harp quickly sensed the birth of a phenomenon that was to be like no other: social as well as technological, fun as well as serious. One look was enough. She was in.

Harp and Ely went into high gear. Two days later, they had incorporated, called in an accountant to set up the books, and turned the Harps' downstairs bedroom into an office, factory, and warehouse. They threw themselves entirely into the project, working from early in the morning until late at night.

Harp and Ely instinctively used to the best advantage methods that are no secret in most industries but that had been completely ignored by the hobbyist suppliers: heavy advertising and customer service and support. And it didn't hurt that the two principals were women. "We really capitalized on it," Harp says. "Everyone wanted to help 'the girls.' " And Vector Graphic, Inc., took the computer hobbyist market by storm.

Jacqueline Morby: Discovering Her Own Worth

Like Harp, Jacqueline Morby also spent a number of years as a well-off housewife, but that's where the similarity ends. Highly intelligent but basically shy, Morby instinctively avoids the limelight. Her strength is the quiet kind, and she's got plenty of it.

As a housewife, Morby was not terribly bored, but she was not typical either. After a few unfocused years of work following college, she left the business world and she and her husband adopted an infant son. Then in 1969 her husband's work took the family to South America, where they lived for five years in fascinated contentment. The experience satisfied Jacqui's intellectual curiosity and sense of adventure. "I never wanted to be ordinary," she says. "I always wanted to do something special. I didn't want to have things pass me by."

There certainly was no dearth of excitement in Argentina, where Jeffrey Morby was overseeing the Bank of Boston's South American operations. Jacqui characteristically approached the experience not as a holiday, but as an education.

"In South America, I was determined to speak the language better than anyone else and to become completely involved in the culture," she recalls. "I didn't want to be an American who went out and played tennis every day. I wanted to understand Argentina and Brazil."

While most Americans in Argentina led insulated lives in the suburbs, the Morbys lived in the capital city of Buenos Aires. "Almost all our friends were Argentines," Morby says. So much a part of the culture were the Morbys, that they adopted their second child there, an Argentine girl.

Continuing an earlier propensity for volunteer work, Morby assumed the presidency of the University Women's Club, a decades-old, English-speaking cultural institution in Argentina open to all nationalities. "It was an interesting intercultural experience," she says. "The group provided people with the kind of intellectual stimulation they'd get in Boston or New York."

What she had first noticed in volunteer work in the United States again became apparent: It was clear that she was better than the rest at slicing through to the guts of an issue, deciding on a course of action, and taking it. "I was surprised to find that I seemed to be better [than the others] at many parts of the things we were doing," she recalls. "I could think more clearly, accomplish more, and present things better. I'd always rise in those situations. I had never thought of myself as a leader at all, but I began to value myself more."

She also discovered that she's no coward. Toward the end of the Morbys' stay in Argentina, things began to heat up politically. Terrorist acts—particularly against Americans—were rampant and on the increase following the return in June 1973 of the long-exiled, and about to be reelected, Argentine President Juan Peron.

There had been a number of kidnappings of American business executives, with ransoms amounting to many millions of dollars in each case. As head of the Bank of Boston, Jeffrey Morby stood a good chance of being snatched off the street. "We were careful if we thought we were being followed," Jacqui says, "and we would change our hours regularly." They also had four armed guards at their home.

In spite of the real and serious danger, they regarded the whole affair as no more than an annoyance. "We weren't afraid," she maintains. "We were careful and wary." Even death threats—delivered by telephone in the middle of the night and by carefully typed letters inserted in the Morbys' utility bills—were not taken that seriously.

That is, not until an automobile company executive in another city was gunned down while driving in his car. "Until then, people had been kidnapped but not killed," Jacqui explains. "That's when we realized it wasn't for us—Jeffrey could easily get killed."

They left in September 1973. "Within a month, every foreigner was out of there," she says. The Morbys had been back in Boston only four months, however, when problems in the bank's Brazilian operation forced them back to South America for nearly another year.

When the experience was over at last, bystanders at the Morbys' arrival in New York must have wondered at their five-year-old son's first question: "Where are the guards?" He missed the armed men who had become his playmates. The whole family, in fact, took about a year to readjust to life in a freer society; they had grown used to being watched and actually felt insecure with their total freedom.

Jacqui Morby's growing recognition of her own capabilities had let loose a trickle of ambition. Now that she was back in Boston, she realized that she wanted to do "something worthwhile." That impulse—which didn't hit until her late thirties—was not out of a desire to escape any domestic malaise but rather evolved from her very gradual realization of her own worth. She had not been secretly burning with ambition, and she entertained only a silent and tentative belief in her own abilities until she blossomed in Argentina. Unlike Harp, who quickly disdained volunteer work as "meaningless," Morby found in it the irrefutable evidence she needed of her own potential.

Born June 19, 1937, Jacqui Collins came of age in an era when women were not expected or encouraged to have careers, and she blindly followed the prevailing wisdom. At the same time, those close to her sensed a subtle but strong determination within. "Don't misread Jacqui," her late mother used to say. "She may be quiet, but you can be sure she'll get her way in the end."

Although her academic family had high regard for education, she was brought up with the idea that even women who went to college were expected only to get married, have kids, and take care of their husbands. An education would merely make them better wives and mothers.

"It didn't occur to me to do anything else," she says. "My parents were both proud of me, but neither one expected me to do anything. It just wasn't in the culture." Still, because she was very bright and came from a family of educators, she always assumed that she would attend college. Although there wasn't a lot of money around, her family sacrificed to send Jacqui to Stanford University.

Always at the top of her class, but quiet and shy, Jacqui did not assume a leadership role at college but did have "an awfully good time." She also found an appropriately ambitious husband. True to expectations, she married classmate Jeffrey Morby soon after they graduated in 1959.

Jacqui then made a brief foray into the business world, first writing government accounting reports for a now-defunct company owned by Harvard and MIT, while Jeffrey attended Harvard Business School. After Jeffrey graduated in 1961, they moved to Los Angeles, and she took a job at Hughes Aircraft that convinced her business was "very boring." She decided to try teaching.

After two years of substitute teaching in Los Angeles, with many assignments in some very rough neighborhoods, Jacqui began thinking maybe business wasn't so bad, after all. Her sentiments echo Mecca's: "Teaching is one of the hardest professions there is," Morby says. "I was far more exhausted then than I ever am now."

In 1966, Jacqui took a market research job with a very small foreign import company, Athena Scientific. "That got me interested in products, markets, and marketing. It gave me more background for what I do today than I'd gotten before," she says, "but I still had no particular interest in doing anything significant."

At the same time, she was doing lots of "typical volunteer work," for groups like the symphony and the Los Angeles Art Museum. Like Harp, she discovered that she was on an entirely different stratum than most of the other volunteers. Unlike Harp, she enjoyed the feeling.

Still, it would take another 15 years before she would really come into her own. In late 1975, after returning from South America, Jacqui considered getting involved in a political cause or the museum work she enjoyed so much. She soon became active in Boston's Institute of Contemporary Art.

But when a friend told her about the Simmons College Graduate Management School, it was all she needed to hear. "The six years I'd been out of the country, a lot had happened—Watergate, Vietnam. I had no idea women were even in business school," she recalls. There had not been a single woman in Jeffrey's 1961 graduating class at Harvard Business School.

"I'd always been interested in the stock market and I liked the market research I'd done. I figured I'd use [Simmons] as leverage to get into the business world. It seemed perfect." Her daughter was two and a half when Jacqui discovered Simmons; in two years, going part-time, she'd be finished. She enrolled.

In her last year at Simmons, Morby had to decide on an internship program. She rejected banking for two reasons. Because her husband was a banker, she didn't want to have to compete with or try to avoid him professionally. Secondly, she was too old for the banker's timetable. "I'd be getting out of school at 40, and it would be too late to go through the training and work my way up. I needed a fast start."

She finally zeroed in on the then-obscure field of venture capital and talked to everyone in Boston who was connected with it. "Venture capital is a natural thing for my temperament," she found. "I like people and I like new and interesting experiences and situations. Discovery is a lot of what we do."

In her last year at Simmons, Morby became an intern at TA Associates, one of the oldest and largest venture capital firms in the country. When she graduated in 1978, TA welcomed her as an associate. After working on some mainframe software investments for TA, Morby began investigating the area of microcomputer software, which was also obscure then. (In 1979, even Apple Computer Inc. was still small potatoes. And the handful of micro software companies destined to become the market leaders were still fledgling.)

Morby, incisive and intuitive, sensed what now seems obvious but at the time most people totally missed: the enormous potential of that market. "Many people tended not to understand software, especially investors and bankers," she says. "Because it was something you couldn't see, you couldn't touch, you couldn't hold, it was a frightening thing to them."

But she did understand it and she managed to convince TA to make what many at the firm saw as too-risky investments very early on. Controversy turned to congratulations when the micro market took off in a blaze of glory. Her instincts proved to be right on the mark.

Portia Isaacson: Ambitions of a Misfit

"The first step in getting there is wanting to be there," says Portia Isaacson. But unlike Lorraine Mecca, Lore Harp, or Jacqueline Morby, Isaacson's desire "to be there" started astonishingly early in life. Even as a child, Isaacson was sustained by a goal. Her overriding, lifelong dream of being a scientist was born only four years after she was.

"Even before I started school, I used to play with bottles, pretending I was a chemist," she says. But where did a four-year-old learn about chemistry? When her parents rented a "teacherage" to live in (the teacher's quarters in a one-room country school), little Portia had nothing better to do than wander into the classroom and attend classes.

"I was really lucky because back then there was no such thing as kindergarten," she explains. "So I think I got some good stimulus really early, particularly since grades one to eight were all in one room, so I got to listen to all the grades."

There was never any danger that she'd be kicked out, either. "I was probably this really funny-looking, slightly chubby little girl with huge, thick glasses who was really smart," she says, "so I was nearly always kind of adopted by any teacher."

With science as her dream, Portia soon fixed on Marie Curie, the discoverer of radium, as her heroine. "I was impressed with her single-minded focus and drive," she says. Even today, Isaacson bemoans the fact that her own contributions to the world have not yet been as clear-cut as Curie's one great scientific discovery.

Inspirational as it was, having Curie as a role model "gave me some very odd ideas that it took me most of my life to get rid of," Isaacson says. "It meant you had to be extremely poor and suffer excruciatingly in order to contribute to science." Isaacson met the first requirement from the start and seems to have lived the next few decades in an attempt to qualify for the second.

Isaacson's personal reputation today is of a tough, driven woman who doesn't take flak from anyone. She has been described as obnoxious, domineering, and, in the vernacular, "a real bitch"—a sobriquet often leveled at strong women.

Isaacson is well aware of these unflattering opinions of her and regards them with some amusement . . . and a little pain. What others perceive as a haughty attitude actually masks the remnants of her long-held view of herself as an outsider: at once better than most and disdained by many.

"I wasn't fully socialized until I was 35," she admits. Her many lofty goals, always designed to elevate her above the common man or woman, were born of a profound sense of insecurity that continues to haunt her. In spite of her many accomplishments, Isaacson admits that she still feels inadequate. "At the end of every day I add up everything I've done and evaluate my performance," she says. Her insecurity unfailingly convinces her that she hasn't done quite well enough. She claims that she used to "take IQ tests for sport," just to see a high score set on her own worth.

Paradoxically, as deep as her insecurity runs, so does her unquestioning recognition of her own talents and intellect. "I've known it for a long time, now you know it," is her silent, bitter reproach to the (cruelly unappreciative, she felt) people of the Oklahoma town that was her childhood home.

The disdain the townspeople felt for her family because it came from "the wrong side of the tracks" was the major source of Isaacson's insecurity. But in spite of the pain and humiliation she endured from the outside, her intellectual gifts and determination gave her considerable inner strength. And in fact, the anger she felt at the incongruity of her inner and outer circumstances kept her going at full tilt for years.

Although in many ways hardship has been her driver, for Portia Isaacson "wanting to be there" had its genesis in a confused compulsion to escape and at the same time to endure suffering, and ultimately to learn, to excel, and to make a major contribution to the world.

She grew up on an "Okie" farm—poor, abashed, and strictly a loner. During the catastrophic Dust Bowl period, her parents had joined the many farming families who migrated to California to work in the war factories. There Portia was born, in Oakland, on September 7, 1942. A year later, tired of California, Allen and Virginia Midgett brought their first child back home.

They didn't get a very warm welcome. "Even though the whole town of Stratford, Oklahoma, was poor, they regarded us as one of the less desirable families," Isaacson recalls, "because we were a little bit migrant and we didn't always pay our bills."

Not that they didn't try. In 1947, Allen Midgett invested in 360 untamed acres. By singlehandedly clearing that land, Midgett created what he hoped would be the basis for a pretty good living. "My dad tried quite a few different things—dairy, chickens, mostly animals," Isaacson says. "Nothing ever worked."

Midgett's uncomplaining response to almost constant adversity was not lost on his daughter. "He always had another job. In fact, my dad was an entrepreneur in the sense that he did anything there was to be done where he could make a little money."

His kind of determination in spite of setbacks, and his willingness to keep trying something new, are what Isaacson feels lie at the heart of her own entrepreneurial nature. "An entrepreneur isn't someone who thinks and plans and schemes for 20 years and has this one great idea and does it, and it succeeds really big," she says. "What an entrepreneur does is 100 things and 99 of them fail—usually in such small, minor ways that the world doesn't even notice they were ever trying anything. And finally they get one of them right." This is certainly true for Isaacson, who before she was 40 had known more failures than most people know in a lifetime.

The long days of Isaacson's girlhood began and ended with farm chores, which varied according to the type of farm it was at the moment. When the homestead tried raising chickens, eggs had to be gathered and gullets had to be filled. "This was not going out to a little place and tossing out some stuff," Isaacson says. "I mean this was 20,000 chickens. This was lugging bags of feed and gathering in thousands of eggs."

There were often crops to tend as well. "A lot of times I'd drive a tractor several hours a day to plow the crops," she says. In the fall, shortly after school started up, it would just as suddenly close down for an entire month and all the school kids would pick the harvest of pecans or sweet potatoes to make a little money. The season of harvest always accomplished three things: it got the produce to market, it brought in a little cash, and "it made your hands black."

On the dairy farm, she spent two to three hours every morning and again at night on horseback rounding up 30 cows that dumbly wandered the entire 360 acres. "You round them up, herd them to the barn, then when you get there you find out, 'Oh, shit, I've only got 24!' so you have to go back and find the other six," she remembers.

But while Isaacson's body was out working the fields or caring for the animals, her mind was frequently somewhere else. While on horseback ostensibly rounding up the cows, for example, she usually had a book hidden under her shirt. "I'd get out of sight of the house and start reading my book and sometimes lose track of the time while my dad was waiting back at the barn for the cows," she confesses. "I was known as being very absentminded and not very responsible about my chores."

But Allen Midgett was perhaps a bit more indulgent than he appeared to his daughter. "I knew she was smart. She always had a book, all the time, sure did," he recalls. "She had a horse that knew where the cows were. He'd run under a rail to go get a cow and knock Portia right over but she'd get back on with her book and go again," he laughs.

Here was a girl with an IQ "through the roof," in her words, with deep ambition and "competitive from Day 1," spending several hours every day on farm chores and always, in the back of her mind, searching for something worthy of her abilities. It must have seemed that there had been a terrible mixup in heaven for her to have landed where she did on earth.

After about five years of working the farm, her parents got divorced in the early 1950s, when such a step was still relatively uncommon. When the devastation of the divorce hit, Portia was about ten. "I thought it was awful and I thought it was my fault," she recalls. "I became very inward. I really didn't like my life, so

I read all the time and ignored my family and everything around me."

At school, however, it was quite a different story. Portia was busy taking top honors in sports, competitive debating, and academics, particularly science. "I felt my only really positive experience was at school. Any kid needs strokes, so I did whatever the teachers wanted to get strokes."

If Isaacson's life were a Hollywood movie, winning lots of prizes would have gained her the respect and acceptance of her classmates and she would have been carried triumphantly down Main Street on their shoulders. But instead it was Oklahoma real life, and Isaacson clung to her aloneness as a refuge. "I was a misfit, there's no doubt," she felt. "I was a star basketball player and captain of the team but I was never invited to the parties after the games."

Having positioned herself as the local unapproachable child prodigy, she was stuck playing the role. "It probably didn't have to be that bad," she admits. Still, she had virtually nothing in common with anyone in the town, where students frequently quit high school to start working at dead-end jobs and where girls often were married by the age of 16.

Furthermore, she was extraordinarily idealistic as a teenager, "even more than most kids are at that age," she says. And she was outraged at the overt racism practiced in the Oklahoma of the 1950s. "Black people were locked up if they were seen in my town after dark," she remembers. In her competitive speaking, she frequently railed against such injustices—and while her logic was flawless, her opinions were very unpopular.

So Portia lived for years in emotional exile, angry at her family, the town, and everyone in it, all the while suffering an underlying helplessness about how to get where she wanted to be. "My big dream was to go to college, but I didn't think I could do it," she says. In those days, she didn't know how to catch a bus, much less pay for the trip.

Her one hope was her pure intelligence. Isaacson's academic performance was so outstanding that she was recruited by many top colleges with offers of scholarships. In the post-Sputnik era, she had scored very high on a test for the Westinghouse Science

Talent Search and through that had applied for and gotten a scholarship to MIT.

Yet she couldn't seem to bridge the enormous gulf between Stratford, Oklahoma, and the rarefied Cambridge air. "I was scared to death of the idea of an MIT, or even college," she remembers. "It's like dreaming you want to be something but being in way too much awe of it."

She was a little less scared of the idea of Oklahoma State University (OSU), where she'd spent a high school summer studying biochemistry, but ignorance still held her back. "I tried to figure out how to go to school at OSU, but I didn't know you could get a loan, or even that you could get a job," she says, "and I couldn't even formulate the questions.

"You can't imagine how culturally remote the area is where I grew up. It's like the Ozarks. You don't even know what to ask. You're just incredibly ignorant about the ways of the world," she explains. "The truth is I *could* have gone to college from there, but I didn't know how and there was no one around to tell me.

"I still get upset about it," she says now. So angry and upset was she at the time that, the day after fulfilling her obligation as valedictorian of her high school class, she took all the money to her name—$25—and hopped on a bus to Dallas. Without batting an eye, she left her family and everyone else behind. "Now, that's angry," she adjudges.

After two weeks of working as a carhop in Dallas, Portia (still just 17) took her first real job, as a chemical assistant and secretary in an industrial laboratory, and immediately set out to fulfill her goal of going to college. Dismissing her scholarship to MIT as an unclaimable prize, she enrolled in the night-school chemistry program at Southern Methodist University (SMU).

Although it's likely that SMU would have given her a scholarship, Portia didn't even apply for one. She was a young woman alone in a big city for the first time in her life, and her major focus was "living day to day," she says. "You don't think clearly at 17, even if you're smart. Smart has nothing to do with it. We're talking common sense here."

Besides, here was an opportunity to tough it out, in the finest Curie tradition. "I was determined to do it on my own," Isaacson says. As a part-time student, working full-time to pay her tuition, she envisioned a satisfyingly hard road ahead, but didn't conceive just how hard until she sat down one night and did a little math. "I figured out that at the rate I was going, I'd graduate at age 82."

That thought was disheartening enough, but Portia was also becoming painfully aware of her own personal inadequacies. "Every day I had situations I was really very uncomfortable with. I felt the clothes I had were very 'not right' to wear to work, but I didn't know what to do about it," she says. "And there was no one I could trust who could help and guide me."

She felt like the misfit she thought she had left behind. "Even the social aspect of work was hard, meeting people I didn't know how to deal with or handle," she remembers. "Everything was so totally different from anything I'd ever experienced before. It was a scary time."

Totally unequipped for life in the big city, Portia did the only thing reasonable. She joined the Army. Fort Sam Houston, San Antonio, Texas. Although that move took her lightyears away from her academic goal, it served as a crash course in The Real World.

"It was really an escape," she realizes. "Many young people join the Army because it's an escape and then it takes care of you. You don't have to make all those decisions, and I'm sure that's why I did it."

It turned out to be an excellent move. "I loved basic training," she says, and she was a quick study. The Army taught her how to manage money, how to get a loan, and generally how things work. She got plenty of positive reinforcement, too, since she aced every course she took and got the highest score ever recorded on her WAC test.

The worldliness of the people she met was an education in itself. "I was exposed to life," she says. Continuing her flight from the painful memories of her youth, she ran at breakneck speed into adulthood.

After a two-year hitch in the Army, Isaacson got married at 19, to a man she'd known for only a couple of months. "That's how naive I was," she says. She moved with her husband to

Louisville, where he was stationed, and six months later he walked out on her.

Because she "didn't know the foggiest thing about birth control," she says, she had gotten pregnant right away. Isaacson found herself alone, six months pregnant, unemployed, and hundreds of miles from home. So this was Real Life.

She actually welcomed her husband's leaving, though, since by then she was extremely unhappy with the marriage, if it could be called one. "Actually, I hardly even knew him," she says. "I lived in Louisville and almost never saw him. He lived on base and visited occasionally. And he was disenchanted with me when I was pregnant, so it wasn't a big loss."

After her husband left, she lied about the baby's due date to get a job as a typist, and worked until the day of the birth. "After Allen was born, I took a two-week vacation, packed up the car, and headed for Oklahoma." Three months after she got back home, she learned that her husband had been killed in a car crash. "Not soon enough," she says. Whatever was still soft inside Portia was hardening nicely.

Back in the Oklahoma she had so gladly left, Portia was now faced with more problems than she could even have imagined before. She was a new mother with no husband. She had no money, no job, and, worst of all, no education.

"My father was really upset that I'd failed already at 20, with no husband and no support, but I didn't feel that way." Failure is in the eye of the beholder and Isaacson has always been masterful at turning bad situations into good ones.

Like Lorraine Mecca, Isaacson discovered early in life what are now popularly called "visualization techniques," which she instinctively used back before they had a name. "It's extraordinarily effective," she says.

Isaacson has been using the technique for as long as she can remember. "I know I did it in all competitive situations," she says, "like if I was competing in some speech contest or some basketball game, I would visualize winning—in lots of detail—and daydream about it."

Naturally, it doesn't always work. "Not all goals are possible," she acknowledges. "You do sometimes fail, for whatever reason." Nevertheless, back in her old digs, Isaacson was busy visualizing a college education. She took a job as a medical records clerk in a hospital emergency room, determined to support herself, her baby, and her schooling.

College, however, was not the only thing on her 20-year-old mind. In her meager spare time, she hooked up with "a marvelous young man who'd grown up near me," she says. "He was very attractive, sexy, lean, tall, and fun—an Oklahoma truck driver. Dad approved."

Again she got married and again she got pregnant. With a babe in arms and another one on the way (two, as it turned out), she did something her new husband found incomprehensible: She enrolled at East Central State College in Ada. She was 21, her husband was 20.

She acknowledges that going back to school at that point was "completely unreasonable," considering all the responsibilities she already had. Even though her husband—normally "very reasonable"—was developing a "serious drinking problem," in her words, she went ahead with her plans. "To achieve my goal of being a scientist it was necessary for me to go to college," she explains. "I had figured out how to enroll, how to work, how to get a scholarship, and so on. The kids didn't bother me; that was just a management problem. It never occurred to me not to go because of them," she says. "It occurred to my husband, but I didn't see what kids had to do with it. He was right," she admits now, "but right has nothing to do with an obsession.

"He just didn't relate to my ambition," she says, "and we fought all the time." After the births, in a move that let her escape the discord but also inspired more of it, she returned to finish the semester while her premature twin boys were still in the hospital.

Portia's determination, while impressive, still looks a lot like extreme selfishness—and she agrees that she was as self-centered as they come. "Only in recent years have the people around me taken on any importance whatsoever," she admits.

Meanwhile, her second marriage was hurtling downhill like a runaway baby carriage. "Finally I moved out and took the three babies with me to college housing." So there she was, a 22-year-old physics student with a 2-year-old boy and six-month-old twins. She remembers thinking, "I'll never be able to feed these kids!"

Fortunately for Isaacson, the 1960s had rolled around, bringing with them plenty of social welfare programs.

In her case, being a welfare mother didn't mean long days at home doing laundry and changing diapers. It meant that there was federal money to pay for baby-sitters, food, and other expenses while she attended classes. She also got several small scholarships from the school. "The school really liked me," Isaacson brags. And no wonder. In spite of crying babies and constant financial worries, she managed to get a 4.0 grade point average.

And she was supremely happy. She was putting in her stint of Curie-like suffering and loving every minute of it. "I was so excited about what I was learning, and I was doing what I wanted to do," she explains. "It was a very rewarding time in my life."

Her dedication, enthusiasm and intelligence attracted a large network of supportive friends who lent a belated warmth and richness to her life. No longer was she an outcast. Her friends helped take care of the children while she attended classes, and at night she tutored other students at a bar where she worked, between customers. "It was the only bar where you could drink beer and learn physics at the same time," she laughs.

The babies caused her hardship, certainly, but they were also a strong motivation. "I wanted to get out of the poverty situation before they remembered it," she says, "and they don't." One of the things they don't remember is that after three years of living on the edge of poverty, Isaacson found herself completely broke, and she still wasn't quite finished with her studies.

During those three years of study, her circle of friends had gradually scattered, as academic associates tend to do, so she no longer had many outside resources to call on. With 20 course hours to go but no money to get her through the home stretch, Isaacson heard that she could get a job teaching high school physics without a degree in Texas. That was all she needed. Into the old Renault went the three kids and off to Pampa, Texas, they all headed.

The Renault had only a driver's seat and was jammed full of Portia's earthly belongings, stuffed in among babies. Seats weren't all the car lacked: It didn't have much of an engine either. What little engine it did have blew 30 miles out of Pampa, in the middle of the hot, empty Texas prairie.

After being rescued from the roadside by strangers, she quickly put her new life together: She found a house, a car that ran, and a baby-sitter, and she started teaching. Unfortunately, she was teaching only one physics class and four remedial math classes. She loved her physics class but detested the remedial math. "Not only did I hate it, but I couldn't handle it," she says. "These were classrooms of 40 students, all six-foot-tall guys walking around the room who couldn't add, and I couldn't even keep discipline in the classroom." After only a month, miserable and increasingly frustrated, she quit.

Once again she packed up the car and the kids and went back to East Central State, intent on finishing up her last 20 hours even though she was still essentially broke. She got her tutoring job back, and enrolled in every course she needed to get her degree that semester—so she thought.

Having been advised all along that the school would accept two of her course credits from the Army, she was crushed to find out toward the end of the term that the registrar had changed his mind and she needed yet another course. "It just killed me," she says. "I came a little bit unglued. I just felt at wits' end and I absolutely didn't know what to do. I just gave up." For the first time, she was at a complete loss and her former support systems were now too thin to help her out.

Isaacson appealed to the wisdom of one of her physics professors and followed what she now calls some "very bad advice." He thought she should leave her children with her father and then-stepmother and check into a mental hospital in Oklahoma City. And that's exactly what she did.

"I don't blame him, poor guy—he didn't know what to do," she says. "But all I really needed was four days of rest. I didn't need mental treatment. I was just emotionally exhausted. In fact, after two days the hospital told me they didn't think there was anything wrong with me."

In spite of that sanguine conclusion, the doctors announced that they had decided to keep her there four months. Because she had voluntarily entered the hospital, Portia now stood a chance of losing her kids. "At that point, my stepmother had started legal action to get my children from me," Isaacson recalls bitterly. "She thought I wasn't providing them with a very good livelihood, which was in fact true. It wasn't that I didn't take good care of them, but she thought she could better provide for them, which was undoubtedly true. I didn't know what she could do legally and I was afraid she might have a case." So Isaacson took direct, dramatic action. "I went into survival mode," she says.

Five days after she had entered the hospital, and without telling anyone, she walked out, snatched her kids, and crossed the state line with them, back to Dallas. "I didn't break any law whatsoever in the process, but I thought I had. I didn't even know that I could leave the mental hospital, so I was scared to death."

Back in Dallas and deeply in debt, she immediately started looking for work. "Here I was a physicist except for one course, but I had to get any kind of job that paid well, so I did the awfullest thing." She flashes an enigmatic smile. "I took a programming job."

Her title at Bell Helicopter Co. in Hurst, Texas, was "engineer," but she was hired specifically to do programming. Feeling exceedingly compromised, she took the job "because it was the only thing I could do, even though I felt programming was kind of like typing—certainly nothing a physicist would do." She had done some programming for the physics department at East Central State College and had found it tedious and not at all interesting. Unhappy at having sunk so low, at the same time she felt lucky to get the job, since she desperately needed the money.

She was lucky to get the job in more ways than one. Women in computing were exceedingly rare at that time, but because the company was a major government supplier, and thanks to the nascent women's movement, Bell had a gender quota to fill. Isaacson was one of the first two female engineers the firm hired.

Her "sacrifice" in accepting the job turned out to be the single best thing she had done up to that point. "As soon as I got my hands on the computer, I realized I loved programming." Since she was solving complex problems of vibration analysis for helicopters, her job was much more complex and challenging than the programming she had previously done.

Everything else in her life started improving too. She met and married Jimmy Isaacson, a numerical analyst at Bell and "a wonderful, wonderful man" whom she considers her first husband, though he succeeded two others. He adopted her three kids and "he really is their father," she says.

There would be a few more setbacks, to be sure, but Isaacson had managed to set herself on a path that would lead her to the microcomputer, soon to prove the most compelling factor in her life.

Ann Piestrup: "I Wanted to Make the World Better"

Just ten months after Portia Isaacson was born in California, Ann McCormick started life on July 9, 1943, on an apple farm in Youngstown, New York. Not only were the two separated by the expanse of a continent, but also by the different circumstances of their lives. From the start, Piestrup's environment was far easier and more supportive than Isaacson's.

And yet, beneath dichotomous exteriors, Isaacson and Piestrup shared a singular degree of idealism. Isaacson's early dream of a Curie-like contribution was matched by an innate spirituality in Piestrup that evolved into a desire to make the world better through education. And, like Isaacson, Piestrup sensed an inner strength and power even as a child.

"I was a very intense little girl," Piestrup says. "I was looking for the meaning of life, and I wanted to make the world better." She decided at age five, while just in kindergarten, that a good way to do that would be as a teacher, following the example of several of her aunts.

As a small child, however, she started out in business. That is to say, she accompanied her father every day on his job of selling insurance and mutual funds during her school vacations. Because Gordon and Ruth McCormick had divorced, Gordon cared for his son and daughter during school vacations, and chose to take them to work with him instead of hiring a baby-sitter.

His career eventually led to his buying and selling insurance companies and banks. "He took me to the negotiations for those deals," she recalls. "From the time I was eight, when my dad went to lunch to talk big deals, I was there. I didn't know I was learning, but I heard the conversation, the patter, and later on I saw myself as more able to do that kind of thing, because I'd done it since I was a little girl."

Even though her father stepped through big deals in his work, he was not personally rolling in cash. Still, despite having divorced parents and not much money, Piestrup feels her childhood was advantageous in many ways, largely because of each parent's attitude toward life.

"My mother saw herself as powerful, as someone who could do what she wanted to do," Piestrup says. After her divorce, Ruth McCormick felt keenly the inequality between the sexes in the business world. She got a secretarial job at Bell Aircraft in Niagara Falls, then in the midst of its post-World War II boom, and spent two years there.

But because of the prevailing attitude toward women in the workplace—that they "didn't really need the money"—she had trouble supporting her children. "I spent two years at Bell waiting for a 10-cents-an-hour raise," Ruth Clinton (she later remarried) recalls.

Clinton saw that her salvation lay in getting off the secretarial track and finding more enlightened management to work for. So she methodically studied all the major cities in the United States to find one not only where she might be able to make a good living, but also where her children would get the best education. Seattle won handily.

The move proved to be a good one. Clinton found just what she was looking for at Boeing Aircraft. At Boeing, she was paid well for her creativity: She began in a clerical job but astoundingly, after only six months, she was given the classification of "engineer."

"I didn't know anything about engineering, particularly, but I could spell and write proper grammar and that was something most engineers weren't good at then," Clinton explains. What she couldn't do was type. "I might have been a good executive secretary if I'd ever learned to type or take shorthand. But I hadn't learned because I hadn't really planned to go back to work." Later she would tell Ann, "Never admit you can milk a cow or type, or you'll end up having to do it."

At Boeing, Clinton's boss was an astrophysicist who gave her "wonderful" assignments, she remembers. One was to survey all the existing literature—ancient and modern—that made reference to moon travel, in conjunction with a project that proposed establishing a moon colony. Very heady stuff. And this was when space travel was still just a dream. Piestrup remembers feeling "really proud that my mother worked on space projects."

Ruth Clinton also treated her children with respect. "She shared with us everything about the finances of the family, so we were privy to information that's often kept to adults." So, from both quarters—on the road with her father and through conversations with her mother—Piestrup was more exposed to the adult world than the average child.

That may partly explain her decidedly serious approach to life. By the age of 15, Piestrup was looking for some real meaning in life and started studying all the major, and some minor, religions. "I was looking for the ultimate," explains. "I was just that way about my life. Like if I got a prom dress, it had to be *the right dress;* it couldn't just be any old dress on the rack. It was a philosophical thing to me."

Where did Ann's spirituality come from? "It came from inside myself that I wanted to know the truth about God and the world, just as many teenagers do," she explains. "A lot of people either have a crisis in faith at about 15 or change religions or find religion. It was the same kind of quest, looking for meaning in life, as people who join the Peace Corps."

It was not the Peace Corps, however, that Piestrup joined, but the Catholic Church. Not only did she join the church, but in a typically intense move, Ann became a nun after graduating from high school. At 18, she entered the order of the Sisters of Saint Joseph of Peace.

From 1961 to 1967, Piestrup was a teaching nun, though still not a full-fledged teacher. In 1967 she got her B.A. in social sciences from Seattle University, and that fall she took a job in Buffalo teaching poverty-stricken fifth-grade students.

"That had a very great impression on me because I had brought with me all the convictions I'd had about wanting to give the best possible education to children and wanting to make the world better," she says. "The cold reality was that, in many cases, the kids didn't even have the basics—they weren't fed—and there was great turmoil in their lives.

"I determined that I wanted to do something about that on a broader scale," Piestrup explains. "The convent was a little confining for the ideals that I had, as far as pushing education to a further point. I really didn't know very much about convents when I went there, but I played it out. I decided to really stay and find out what it was like.

"After six years I decided that, though I had very warm friendships and I was deeply a part of that life, that wasn't where I could find the expression for what I wanted to do in the world. It wasn't enough just to be a sister teaching in one classroom in a Catholic school in Buffalo," she recalls feeling. She knew she would have to broaden her sphere of influence far beyond a single classroom. She also realized that she had a lot more to learn if she wanted to make the global changes she had in mind.

At 24, she was also thinking about having a family, "although that wasn't in the forefront of my mind at the time," she says. "I had really lived according to the [convent's] rules." It was, finally, her changing views of herself and her role in society that made her decide to leave the convent. "I couldn't carry out the dream I had when I went there," she says.

Ann quickly mapped out a different approach toward her goals and followed it with characteristic zeal. Wanting to learn from the best possible sources, she pinpointed the University of California at Berkeley as the premiere graduate school in the country and enrolled there.

It was a long way from the convent, emotionally as well as physically. While at Berkeley, her personal circumstances changed dramatically when she met Mel Piestrup, then a doctoral student at Stanford University. They were married in 1972.

Ann's 1973 doctoral dissertation in educational psychology, on "The Black Dialect and Reading in the First Grade," shed light on the often unrecognized fact that the speech patterns of blacks in the United States constitute a separate dialect.

"The dissertation talked about what was really going on with children, rather than something esoteric," Piestrup notes. "It wasn't just abstraction. It was gutsy, real things, which has always been my approach: to ask what will really work on a practical level instead of a theoretical level."

At Berkeley, Piestrup also indulged a fascination with visual media. Not only did she do videotaping to earn money, but her dissertation *was* a videotape. "I've always been interested in controlling media, and I used the television equipment at the School of Education at Berkeley more than anybody in the school's history," she claims.

While working toward her doctorate, Piestrup was called upon to test her mother's theory of women in business. "There was a point in my career when suddenly I didn't have any financial support for graduate school," Piestrup recalls. She went to the college placement office looking for a job and, remembering her mother's counsel, claimed she couldn't type.

"I in fact could type—my own papers. But I would not put myself in a traditional female secretarial role," she says. "I just saw that as stopping me." The placement office's response was, "Well, if you can't type, then you'll have to clean house," she recalls.

"So I said, 'Well, then, I'll clean house.' " But somehow the Berkeley placement people couldn't allow one of their doctoral candidates to (literally) stoop so low. Ruth Clinton's advice worked beautifully: Ann instead got a federally funded job as a researcher at the American Institutes of Research.

It couldn't have been a better match. Piestrup began ten years of government contract research work, at not only the American Institutes of Research, but also SRI International and RMC Research Corp. The focus of the research was to find ways of working effectively with poverty-area children, the very subject that interested her most.

"It's been like that all my life," she says. "Whatever it is I want to do happens to me. But I was also willing to work. During the time I was writing my dissertation, I had to commute 50 miles every day to do that work."

One project she worked on was a study of 2,000 so-called exemplary educational projects throughout the country. "Of those 2,000, we found six that could prove they really made a difference in terms of test scores," she recalls. And Piestrup all too frequently found flaws even in the most successful programs.

"Often the teachers made it hard instead of making it easy," she observed. "They would, for example, have the philosophy that learning should be difficult, so they'd make sure to give kids work that they'd get 60 percent or 70 percent wrong, instead of 90 percent correct, so the kids would be discouraged and not try because they felt they couldn't do it.

"It's a real crucial thing in learning," Piestrup maintains. "The theory is to make learning manageable—give the students just enough new information that the material is interesting, but they feel competent. Building that confidence is so key.

"It's so simple and yet, even if research says students should feel successful, teachers often don't apply it," she found. "Teachers often did things in kind of a punitive way. One person said to me, 'They've got to realize learning is hard.' "

Punitive is one thing Ann Piestrup is not. She has always approached children more as a comrade than as an authoritarian. "Even before I had a child, there were always lots of kids at my house," she says. "I was the nice lady in the neighborhood."

In fact, she thinks of herself as childlike in many ways. "I'm very playful. It keeps the creativity flowing," she feels. The child within her has a toy collection, ostensibly for the kids she knows, that includes exquisite handmade wooden toys. "They're really mine," she admits.

It was after her own daughter, Sarah, was born in March 1977 that things began to jell for Piestrup. In the name of motherhood she took some time off from working. During that period, everything she had learned and observed about education, as well as her own heartfelt desire to improve it, gradually came together.

"I started to think about computers," she recalls. Piestrup had used mainframe computers back in the sixties for analytical number-crunching in her doctoral work, but only in the very removed way peculiar to mainframes. "I put little punched cards into cubbyholes and printouts came back," she says. "It was all like a cookbook version of statistics. It was not that I deeply understood computers at all. I'd never touched one because they were way back there in the computer center and they were a very precious medium, at that."

But by 1977, the microcomputer revolution was just heating up and Piestrup happened to be geographically right in the middle of it, in what was becoming known as Silicon Valley. Piestrup remembers her excitement when she found out that there were microcomputers with color, music, voice, and graphics capabilities. "I thought, 'This is exactly what's needed.' "

She saw the personal computer as a reasonably priced miracle of technology that could supplant all the cumbersome and expensive teaching machines she'd ever seen. "I thought, 'Here's a television that you can talk back and forth with.' " And therein lay the key to successful teaching, she was convinced. "I'm not saying that machines are better than people, but it was certainly better than books or blocks or filmstrips or anything there'd been before because it was interactive." And she realized it immediately.

Piestrup sensed that a revolution was within her reach, and as soon as she got her hands on a microcomputer all her ambitions crystallized. "It just changed my whole career and lifestyle and everything to have that device," she says.

Piestrup felt she had been given the means to accomplish her goal. "I wanted to capture the essence of wonderful instruction that has a positive approach, where children can succeed and feel confident in themselves and yet learn the very basic, fundamental things, and not have the process interrupted by anybody getting in the way. I wanted to really make a revolution in children's possibilities."

Joyce Wrenn: Making Every Minute Count

Pivotal events in a person's life can happen in a second, sometimes very quietly. At one particular moment Joyce Wrenn made a conscious decision to "make every minute of my life count." When this thought came to her she was 13. "I decided I was going to do what I wanted to do with my life and it needed to be important to me. I wanted to make a contribution."

In Wrenn's case, the decision did not come so much like a sudden lightning bolt as the subsequent low rumble of thunder. What *had* come out of the blue, inspiring her resolve, was a full four-year scholarship to Cincinnati's private and very exclusive Sacred Heart Academy—an award that elevated her above about 100 other eighth-grade girls citywide who had taken the qualifying test but fallen short of Wrenn's performance.

The scholarship also served to pluck Wrenn right out of her comfortably humble surroundings and set her down in what might as well have been a foreign country. Not only would she physically leave behind all her old school friends, but she was leapfrogging several socioeconomic strata to enter an unknown world of affluence. "Going off to a very exclusive school was a bit frightening," she admits. "The girls there were very, very wealthy."

Wrenn was not. "We always had plenty of love and affection in my house but not a great deal of money," she says. Her mother officially stayed home but constantly took on extra jobs to help out. Joyce intuited early that eventually she was going to have to make it on her own.

Born Joyce Smith on December 18, 1935, Wrenn grew up in a three-generation household in which family took precedence over all. Because her only brother was old enough to have joined the Navy when she was just in kindergarten, her parents often remarked that it was as if they'd had two "only" children.

By the time Joyce was the "only child," her maternal grandparents had moved into the house. During her childhood Joyce flourished under the abundant adult attention and was unusually alert to its wisdom. "I went everywhere with my parents and grandparents and was always included in adult conversations, so I listened attentively to what they were doing with their lives and where they had done well."

One bit of oft-repeated advice from a favorite uncle became somewhat of a theme for Wrenn, and still holds up well, she feels. "He said there are opportunities every day, and just because you missed one last year doesn't mean there isn't a good opportunity today," she recalls. "You need to look for it."

Like Piestrup, Wrenn got a good strong dose of business life even as a child. She spent many hours with her grandfather, who years earlier had been a livestock commission merchant. "We used to go out to all the local farms since he still [represented] the farmers at the Cincinnati Stockyards," she recalls. On those trips Joyce admired the weave in the fabric of dozens of business relationships.

Her parents gave Joyce a lot of support but at the same time held high standards for her. "My father, especially, expected perfection out of me and encouraged me to be whatever I could be," she says. "If I got a 99 in math, I never got a congratulations. It was always, 'Why isn't it 100?' " she recalls. Wrenn feels her parents' attitude helped her develop her full potential. "I tried to live up to their views of me."

As Joyce's girlhood gave way to adolescence, the other members of the household were also growing older, and with age came illness. "I can remember at the age of 12 and 13 not being surprised anymore to come home from school and find an ambulance in the driveway," she says. "In fact, my question at that point was, 'Who's going to the hospital today?' " Neither her parents nor her grandparents escaped serious ailments. During those years she spent most major holidays keeping watch at hospital bedsides.

Circumstances pushed Wrenn into the role of an adult early. "Whenever anyone was ill, if it wasn't my mother, she'd be at the hospital with the person, and therefore I was expected to run things at home," she remembers. "I learned to cook—not very well, but I learned it—and I learned to help out in whatever else was needed at home."

By the time Wrenn won the Sacred Heart scholarship, she had given more than her childish share of thought to the question of what really mattered in life. She understood with exquisite clarity that it was essential to be independent, not to waste a drop of precious time, and to make a significant contribution to whatever situation she was in. She has since lived her entire life according to those ideals. "I got in the habit every day of looking at what I was going to do with that day," she says, "and seeing whether that made sense with what I wanted to do with that week and that month and that year."

The scholarship meant making a formidable transition to a completely unfamiliar environment, but Wrenn was determined not to let her new setting throw her off balance. She fixed her mind on success. Although she hadn't studied hard at all in grade school, she vowed to apply herself totally to the high school curriculum. "I thought, 'Now's the time and I'll really work hard,' " she recalls.

She took full advantage of the Academy's very small classes and the resulting luxury of individual attention. Although she didn't have the kind of money her classmates did, she most certainly had an abundance of talent. She excelled scholastically, even while devoting time to baby-sitting and house-cleaning to earn extra money. Also out of necessity, she sewed most of her own clothes.

Joyce could easily have parlayed her school associations into a very comfortable future, since she inevitably met and mixed with a number of wealthy boys. But instead she made a conscious decision early in her teenage years not to marry anyone with money.

"I had observed a number of gals who were kind of decorations on the arms of their husbands and I didn't want that," she recalls. In the 1950s of Joyce's adolescence, most girls were looking for nice boys to marry who would be able to support the family they planned on starting immediately. "Most of my friends were preparing for marriage and motherhood and really weren't thinking much about careers. I thought if I married someone who economically was somewhat in need, then by definition I could make a contribution," she says. "It wasn't so much a career orientation, it was just something that, to me, seemed to make sense."

She would be put to the test on that point, and she passed with flying colors. "During those teenage years, if I found that a fellow I was dating had a fair amount of money, I became disinterested very quickly," she notes. "I think that decision really made a difference."

On another front, Joyce had to stand her ground against her teachers and advisors, who also subscribed to the prevailing expectations for women. Because she had demonstrated a natural aptitude for art, English, and literature, her teachers tried to channel her exclusively into those areas. Joyce had other ideas.

"Back in the fifties, it wasn't clear to anyone what kind of career opportunities there were for women," Wrenn recalls. "I figured that I would be able to earn a reasonable living if I concentrated more on the sciences and math, and I really stuck to my guns on that." So while she enjoyed almost all her subjects, Joyce stubbornly focused her attention on those that she felt could later support her. After graduating as valedictorian of her high school class she went, again on a scholarship, to a small Catholic college in Cincinnati.

In keeping with her desire not to marry for money, she found herself in love with an ambitious but impecunious young man whose father had died and whose mother had helped put him through college. Halfway through Joyce's junior year, Bruce Wrenn got his military orders for Germany, so they decided to get married right away and go overseas together. They married in February 1956 and Joyce spent the next two years as an officer's wife. "According to the rules at that time, I couldn't work or go to school," she explains, "so I just had a ball traveling around Europe and having my college friends visit me."

Back in the United States, Bruce went to work at Du Pont Corp. in Delaware, and Joyce finished college at the University of Delaware, graduating in June 1959 with a B.A. in math.

It was the post-Sputnik era, and Bruce went from Du Pont to Thiokol Chemical, where he was in charge of the third-stage rocket for the Minuteman space project. On a business trip to California, he was so impressed by the pleasant climate that he decided to get his master's degree there.

While he attended USC and worked part-time under a Hughes Fellowship, Joyce worked full-time as a systems programmer at Bendix Computer in El Segundo, California. At night she studied for her master's degree in math at UCLA. But Joyce eventually had to drop out of grad school. "I just didn't have the time," she says. "Because I was working full-time, I couldn't handle the work for graduate school and run the house, too."

It was an era when the husband's career usually came first, and that was fine with Joyce. She wanted to work hard, she wanted to make a solid contribution, and she wanted to help her husband. Although such purity of motive undoubtedly is its own reward, in the business world Joyce Wrenn's efforts couldn't help but pay off in other ways. "By the time I had put him through seven years of school, I had established a career," she notes, "and that's really the way my career came about."

After Bruce earned his master's degree, he got a doctoral fellowship at Stanford University in Palo Alto, so Joyce naturally looked for a job in the Bay Area. In 1961 she became a programmer in IBM's Advanced Systems Development Division.

In 1961, of course, "computer" was still an exotic word, commonly linked with science fiction scenarios. The computers of the day were still impressively large, and programmers were generally regarded as a mysterious breed—almost alien, with their own language and esoterica. "People never really understood when I told them what I did," Wrenn recalls. "It's so refreshing today. I can say I work on software and they understand."

Besides astounding changes in the computer itself, the last quarter of a century has also seen marked changes in the realities of programming. Instead of typing instructions directly into the computer using a keyboard, as even six-year-olds nonchalantly do today, software programmers wrote by hand on coding sheets, which were then keypunched onto thousands of punched cards or a long paper tape to be fed (excruciatingly slowly, by today's standards) into a card reader to the "brains" of the computer itself. The results were likely to come back to the programmer days later.

Still, compared with the electromechanical adding machines that preceded it, the computer was regarded as fleet-footed in its youth. Above all, it was mysterious. In those early days, the big computer was locked away in a back room, attended by experts who alone could unlock the secrets of computing. It was into this elite coterie of the early programmers and its outwardly strange atmosphere that Wrenn was admitted.

Her seriousness of purpose, high energy level, and intelligence soon pushed Wrenn out in front; after only four years at IBM she had jumped into the ranks of management. "In 1965 there were very few women in management, and I was competing with male managers," she recalls. "I interviewed men [applying for jobs] who had never been interviewed by a woman before. In those years it was a subject I always addressed in terms of their level of comfort in working for a woman, and I thought we should address it up front," she explains. "With most of them it was not a problem, but with some it definitely was a problem and it was better to recognize it right at the beginning."

In 1967 Wrenn was named financial applications development manager in the Service Bureau Corp., then an IBM subsidiary. From overseeing a staff of about nine people, Wrenn suddenly had 30 to 35 people reporting directly to her. "To manage that number of people and get the right kind of product out the door was the greatest challenge I'd faced up to that point," she says.

Of course, that was just the beginning of her steady climb up the IBM organization chart. "Every time I got a promotion I had more and more people reporting to me," she says. And the promotions came as predictably as the tide.

Whether sewing her own clothes in high school or programming IBM mainframes, Wrenn has always derived deep satisfaction from her own creativity. In the early sixties, she invented the application customizer, a software program that allowed users literally to "fill in the blanks" in creating their own commands to get a customized-application software package. Although commonplace today, in the early sixties that software technology was "pretty far-reaching," she says. IBM, often slow to announce its own new technologies, finally announced the application customizer in 1970 and applied for a patent for it.

The application customizer is one of the achievements of which Wrenn is the proudest. And, true to its reputation, IBM was very generous in its praise. Wrenn was honored at an awards dinner and got "a nice check, which I promptly used to go off to Australia and New Zealand for a six-week vacation with my family."

Wrenn also holds dear another, less obvious, distinction. "Everything I've worked on at IBM has seen the light of day," she says. "I haven't worked on major projects that were killed, and that often happens in a development environment."

It would be almost 20 years after Wrenn joined IBM that Big Blue would reevaluate its commitment to strictly powerhouse computers and embrace the infant microcomputer. Wrenn would be right there, bringing her expertise with the big machines and her fascination with the small machines to IBM's legendary development team in Boca Raton, Florida.

Therese Myers: The Need to Achieve

Sometimes it is one's surroundings that gently—even imperceptibly—prod a person in a particular direction. Therese Myers claims to have had no particular goal in life as a child and to have done nothing that would remotely suggest what she's doing now.

There is some evidence, however, that her interest in business came from her family, which was populated with businesspeople. "My mother's and father's families always had their own businesses," she says. Her father, for example, had a small auto parts chain, and her uncle owned a steel-sheet-metal company.

McKeesport, Pennsylvania, a small and rather uninspiring steel mill town just outside Pittsburgh, is where Terry Myers spent her girlhood. The memorable movie *The Deer Hunter,* filmed in a neighboring town, gave a harshly accurate depiction of the area. Although today the mill of McKeesport is silent, during Myers's childhood it was the very heartbeat of the town. "You always saw the red sky," she recalls.

Moviegoers may remember soot and grime as the chief characteristics of Pittsburgh's environs. But Myers's early life was not nearly as grim as the lives of *The Deer Hunter*'s characters. She was lucky enough to be born into a relatively well-off pocket of the community, where most of the adults were college-educated (as would be most of their children).

Myers even managed to squeeze the bucolic out of a landscape that pressed its nose against industry. A few miles from the hissing steel mills was a 600-acre farm where Terry kept and rode a horse. "It wasn't like here in California where they have all these nice riding rings and you see little kids in riding outfits," she's quick to point out. "They were actually farming the land and I just had my horse there."

Born July 1, 1944, Terry was the only child of Harold and Eleanor Myers. When Terry was 13, her father died, leaving a painful void emotionally, but giving mother and daughter the financial means to enjoy life in a way Terry had never dreamed of. "After my father died, my mother and I went somewhere every summer—to different places in Europe and South America," Myers recalls. "It was so incredible because I met people all over the world and they were all so interesting."

This was a far cry from the general populace of McKeesport. Suddenly, she was not spending hours with the farm kids, but rather with very sophisticated adults. "The exposure to the world changed my life," she says. "The exposure to Europe, to ideas, to different cultures was just enormous, just absolutely marvelous."

She was always an excellent student, but her travels added a further rich dimension to her education. In school, however, Myers didn't consider herself competitive or ambitious, but rather "an achiever." Even now, she says, "I'm much more interested in the product: the process of getting a product to be a hit."

Myers never held a job until the summer between her two years in graduate school at Pittsburgh's Carnegie-Mellon University. But the first job she took was to have a profound influence on her career.

During Myers's first year of studying industrial administration in grad school, an assistant cashier from the overseas division of Citicorp—the holding company for Citibank, the nation's largest bank—went to Carnegie-Mellon looking for summer recruits. John Reed, who eventually became Citicorp's chairman, interviewed Myers and asked her to come work with him.

"The day I got to work, Walter Wriston was promoted to president of Citicorp, John went with him, and Tony Nicholas took John's job," Myers recalls. So it was Tony Nicholas she worked with in the overseas division, in a twist of fate that would follow Myers long after the summer ended. "My whole career was influenced by Citicorp," she says now.

And within Citicorp, Tony Nicholas's effect was most profound. While she had "quite a few" mentors at Citicorp, she says, "Tony was unique. Citicorp was hiring a lot of young people then and Tony included me in everything." Being privy to the style and substance of an experienced manager was invaluable to the young up-and-comer. "He was wonderful," she says. "I learned a lot from seeing his way of dealing with people."

After her summer at Citicorp, Myers went back to school as planned. She graduated from Carnegie-Mellon in 1968, then went back to New York to work for Arthur Young & Co. as part of its experimental and exceptional Non-Accounting Major Program, under which she and 29 others from nonaccounting backgrounds were selected to learn accounting, at Arthur Young's expense.

Arthur Young sent the 30 recruits to summer school for two consecutive years at Northwestern University in Chicago, and they all emerged with master's degrees in accounting. The rest of the year, Myers was on the firm's audit and consulting staff, where she specialized in designing management and accounting systems.

So noteworthy was Arthur Young's experiment that, during Myers's second summer at Northwestern in 1970, the program was written up in *The New York Times* in an article that featured Myers. When Tony Nicholas picked up the newspaper that day, he saw Myers's picture and found himself reading about his former protégée. What he read he liked.

A phone call later, he had convinced Myers to go work with him again. At that time, Nicholas was heading up Citicorp Leasing in New York, "so I went in [as an assistant vice president of Citicorp Leasing] and helped him set up Citicorp's middle-market leasing organization," she recalls.

Nicholas left that division in 1971 to work again for John Reed, who had bought a company in Los Angeles for Citibank and set it up as a subsidiary called Transaction Technology, Inc. (TTI), to develop on-line systems for Master Charge (now MasterCard) credit evaluation and Citibank check-cashing services. Nicholas and Reed both remained based in New York.

It wasn't long before Myers's phone rang again with another offer from Nicholas. "Tony asked me if I wouldn't like to go to California for six weeks." She jumped at the chance. "My roommate at Carnegie-Mellon had moved to California and married a wonderful person, so I thought, 'I'm gonna go there!' I had no intention of going back [East]." And she didn't have to. After the six weeks were up, the firm asked her to stay on.

From 1972 to 1974, still an assistant vice president, Myers oversaw TTI's administrative and financial operations. While there, she met Gary Pope, who would later become Quarterdeck's co-founder and her closest partner, in a rather unusual encounter.

In 1973, TTI decided to test the security of its automatic-teller credit card system by sponsoring a contest, open to California Institute of Technology seniors only, challenging them to defraud its credit cards. Myers would act as one of the judges.

"The contest was to prove that credit cards with magnetic stripes could be defrauded," Myers explains, "and to show how easily it could be done." Today, of course, the data on magnetic stripes are encoded, but in 1973 the stripes contained actual, readable information. The banking industry at large was advocating the stripes as a standard, but in reality it was very easy to change the information on a card.

"[The contest] was an intimidating experience," recalls Pope, who was studying math and computer science at Cal Tech. Nevertheless, he managed to "defraud" TTI while its top management looked on. Out of 25 entrants, he won third prize by using a simple $4 item that read the information off the magnetic stripe and made a copy of the data. All the other entrants came up with successful ways of defrauding the cards as well.

Naturally, the company offered many of the entrants jobs. After graduation, Pope joined TTI, which immediately set him to the appropriate task of evaluating the security of various credit card encoding techniques.

Like a television network with a hit series, Citicorp created a TTI spinoff in 1974, when TTI's chairman, Jack Scantlin, left to form a company called Lexar Corp. He took Myers and Pope with him.

"Lexar was 100 percent funded by Citicorp and chartered to do for the corporate bank what we had just done in the consumer bank," Myers explains. "We had full rein to do whatever we wanted to do."

For two years, with Myers as vice president of product design and Pope as software programmer, they worked on developing a Telex encryptor security system for Citicorp's international Telex operations. It was the first time Myers had worked directly with computer technology. Then, in 1976, Scantlin got another idea: that what the bank needed was an integrated voice and data network, consisting of computer workstations with a central digital PABX (private automatic branch exchange) for secretaries and professionals. His team ran with it.

"We were the first ones to go on the circuit to talk about a professional worker using a computer, back in 1976 and 1977," Myers says. That was several years before the general acceptance of the idea that the major market for small computers was the business world.

In 1977, Scantlin convinced Citibank to finance the development of an office automation system. Pope was promoted to manager of system software, and he oversaw the creation of software subsystems for the prototype. By the summer of 1978, Lexar Corp. had delivered the Lexar System 90.

The System 90 comprised 30 workstations, one for each of 15 executive vice presidents and their 15 secretaries. The system, built around a microprocessor very similar to the one that would be used in IBM's Personal Computer three years later, had full integrated software: word processing, electronic mail, a link to mainframe computers, forms design, database management, telephone messages, "and everything you hear of today," Myers says.

That level of integration played into the way executives actually spend their days. Not only do they face frequent interruptions, but they usually perform simultaneous, related tasks, such as analyzing data about a project to write a progress report. Citicorp's managers were overjoyed to have a computer system that had actually been built around their needs. Until that point, they had had to adjust their habits to the computer's functions and schedule. Furthermore, traditional systems were usable only for single-track work; there was no quick jumping around from task to task.

The product was a hit with everyone who saw it. In 1979, three key industry analysts separately ranked the product first or second in price/performance out of the top 15 existing office automation systems. The other comparable system was one from office automation giant Wang Laboratories, Inc.

How did a small group like Lexar get such high marks? "We understood integrated software," Myers explains. That may not seem remarkable today, but 1978 was a full five years before the introduction of the first popular integrated software package, Lotus 1-2-3.

The insight of Lexar's team members has taken them a long way. "Everything we're doing at Quarterdeck today is a derivative of the System 90," Myers explains. She also gives credit to mentor Jack Scantlin for imparting "his high standards of quality."

Citicorp so liked Lexar's work that it decided to buy the company. Citicorp bought Lexar in 1979 and set it up as two subsidiaries called Lexar Corp., to produce a large, digital PABX phone system, and Axxa Corp., to produce the System 90. At Axxa, Myers was a principal, director, and vice president of product management, and Pope was a principal and vice president of software engineering.

Axxa proceeded to manufacture the product and, with high hopes, took it to market in January 1980. No one there could have known that the crucial element of timing was fatally askew. Three months after Axxa brought out its product, a federal banking ruling came down prohibiting banks from selling hardware. There was nothing for Citicorp to do but divest itself of both Lexar and Axxa.

Citicorp sold Lexar to United Technologies and Axxa to the Swedish conglomerate Anaconda-Ericsson. "And we left," Myers says. "But we understood, better than anybody, both whom we were targeting and also the shortcomings of the system we had developed."

The major failing of the system they had created lay in its inflexibility, Myers had discovered. "Many of the users were up on the latest things in personal computing," Myers recalls. "We had to tell them, for example, 'No, we can't add VisiCalc.' " So the system developers found themselves always scrambling to keep up with the users' demands.

They also faced the old familiar problem of mainframe-based systems: inaccessibility. "The managers couldn't get into the system to customize the functions they used," she says. "Even something as simple as a request to 'Move this column over to the other side of that column' had to be handled by a programmer."

After the sale of Axxa, Myers and Pope started thinking about taking their favorite project several steps further. "We said, 'My gosh, this should be running on a personal computer, and it should be software that's operating-system-independent. It should be hardware-independent and, besides that, it should run everybody else's software.' So we said, 'Let's just start it and see if we can do it,' " Myers recalls. It really was the divestiture alone that pushed Myers and Pope out of the Citicorp nest. If not for the fateful federal ruling and Citicorp's necessary response, Quarterdeck would never have been born.

Myers and Pope—along with Axxa colleagues Jill Eastman and Michael Kuppin—formed a partnership in September 1981 to study the feasibility of starting their own company. Eastman and Kuppin both had jobs, while Myers and Pope (the idea people) lived for a year without salaries, working out of the proverbial garage. "That was the best year we ever had in the business,"

Myers laughs. "I'd get on my bike and ride down to this place [the garage] and be there for a couple of hours."

The preliminary studies over, they decided to go ahead, so in September 1982 they converted their partnership into a company and named it Quarterdeck Office Systems. All but Kuppin, who left early in 1987, have remained with the company.

Quarterdeck's timing was perfect. The year 1982 still meant a bonanza for high-tech start-ups looking for cash, and within a month Quarterdeck had easily attracted $800,000 from three venture capital funds to finance the development of a prototype. From Axxa they lured another seven employees and now they had a talented team that had worked together since 1977. Young and innovative, with a good product and the ability to attract venture capital, Quarterdeck was suddenly a company to watch.

Janelle Bedke: Ready to Take a Risk

Janelle Bedke embodies perfectly the attitude that begets success. In 1980, after ten and a half years with the established, well-respected Hewlett-Packard Co., Bedke left her very secure and high-paying position to start Software Publishing Corp. (SPC) on a shoestring.

Although she was leaving a fast-track career for an uncertain future, Bedke didn't even grit her teeth. She was feeling increasingly dissatisfied with the corporate experience. "HP got to be a large company and it was difficult to see any direct results," she says. "Things bubbled up into the system, and I was never sure I had made a difference. It was frustrating.

"I didn't have a lot of fears and doubts because part of me was so sure that if Fred [Gibbons], John [Page], and I couldn't do it, who could?" she says. John Page was a 12-year veteran of HP and a database-management software expert. Fred Gibbons, then a marketing manager, had been at HP for five years.

Bedke really wasn't worried. "I don't have a big fear of failure," she says. "Somehow, some way, I wouldn't let it not work. I don't know why I feel this way; possibly it's from my parents. Or if, in the history of a life, someone has endured many failures, maybe that person is gun-shy or not trying hard enough."

Although Bedke took a big risk indeed, she can't take credit for the idea itself. "It was really not until 1979 when I met Fred and began to talk to him about some of his ideas that the idea of leaving HP and starting out on my own really occurred to me," Bedke says. "He was the catalyst for me. I don't know that I would have done it without him."

As for Gibbons, he was sure it was Bedke he wanted as a partner. "It was very clear to me that she was an outstanding doer," Gibbons explains. "By that I mean that she had complete command of the technical details of the projects she had worked on, complete command of the execution details of taking a product into manufacturing and getting it out to the customer, so she just was an exceptional doer."

Once catalyzed, Bedke was the first of the three cofounders to take the plunge. She quit her job and, drawing no salary for a year, she started Software Publishing in her living room, working many 16-hour days. "It was a long decision [to leave HP], but once I made it, it was really easy," she says. "I never regretted a moment at HP and I never regretted leaving."

Where did Bedke get her deep belief in her own abilities? Part of it, as Lore Harp suggests regarding herself, was the positive reinforcement she got from every success she ever achieved. Another part of it started long before Bedke had a chance to show anyone her stuff.

"My father encouraged us very strongly academically," she says. "There was no doubt I'd go to college and have a career." Janelle and her three sisters listened well: They were all excellent students and are now very successful. One is a physician, one is a pharmacist, and one does technical support for a small computer company.

Janelle was born in Sacramento, California, on November 20, 1948, the third of the four daughters. In one of the obscure coincidences of the industry, Bedke lived in Germany for a time as an "Air Force brat" while Lore Harp was growing up there.

The Bedkes also lived in Washington, D.C.; Hawaii; and Salt Lake City, where they eventually settled. "Every three years there was a new environment and a new school," Janelle recalls. "That allowed me to be flexible and adaptable."

Even constant change did not slow her down academically. "I probably compete with myself more than anything else," she says. "I'm comfortable doing the best job I can." The best job she could do was very often the best job, period.

She was a top student wherever she went, with a particular affinity for mathematics. "It's a beautiful thing," she says of math. "It works. It has a symmetry." Her academic excellence made her senior year in high school superfluous, and she went directly to the University of Utah at age 16.

In her sophomore year in college, she started to wonder what she could do in the world with her beloved mathematics. "Between teaching and research, neither thrilled me," she recalls, although those seemed to be the only alternatives for pursuing math in its pure form.

At the time, the seeds of computer science as an academic discipline had just been sown and, fortunately for Bedke, the University of Utah planted early. "Computer science incorporated the same logical principles that I'd learned in math," Bedke says. "It was problem solving and yet doing it in a real way that got real results. That was the excitement for me."

Although no undergraduate computer science degree existed at the time, she took all the available computer science courses, in addition to the science and engineering courses necessary for a math major. "I was the only woman in most of my classes," she recalls. Only 1 or 2 percent of the hundreds of students in the computer science and math programs were female.

"I was lucky to be an early entrant," she feels. Lucky and smart. By the time her graduation was in sight (magna cum laude, 1969), high-tech firms had started courting the qualified in high style. During her last year at the university, Bedke interviewed with many big-name companies, including IBM, Control Data, Hewlett-Packard, Bell Labs, and General Electric. "I was wined and dined and flown all over the country," she recalls. Very exciting for a 20-year-old.

She decided to go with HP, and immediately after graduating, Bedke flew out to Palo Alto, California. "At HP, I actually touched a computer for the first time," she recalls. It was a minicomputer, the smallest computer she (or anyone else) had ever seen. As a student of computer science, she had written programming code on so-called dumb terminals hooked up to a very large and powerful mainframe computer, completely hidden from sight in some back room.

At HP, her raw talent and ambition meant instant recognition and success. Her first job was as an R&D software development engineer for HP's minicomputer line. For five years her work revolved around software development for minicomputers, and she moved rapidly up through HP's ranks.

By 1974, the company was putting the microprocessor chip into some of its terminals, and Bedke gravitated toward those "intelligent" terminals. She became R&D project manager for HP's microprocessor-based terminal line, the first woman at HP in a management position in the engineering lab.

In this position she was developing the technology of the future. "There's a fine line between an intelligent terminal and a microcomputer," she explains. By the time the intelligent terminal had unquestionably evolved into the microcomputer, Bedke had already realized the true value of the small machines. "The excitement and the intrigue for me were just that the computer became more and more usable by more people."

By 1979 the personal computer revolution had caught fire, and entrepreneurs were itching to throw their logs on the flames. One of them was Fred Gibbons, who had joined HP in 1975 and had held a number of product management and marketing management roles for the firm.

In Bedke he recognized the spirit, intelligence, and determination necessary for the project he had in mind. And in him she recognized a brilliant idea: easy-to-use software designed for business executives. Together they would open people's eyes to a need that most software developers had overlooked.

Ann Winblad: Creating Something Out of Thin Air

"I've never had any problem making money," says Ann Winblad. And "never" means exactly that. Even as a child, she knew the secrets of turning a profit.

Now a young millionaire, Winblad had a happy childhood in a small Minnesota town, in a family that substituted creativity for wealth. Her father was a popular teacher and athletic coach "with a heart of gold" who took on extra jobs to make ends meet. "The most he made was $10,000 a year when I was a kid," Winblad says.

Even in the 1950s, that didn't go so far, especially with five daughters and a son to support. But Wilbur "Soup" Winblad (so named from an early "soup bowl" haircut) was very clever, Ann remembers. "Instead of taking us to the clothing store, where we'd see the most expensive dresses but couldn't have them, he'd bring home ten little dresses each for two of my sisters and me, and we'd pick out the three we liked best." So, in place of feeling disappointment or envy, "we felt very wealthy," she says. "We had lots of choices and we felt we got the best dresses." Soup Winblad was demonstrating perfectly the Isaacson-like knack of turning a bad situation into a good one.

And Ann proved herself just as creative in solving problems. To earn money one summer for her childish needs, she didn't mow lawns or wash windows; she drew pictures. "I was a good artist," she recalls. "I drew 100 pictures, got my sisters to color them, and held an art fair, where I sold them for 5 cents each."

In the 1950s Barbie dolls were the rage among little girls, but instead of joining the madness, Winblad took full advantage of this weakness in her compatriots. "On the sewing machine, I made clothes for Barbie dolls and charged exhorbitant prices for them. Even my sisters had to pay." She wasn't totally money-hungry, she insists. She let her sisters earn money by helping her in the shop.

A couple of years later, at age ten, she got her first official paying job, picking strawberries at a nickel a pint. After working in the strawberry fields, Ann would spend her nights sewing to earn more money for movies and clothes for herself. "I was real busy getting money from the 8- and 9-year-olds," she recalls.

In spite of her hard work, Winblad's childhood was an idyllic existence sheltered from many of the harsher realities of life. Farmington, Minnesota, as its name suggests, was an agricultural community—population 2,000. "When I grew up I thought the entire American economy was based on farmers, nurses, and schoolteachers," Winblad says. "I'd never seen a business in operation until I was in high school."

There was one drawback to this quiet life, especially for an intelligent, high-spirited young girl. "I remember being so bored," Winblad says, "thinking there must be something else, something bigger out there. I have a high energy level—I don't know where it comes from—but when other people are getting tired, I'm still awake."

She was born November 1, 1950, the oldest of the six children. Although she was contemporary with the first generation that grew up "glued to the set," her family didn't own a television until she was eight. "No one had one," she recalls.

Having no television meant that her imagination worked overtime, but it also limited her view of the world. "Living in a small town and searching for possible identities was something like being on an island," she remembers. "Where do you go? You couldn't ask anyone. Most of the people in the town knew what you knew." Like Isaacson, she found that reading was the only way to see past her physical boundaries.

In grade school she read every biography in the town library. "There weren't too many," she laughs. It struck her that the biographies of women—Sarah Bernhardt, Isadora Duncan, Anna Pavlova, and Marie Curie—were inordinately tragic, filled with trials and disasters. She preferred the stories of men. "The Wright brothers, for example," she says, "were so happy and so smart, and they created something out of thin air."

In contrast to Portia Isaacson, who took Madame Curie's tribulations to heart in a most poignant way, Winblad found such suffering unnecessary and somehow disappointing. Winblad preferred to imagine herself soaring above trouble and tragedy like the happy Wright brothers. She, too, wanted to create something out of thin air—like the Barbie doll dresses.

Winblad's innate business instincts began their refinement in high school, when she got a job after school and during summers in a local pool-table factory. She officially was a mail clerk, although she would also fill in for whoever was on vacation. "One week I'd be the accounts receivable clerk and the next week I'd be the assistant to the president," she laughs.

"I got to do every job once," she remembers. "It was like being in a live small business course, where you moved around to each station and in real time you did the job." Naturally, she learned a lot about how a business operates.

Her next-younger sister, meanwhile, characteristically was relegated to wielding a staple gun on the factory floor "while I worked in the air-conditioned business office," Ann remembers. That sort of pecking order seemed appropriate and right to Ann, who from the start assumed a leadership position: first in the family and, later, in school. In high school, Ann was active in many clubs, the school newspaper, and cheerleading, having inherited a great deal of athletic prowess from Soup, a former basketball and football star. She was president of the National Honor Society and valedictorian of her graduating class. She was, in all areas of endeavor, stellar.

At St. Catherine's women's college in St. Paul, she continued her reputation for excellence as one of 25 "experimental students" who were allowed to study whatever they wanted. That meant she could skip many introductory courses and get right to the interesting material, even in subjects far removed from her major of math. "It made you get up to speed very fast," she says.

Most of her math classes were held at St. Thomas College, a male branch of the five-college cooperative that included St. Catherine's. There she learned math alongside "20 unique guys," as she puts it. "We talked about math. No one at [the all-female] St. Catherine's talked about theorems."

By the time she was a junior, she was the only female in her math classes. That didn't bother her except that she "couldn't make jokes with the math students, they were so serious." That's when business caught her eye. "It was like a curtain opening. It was novel, new, and interesting," she says. "It was very much like math, in that it had to do with understanding systems. In fact," she claims, "anyone who's good in math has the potential to be a good manager from what he or she learned in math."

She also fell in love with computer science and became "one of the best programmers on campus," she says. After earning a B.A. degree in mathematics and business administration/management from St. Catherine's and a master's in education and economics from St. Thomas, she took a systems analysis job in

Minneapolis. But sequestered in her cubicle at the elegant Federal Reserve Bank, it didn't take long before utter boredom set in.

"My expectations were pretty high after college," she recalls. Although she earned a very good salary and got frequent promotions, it just wasn't enough. There was no excitement, no challenge. Indeed, most of the people at the Federal Reserve were content to do their jobs "like in a factory, not really thinking about things," she says.

"My cubicle-mate watched *I Dream of Jeannie* [and other sitcoms] every day from 1:00 to 3:00 on a portable TV with a beer in his hand, and then he left at 4:30," she says. "No one ever knew." Winblad became increasingly disenchanted. "It was like a bowling team there: no teamwork, half-drunk, and no strategy," she says. "I wanted to be on a football team."

The last straw was the day the bank offered her a several-thousand-dollar raise for her "enthusiasm." She turned it down, thinking, "Tell me what I've done, then give me a raise." She quit a week later, thereby escaping the disillusionment to which she feels many people succumb. After a year and a half, she had decided not to "settle," but rather to find out whether life had anything better to offer.

"Tons of people come from small towns knowing they can do a lot," she observes. "Their capabilities need to be pushed. But they get into a situation like that and wonder, 'Is this the way life is?' They calm down, acclimate, and just stay there instead of looking for other jobs."

Not Winblad. Out of her quest for something more from life, she found a job teaching programming at Normandale Community College and did consulting at the Minnesota School of Business.

Her consulting work included an offer to write some accounting applications for a vocational school. Even though she didn't know the first thing about accounting, Winblad was always one for a challenge. She recruited her then-boyfriend and future cofounder of Open Systems, Dan Webb, to help her. "No one else was willing to do it," Webb says, "and our enthusiasm level was high." For most of 1975, the pair studied accounting. "We were totally unqualified to do the project," Winblad says. "We worked day and night, even sleeping at the school to get an early start."

Having finished it, however, they found themselves very qualified to take on other accounting development jobs. So, with the idea of starting a company, Webb and Winblad recruited two talented friends from the Federal Reserve, Gary MacHalec and Tim Dickinson, both of whom were refreshing exceptions to the sleepwalking rule.

Winblad was excited, but she felt quite alone. "I had no role models in business, and Minnesota is not really an entrepreneurial place," she says. "There was no computer activity there. Everyone thought I was nuts to do this. 'What's computer stuff?' they'd ask." 1976 was still early in the game; at that point, Harp and Isaacson were the only other two of these ten women who were actually involved with the microcomputer.

But at least three people in Minneapolis didn't think Winblad was nuts. The foursome went in on the deal in February 1976 with only $500 from Winblad's and Tim Dickinson's personal savings. Once again, Winblad would create something out of thin air.

Esther Dyson: Intellectual Blue Blood

Talent, inspiration, drive, and hard work notwithstanding, sometimes the very circumstances of one's birth practically guarantee success. Esther Dyson was perhaps the most "favored" of this group of ten women, having been born with the intellectual equivalent of a silver spoon in her mouth.

Her mother, Verena Huber Dyson, is a Swiss mathematician who teaches at the University of Calgary. Her father is English-born Freeman Dyson, former wunderkind and now a well-known physicist and the author of several books, including the autobiographical *Disturbing the Universe.* He is a Fellow at the Institute for Advanced Studies in Princeton, New Jersey. They divorced when Esther was seven, and the children lived with their father.

The eminent physicist Hans Bethe once said of Freeman, "Here was a man who could do everything with his left hand, and spend the rest of the day reading *The New York Times.*"

Freeman's father was Sir George Dyson, director of the Royal College of Music in London.

When Freeman and Verena met and married, she was a young mathematician and he a young physicist at the Institute for Advanced Studies. There at the same time was the legendary Albert Einstein, then a very senior member of the staff, until his death in 1955. Esther, fortunate enough to meet one of the most creative intellects in human history, was regretfully only two or three years old at the time.

Although Esther has not followed precisely in her father's scientific footsteps, she has deep respect for him and feels that she has inherited his drive. "He expected I'd do something worthwhile," she says, "but he never expressed that he'd be disappointed if I wasn't famous for anything."

Is she in any way in competition with her famous father? "No, I've carefully avoided that, in one sense," she says. "I grew up thinking I'd probably be a novelist or an astronaut. Then at one point I thought I'd be a physicist. I think it was because he was a physicist that I thought maybe I *should* be one," she explains.

"I took physics in college, but I really wasn't very interested in it. It seemed very dry. I like parlor-game math and I'm good at it, but I'm just too fascinated by people and uncertainty, and I'd much rather design an expert system than a theorem. And then I decided . . . certainly I decided there was no way I'd ever be as good as he was and, not only that, but I wasn't even good at it at all," she says. "I wanted to understand how the world worked, and I decided the way to understand that was through business, so I majored in economics."

Although she and her father are in different fields, Esther hopes she has inherited his outlook on life so that she can be described as she describes him, "a dreamer who's awake—someone with no illusions but who is not cynical or bitter and is still able to be passionate and romantic about life."

So romantic and yet grounded is Freeman Dyson that in 1958 he went on leave from the Institute to join 40 other scientists in La Jolla, California, to work on Project Orion—the design of a nuclear-powered rocket. Dyson's dream was to personally travel to Mars by 1964 and to Saturn by 1970. In the post-Sputnik era, such dreams were indulged by the U.S. government for several years, until the mood of the country gradually shifted.

Like her father, Esther has her eye trained on the cutting edge of a technology that has irrevocably changed our world. And her perceptions and analyses of that technology have helped shape an entire industry. "She was always very much an original," Freeman Dyson says. "She liked to do everything her own way. It was clear she wasn't going to follow the beaten path."

Dyson was somewhat of a child entrepreneur, just as Winblad was, although not out of a desire to make money. Dyson started her first newspaper when she was eight years old. Although its subject matter and readership did not extend beyond the bounds of her family home, the *Dyson Gazette* proved to be a portentous enterprise.

"I don't remember all the motivations behind it, but clearly I enjoyed writing and journalism and things like that," she says. The project lasted about eight issues, all of which she wrote in ballpoint pen, using "lots of carbon paper." Circulated for free among family members, it described such homely events as, "Dorothy lost a tooth" and "We got a new cat." Esther's hard-hitting analyses came later in life.

Esther Dyson was born July 14, 1951, in Switzerland, her mother's homeland. As a child writer, it was natural that Dyson was a reader as well. In the first grade, she was regularly sent out into the hall—not because she was a cut-up, but so that she could study material ahead of the rest of the class. She skipped fourth grade altogether. At 15 she was accepted by Harvard University.

In spite of her obvious intellectual gifts, she was not considered precocious, at least not at home. "Certainly not in my family," she says. "We never felt extraordinary at all." And the home atmosphere, she assures, was not esoteric. "We didn't sit around talking about physics," Dyson says.

On the other hand, they didn't sit around watching television, either. "We didn't have one and we didn't ask for one," she remembers. "When my father was on TV once, we went to the neighbor's house to watch him." It wasn't a question of money as much as attitude, although her father's alimony payments necessarily took something away from Esther, her younger brother George, and their four younger half-sisters. "There was a self-imposed frugality in the household, a general prejudice against spending money," she recalls. "I'm like that now. I'll take the subway instead of a taxi."

In place of opulence, there was what Dyson calls "a wealth of experience." As a small child, for example, she traveled to Europe several times with her family. When she was seven, Esther lived with her father in California for a year (while he worked on Project Orion), and she lived with family friends in London at age 13 while attending the English equivalent of public school there.

She has continued traveling as an adult, with almost constant business trips within the United States, as well as to Europe and Japan. "I really love it and I love seeing America," she says. "I just like the feeling that I belong all over the world, that the world is mine to roam around in."

Her serious approach to academics ended with her high school career, which, while impressive, wasn't much fun for her. "I was this very wimpy kid in high school," she says. "I was a real drip. I never went out with boys or anything, but I was smart enough to know that maybe I should, and the only way to do that was to leave home and go to college."

So off to Harvard she went at 16. There she "had a great time" and consequently almost flunked out her freshman year. "They called me in and said I was a real disappointment because they'd accepted me under their early admissions program," she recalls. "I had gotten very lazy. I stopped taking heavy-duty math courses. I just wasn't cut out to be a student.

"I spent most of my time working on the *Harvard Crimson* and went to one or two classes," she says. Esther recalls with amusement her mother's visit in November of that year, when she had an appointment with another mathematician at Harvard. "I said, 'Terrific, I have a class in that building around that time. I'll take you.' And I couldn't find it.

"But it's incredible—once they let you into Harvard, they don't want to admit they made a mistake," she says, "so I actually got mostly A's and B's after my first year without really working."

She saved her best efforts for enjoying life. "From observation, I knew very well how to be a good teenager." So she went about being one. At 17, she paid her own way to Europe and lived in

Morocco for two months with her boyfriend, who was serving in the Peace Corps there. It wasn't that she was a wild child, by any means. "I think I'm probably more straitlaced than your average young single woman," she says. "I know I am. I'm also much more discreet. At 17, I was—whatever you want to call it—I was mature."

Mature or not, her parents refused to bankroll her adventure and made it clear that any untoward consequences would be hers alone to face. "My father said, 'If you want to come back, I won't pay the plane fare,' " she recalls. "And they said if I got pregnant, they wouldn't pay for an abortion."

But she came away unscathed and went back to Harvard. Then at 21, she took half a year off from Harvard to work in London. "It was a fly-by-night news agency, and I had a lot of fun," she says. "I was writing and rewriting press releases—there wasn't much real reporting. I knew I was being exploited, but I didn't care. I wanted to live in London and have a job."

At last, Dyson managed to graduate respectably in 1972 with a degree in economics. From Cambridge she moved to New York City and held a couple of jobs that didn't really thrill her. For nine months she worked for Viacom, writing sales promotions for syndicated television shows. She didn't particularly like it. "I thought I was very lazy."

From there, she went to work for the Bureau of Business Practice, a subsidiary of Prentice-Hall, writing helpful hints for office workers. Such masterpieces as "Ten Tips to Improve Your Typing" were tucked into typists' paycheck envelopes. The job was fun, but at that point she was still "very lazy" about her work, she maintains.

But her laziness completely disappeared when she got a job in 1973 as a research fellow for the Council on Economic Priorities. She was project manager and researcher for a publication called *Help Wanted: Employment of Women and Minorities in Retailing.* "I loved it," she says. "I've been working seven days a week ever since."

While at the Council, Dyson applied for a job at *Forbes* magazine, but the company wasn't hiring. A year later she applied again, "so they knew I was persistent. Also, having been an editor at the *Harvard Crimson* helped." In November 1974, she got a "crummy little research job" at *Forbes* and after six months was promoted to business reporter.

"It always was a great job," she says. In fact, it was *Forbes,* not Harvard, that taught her about business. "Economics has nothing to do with business," she explains. *Forbes,* on the other hand, was the best business education she could have gotten. "The staff was so good that I hardly ever dared to say anything at the weekly staff meetings. Even while it was happening, I remember sitting there feeling very privileged to be a part of it."

After three years at *Forbes,* she moved over to Wall Street as a securities analyst for New Court Securities Corp. (now Rothschild, Inc.), where she followed the stock fortunes of primarily high-tech companies.

Two and a half years later, in 1980, she joined Oppenheimer & Co. as a vice president and continued to specialize in the microcomputer and software industries. Her boss at Oppenheimer was Thomas Piper, who subsequently went to Dillon, Read & Co., Inc.

"Esther was hard-working almost beyond compare," Piper recalls. She once took a vacation trip to Japan, he remembers, but instead of sightseeing, she made appointments with Japanese electronics firms. "She said that would be more interesting for her." On her return to New York, instead of handing around snapshots of her vacation, the information hound wrote up a research report. "The report was so well received that the head of one of our client companies called her up and invited her out to lunch to discuss what she had learned," Piper recounts. "This was someone that some analysts would have beat their heads against the wall to get an appointment with."

It was during this period that she "fell in love with the personal computer," Dyson says. She would soon change jobs and take a big pay cut to become intimately involved with the industry, and would spend the next several years at the very heart of it.

2
The Birth of an Industry

There's a difference between the people who got into the personal computer industry in the very early days, when there was still a lot of skepticism about the whole thing, and those who later sensed the excitement and joined in. The earlier entrants can be considered true pioneers of the technology and of the industry. As Ann Winblad recognizes in herself, "I would have been an explorer if I'd lived 100 years ago."

Winblad and the other pioneers really put themselves on the line with something that was so new that most people had never even heard of it. They're the ones who faced the blank stares of the majority of people who had no idea what a personal computer was, never mind what its larger significance would be.

In spite of being frequently misunderstood and sometimes not taken seriously, they persevered to build an industry that has changed—and will continue to change—the face of business, education, and communications, as well as countless other areas of endeavor.

Ann Winblad: "Lucky Stumbling"

The first time Ann Winblad gave a business presentation was to the brass from Cado Systems Corp. in the back of their warehouse in Torrance, California. She was 25 years old and looked about 19. "I stood on top of a crate and I was being very sweet and nice. I was trying to be businesslike, but I didn't know what that meant," she remembers.

During a break, one of the Cado people pulled her aside. "Ann, I'll only tell you this once. You've got to have a different approach with these guys." He passed on some advice he had gotten early in his career: "If you're gonna run with the big dogs, you have to learn how to lift your leg."

It wasn't at all what she had hoped to hear. "I was horrified," she remembers. Nevertheless, his words rang true. She realized she had to appeal to business people's business sense above all else.

Winblad was the first of the ten women in this book to actually start her own business, in February 1976, although within a few months Portia Isaacson would open one of the first microcomputer stores in the country (in Texas) and Lore Harp would also set up shop (in California).

Besides being the first, Winblad was also the youngest—by a considerable margin—when she started her own company. Only 25 in 1976, Winblad led three equally young cofounders in establishing Open Systems, Inc. in snowy Minneapolis, thousands of miles away from any significant computer activity.

Those who knew anything about computers thought accounting software would be difficult to sell. Nevertheless, Winblad, her then-boyfriend Dan Webb, and former Federal Reserve coworkers Tim Dickinson and Gary MacHalec incorporated as Open Systems. The real difficulty, as it turned out, was in developing the software. "Because accounting itself had already been defined, and isn't a broad subject like word processing, we had to work within the existing definitions, and we had to understand the different market areas very well," Winblad explains.

Inexperienced and isolated from the business and microcomputer mainstream, the quartet operated in something of a fog, yet they were exuberant and optimistic. "The time that was the most fun was when we didn't know what we were doing," Winblad recalls. "There was no success or failure, because we didn't really know what success or failure was. And in those days there was this attitude that it was okay to not know things, because nobody else did either."

"Ann likes to coin terms," Webb says, "and to explain our way of doing things, she used to say that we could figure out what we were doing quicker than others could figure out we didn't know what we were doing."

One of their first and wisest moves was the result of "lucky stumbling," Winblad says. "In the fall of 1976, we happened to stop into a couple of dealerships that were selling Cado computers." Cado Systems Corp. was selling its business-oriented low-end minicomputers as report writers (meaning that they could generate reports from raw financial data). Since the foursome had worked on the design of a mainframe-based multiuser computer system at the Federal Reserve, they talked their way into a contract with Cado to develop multiuser accounting software for its computer, thereby essentially redefining the machine.

Open's first contract set the tone for continuing sophistication in its software development work. Because of the complexity of Cado's Cadol operating system, the multiuser software Open Systems wrote for Cado's machines was necessarily very high-level work.

But after five months of writing software, Winblad and Webb came back from a vacation to find their office burned to the ground. With sinking hearts, they picked through the ashes. "The ceiling had fallen in on the programs—$20,000 worth of work," Winblad recalls. But the ceiling hadn't fallen in on Open Systems. "[The disks] were untouched. We washed them off and they were okay."

At the end of Year 1, spent mostly writing software, the partners took a loss totaling $85. It wasn't a profit, but neither was it what a veteran of the business wars would call devastating. Nevertheless, Winblad recalls, "We were crushed." As soon as they had actual products to sell, however, matters quickly improved.

From Cado, Open Systems crossed the fine line between low-end minicomputers and high-end microcomputers, again writing multiuser accounting software for a proprietary operating system, this time for giant NCR Corp. "This was 1978, before anyone had thought of the implications of microcomputers," Winblad recalls. "We went from one multiuser proprietary project to another."

They also started making money. That second year brought in almost $300,000 in sales. "So we were rolling." Most of their early deals were joint marketing agreements with hardware vendors, under which they sold their software as companion products to hardware systems. In 1979, sales went up to half a million dollars.

Around that time, Open started negotiating so-called original equipment manufacturing (OEM) deals, under which hardware vendors actually reproduced Open's software and put their own labels on it—Canon, Fujitsu, and Lanier, for example. By 1980, before the proliferation of retail computer stores, almost 40 percent of Open's business was in OEM agreements.

And the bottom line was getting fatter—doubling every year, in fact. In 1980 the company brought in $1 million, in 1981 it was $2 million, in 1982 about $3.5 million, and in 1983 sales again doubled to $7 million.

But, while it really was rolling, Open Systems still maintained a low profile, since many of its sales were under someone else's label. Its reliance on dealer support instead of out-and-out advertising also kept its visibility low.

That reticence, while it almost guaranteed Open's profitability, is Winblad's greatest regret. "We set our visions too small," she says, ruefully comparing Open's approach with Apple Computer's flamboyant history. Although it was quickly and steadily successful, Open Systems was never a glamour company like Apple.

Apple Computer started the same year as Open Systems and soon had a large cult following, based on the popularity of its then-groundbreaking machines. Four years later, it went public and made millionaires out of at least 100 Apple employees.

"[Apple founder] Steve Jobs told his people, 'Let's shoot for the moon!' " Winblad says. "We shot for Iowa." She worries that maybe she held her people back when they could have done much better, if given the chance. "The philosophy of a company dictates how far it can grow," she says. "We never said, 'We'll try for $25 million [in sales] and then go public.' We took a very safe path. We just wanted to make it profitable."

At the same time, of course, Open Systems' product was not nearly as accessible as everyman's Apple computer. With ten integrated software packages priced at $700 each, Open Systems attracted customers who were not at all the hobbyists who worshipped Apple, but instead serious business users with sophisticated business needs.

And therein lay something of a stumbling block for Winblad, who simply didn't in any way resemble her own typical customer, or even the industry people with whom she had to do business. As the head of her own company, she was still a demure woman in a business dominated by men. And, like anyone who starts a first business, she had to fight the phantom of inexperience.

Nevertheless, somewhat by default, she became the company's spokesperson. "Tim [Dickinson] is just a brilliant guy who can assimilate a lot of stuff and sort out what really makes sense in a product," she says, "but you get him in front of four people and he's totally tongue-tied and uncomfortable."

Dan Webb was "almost too flamboyant and jumpy to be around large crowds," she says, and Gary MacHalec had no interest whatsoever in being a public person. Furthermore, while her partners' strengths lay in the technical side of things, Winblad considers herself merely "a C+ programmer" compared to them.

So Winblad, inexperienced but cool-headed, eminently presentable and used to getting attention, let herself in for some more. She assumed the titles of director of marketing and chief financial officer. As such, she frequently felt intimidated by the people with whom she had to deal. "I was always saying to myself, 'Just remember, this is just a person,' " she says in describing her first business interactions. "So I'd talk to them as people, about their families and kids. I had good interpersonal skills, but I didn't know how to deal with them as businesspeople."

She also quickly realized the painful fact that she had a lot to learn. "It was hard in the beginning to get out there and be with people who knew more than I did about computers, about business, about everything," she says. "I couldn't learn from books; I tried that. People would challenge my ideas and what could I do?" Without experience to back her up, she didn't have much of a case.

In true entrepreneurial style, she turned a difficult position to her advantage. "Sometimes, when you're not the one who can lead, you can be a sponge," she suggests. "You get an opportunity to observe, you're not on the firing line as much, so you really can gather a basis for knowledge before you get up and start being tough." After a period of trying to bluff her way through, she gave it up and let some real knowledge seep in. Being in the background "was a benefit as long as I recognized it wasn't a deficit."

While she felt keenly that in one sense her youth was a distinct drawback, at the same time her innocent appearance often inspired others to support and protect her. "People would say, 'Let me tell you about this,' or, 'Before you go in there, let me help you out.' I can't see anyone doing that to Portia Isaacson," she observes, "but then I'm a small person and I seem friendlier." Instead of bristling at this apparent condescension, she made it work for her. Winblad learned fast instead of bemoaning the fact that people seemed to be ignoring her.

"I could have gotten really depressed about the fact that no one would listen to me, but there was nothing for me to tell at that point in time," she realized. "I needed to network, I needed to understand business relationships better."

She was fortunate to find a mentor in Cado founder George Ryan. "George is probably the best wheeler-dealer I've ever seen—an excellent sales guy and deal maker," Winblad says. Making deals, selling a product, and negotiating contracts were the keys to Open Systems' business in the beginning, and Ryan taught her how. "I think I've gotten a reputation of being a very, very shrewd negotiator, and that comes from George," she says.

Still, even with valuable experience under her belt, she had to prove herself repeatedly to those who could see only a tiny blonde before them. And, time and time again, she turned their prejudice to her advantage.

She frequently made presentations to established hardware companies to win the contracts for private-label deals. "There'd be five guys in suits from other accounting software firms giving presentations—and me," she says. "Well, the vendors were going to remember me more than those five guys in the suits. I was different, I was unique.

"The vendors would joke around with me. In some cases, they'd challenge my ideas and give me more of an opportunity to present the capability of the company, while they just snored away at the other guys' presentations. So being more challenged because people thought I knew less actually gave me an opportunity to present more."

Being female also helped Winblad get her foot in many doors. "Say you're at a convention and there are 4,000 guys and 10 women. You have a greater opportunity to see the people you want to see because it's nice for them to have a little diversification and see a woman every once in a while. And I don't think it hurts being small and blonde—all those things are not a deficit."

While maybe not a deficit, they were a source of confusion at times. In the late 1970s, the aisles at computer shows often resembled a teeming 42nd Street more than a trade show. The overwhelmingly male audiences swarmed from booth to booth, frequently attracted by scantily clad models who were long in the leg but short in the lingo. When confronted with a serious player like Winblad, many attendees understandably took a wrong turn. "Men would always ask me what I did after I finished my show hours, as if I'd been hired for the convention," she laughs.

None of this bothered Winblad in the least, since it was the business that interested her more than anything else. And Open Systems' success was steady and sure. By 1982, the four founders were collecting $200,000 salaries and the company was still making a multimillion-dollar profit.

Open Systems' multiuser approach would pay off big a few years later, when growing numbers of business users would recognize the need for several people to be able to access the same corporate data simultaneously. By the mid-1980s, Open Systems would be sitting pretty on the work of its early years.

Portia Isaacson: Champion of the Microcomputer

"If you could go out 100 years from now and see a time line of technological contributions, the personal computer will eventually be regarded as more fundamental than it is now," Portia Isaacson believes. "We don't have that perspective."

And Isaacson has believed that since she first laid eyes on a personal computer, back in 1975. The following year, around the time Winblad and company were starting out with minicomputer software, Isaacson and a partner opened one of the first microcomputer stores in the country. By that time, she had been involved with computers for more than ten years—since 1965, when she did programming for her college physics department.

After taking her eye-opening job as a scientific programmer at Bell Helicopter Co. in 1967, Isaacson worked in the mainframe and minicomputer world for the next eight years. From Bell Helicopter, she went on to other programming and analysis jobs at Lockheed Electronics in Houston, Computer Usage Co. in Dallas, and Recognition Equipment, Inc., in Irving, Texas.

Computer Usage Co., based in California, was a "very progressive" software development consulting company in which many women had risen very high. "That's where I really got into computer science, where I was building compilers and operating systems and so on," Isaacson says. "It was a very important company in my development."

Computer Usage was the first company to give Isaacson the freedom and responsibility to manage such challenging projects as "the design and implementation of a test generation and control system for Cobol programs for the IBM System/360 operating under MVT/Hasp," as her 14-page resume discloses. It was complex and she loved it.

Unfortunately, after Isaacson had been there only a year and a half, Computer Usage closed its Dallas office. Because she didn't want to move, Isaacson went to work for Recognition Equipment as a senior systems software programmer. And there she had a rude awakening. "At Recognition Equipment, there really wasn't a prayer for a woman to play any kind of a management role," she says. "If you were smart and a leader, you could be a project leader, but you would never manage anything."

Her answer to that was to arm herself with degrees. Even though technically she was not even a college graduate, North Texas State University in Denton accepted her in its master's program. Besides pursuing her own studies, she also acted as an instructor in computer science for the school and did consulting work for Recognition Equipment. Isaacson has always been a tireless worker, usually pursuing two or three ambitious projects at a time.

When she was only a thesis away from her master's degree, at age 30, she received a letter from good old East Central State College granting her the undergraduate degree that had eluded her for so long. It took nothing less than the death of the registrar who, six years earlier, had refused to accept her Army credits. At last she was officially a college graduate with a degree in physics and mathematics. Within a few months, she had a master's in computer science as well.

Isaacson's master's degree only whetted her intellectual appetite, and fortunately her husband understood her thirst for knowledge. With Jimmy Isaacson's encouragement, she enrolled at Southern Methodist University (SMU) in 1972 and earned her Ph.D. in computer science two years later at the age of 32. During that period, she also taught at North Texas State University and, six months before getting the Ph.D., took a job as an engineering specialist for Xerox Corp. in Dallas.

Portia's unrelenting pursuit of degrees, knowledge, and intellectual challenges in general satisfied one of her deepest needs, but at a high price. Her awesome determination is a two-edged sword, and razor-sharp. "It's good news and bad news," she says, "because that same degree of focus on what I'm trying to accomplish means that there's almost nothing else in my life at the time." At that point, her third marriage became the sacrifice.

"I screwed it up," she admits. "I was never home. For two years Jimmy and the kids probably never saw me until 2 A.M." After eight years with a man Portia calls "wonderful," she had to admit they had become virtual strangers. "Besides, Jimmy had decided to marry my housekeeper, who was really super." And he did.

Once again, Portia Isaacson was in a tailspin. She wasn't psychologically prepared for the divorce and she hardly knew her own kids. She had no choice but to leave it all behind. For the next two years, she paid Jimmy child support while she tried to put her life back together and get reacquainted with her sons. "Jimmy really raised them through their formative years," she says.

Meanwhile, she moved in with David Wilson, a close friend from SMU. Emotionally bankrupt as she was, she enjoyed the peaceful, low-key relationship they shared. Technologically they were kindred spirits and, when the historic Mits Altair do-it-yourself computer kit appeared on the cover of *Popular Electronics* magazine in January 1975, Isaacson and Wilson immediately sent in their $397 each, pouncing on the chance to own a computer.

Isaacson couldn't know then that she was one of thousands of anonymous enthusiasts around the country, all quietly fascinated by an obscure technology, who had yet to find one another. Who would have dreamed that there were so many people secretly wishing they could own a computer?

But the proof was in the overwhelming response to the Mits Altair. Its tiny Albuquerque maker with a big name, Micro Instrumentation Telemetry Systems (Mits), went from being $400,000 in debt to $250,000 in the black in the weeks right after the article appeared. And the personal computer industry was officially born.

As for Isaacson's and Wilson's relationship, "David and I didn't make too many demands on each other," Isaacson says. "We each built computers in separate rooms and basically went our own ways." After a few months, however, things got much more serious.

In the mid-1970s cohabitation was nothing shocking, but for the elder generation it could be an uncomfortable situation. "David's parents were upset about it, and I was feeling needy," Isaacson explains, "so we decided to get married."

That's when the trouble began. As friends, they had had a "fantastic" relationship. "Almost as soon as we got married, I began to have expectations about 'acting married' and being together," she says. "That was awful and there was a lot of conflict." Nevertheless, they bought a house together and her boys left Jimmy's and moved in with Portia and David, who is "super with the kids." The marriage lasted a year.

"Six months after we were divorced, we were back to being best friends again," Portia says. They are best friends to this day. Wilson is still very close to her sons, and in 1984 he joined Future Computing as the resident expert on integrated circuits and robotics.

In the midst of her personal turmoil, Isaacson's professional star began to rise. While most people in the mainframe world generally scorned the tiny micro in the mid-seventies, Isaacson wholeheartedly embraced it. She not only embraced it, she promoted it ceaselessly. She became, in fact, probably its greatest spokesperson.

To get the word out, Isaacson volunteered to work for many computer industry associations, wrote scores of articles, and made speeches all over the country. Her message was that the personal computer was possibly the most important technology ever developed. Yes, *ever.* Isaacson felt she had finally discovered something with the potential impact of Curie's radium.

"I became very taken with the idea that, 'Oh my goodness, this is really lucky and I have to go with this,'" Isaacson says, "because how often does a scientist, which I then regarded myself as, have the opportunity to be involved in the birth and bringing to fruition through free enterprise of this most important technology?"

Isaacson wanted to open the world's eyes to what she saw as a wonderful invention that was being ignored by people who should have known better. She wanted to make the micro revolution happen. Although at first her ideas seemed downright curious—even laughable—to the mainstream computing community, her reputation grew steadily. Not only did people begin to recognize her name, but they eventually started listening to what she was saying.

Because of her increasing visibility, "and because the first 100 people they asked refused," she jokes, Isaacson was chosen in 1975 to chair the 1977 National Computer Conference (NCC), the computer industry's oldest and biggest annual celebration of itself. Started by the American Federation of Information Processing Societies (AFIPS) in the early 1960s, NCC grew as the industry grew, continuing to attract crowds the size of respectable cities, even during the computer industry slump of the mid-1980s. In 1977, NCC attendees numbered 36,000. Even in 1985, a bad year for the industry, it attracted 80,000 people.

"The choice was a little radical on AFIPS's part," she says immodestly, since "most NCC chairmen were very forgettable." Isaacson, however, was anything but forgettable, on the basis of her vital statistics alone. She was the first female ever chosen to head the event and in 1977 she would be 34, making her the youngest as well.

AFIPS's invitation was an offer she couldn't refuse. "I knew I'd meet the most important people in the computer industry, make a lot of connections, get some visibility and some real management experience, and have a lot of authority." Those encounters were exactly what she needed to accomplish her goal of making a revolution in personal computers.

Chairing the NCC for one year was far more complicated than it sounds. "It takes three years of your life at least, one of them full-time," Isaacson says. "It's a little like chairing the Olympics."

During that period, Isaacson was in every way on the cutting edge of technology. In March 1976 she and Wilson (then still married) set themselves up as Binary Systems, Inc., and in May opened one of the first computer retail stores in the United States, The Micro Store, located in Dallas.

The Micro Store sold sophisticated small systems to engineers and offered heavy technical support, to the tune of about $1 million a year in sales. While Wilson actually handled the details of running the store, Isaacson took another first step toward her future.

She considered the growing publicity from NCC as bankable as cash. Fame is perhaps the most valuable criterion for setting oneself up as an expert, and fame was burning a hole in her pocket. So Isaacson became a consultant. "At that time, I was already trying to start a company like Future Computing," she says. "I had a little office up above the computer store and a secretary. But the big companies really weren't interested yet in getting into PCs, so there wasn't enough business to make the company grow."

And, though it's important, renown won't pay the bills. Wilson—by then her ex-husband, ex-partner, but still best friend—agreed to support her with money from the computer store so that Isaacson could concentrate on making the most of her situation. That meant marketing herself like any other product. "I didn't make a lot of money at first, but I consolidated my visibility and reputation as *the* expert on personal computers," she explains.

As a consultant, she advised business clients on their plans relating to personal computers, ran seminars, wrote articles, made frequent speeches, and became very active in a number of computer societies. More and more often, her reputation preceded her. "I was very visible on this kind of lunatic-fringe subject of personal computers," she says.

Typical of her message was her guest editorial in *Byte* magazine in February 1976 entitled, "Personal Computing: An Idea Whose Time Has Come." That was only one year after the Mits Altair's debut, and most people still had no idea there was such a thing as a personal computer. As early as April 1977, she was predicting "A Computer in Every Home," in the pilot issue of *Abacus*, an AFIPS publication.

Meanwhile, she was trying to pull together the massive confluence scheduled for June 1977. The major problem she faced as NCC chairman was that the event was to be held in Dallas. "AFIPS was afraid no one would come," she explains. "It had always been held in Anaheim [California], New York, or Chicago, never in the South before, and there wasn't enough population around Dallas to ensure the attendance." When AFIPS's negotiations with Chicago had broken down, it was forced to go with what it saw as a less desirable alternative.

But Isaacson had a plan, one with completely ulterior motives. Seeing NCC as a highly visible platform for her ideas, Isaacson proposed holding a personal computer fair—the first time a microcomputer had ever been displayed at an NCC. For 15 years, the focus had been on mainframes and minicomputers.

"In 1976, before there was any real visibility in the industry about personal computers, I had to convince AFIPS this was a good thing to do," she recalls. "I made a case that by appealing to the computer professionals' curiosity about owning their own computers, we could get them to want to come, and they'd talk their companies into paying their way to NCC, as usual, even if they had to travel further."

As it turned out, she was absolutely right. "Events happened in my favor," she explains. "From 1976, when we decided to have the PC Fair, to mid-1977, when NCC was held, the PC industry had started becoming big news even if it wasn't quite accepted. It was still controversial but it got an awful lot of press.

"There I was, chairing the most serious, straitlaced computer conference in the world," Isaacson says, "and all I wanted to talk about was personal computers, which everybody thought was very entertaining and not business at all at the time. So there was a lot of curiosity, we got a lot more prepublicity all over the world, and the whole thing did work."

About 100 micro companies exhibited their wares that year, in the bargain basement of the convention hall. "We sold very inexpensive space to them and they exhibited literally on tabletops," Isaacson recalls. This was in stark contrast to the flashy booths upstairs paid for by the Big Boys.

For many hard-line mainframers, the PC Fair was regarded as nothing more than an impertinence, but thousands of others didn't seem to mind its remote location or drab decor; the excitement for them was on the tabletops. "The exhibits were absolutely packed," Isaacson says. "That was the most trafficked area of the whole 1977 NCC."

Just as micros emerged as potent forces from that humble introduction, so Isaacson emerged along with them, first urging them onward and then carried forward by the success she helped them achieve. Within a year after the NCC, *Output* magazine named Isaacson as one of ten people in the industry whose names were the closest thing to household words.

And just a few months after "her" NCC, something happened that convinced Isaacson she had finally arrived. She was singled out by her long-time industry heroine and role model, then-Captain Grace Murray Hopper of the U.S. Navy, to take Hopper's place as the keynote speaker at Motorola Corp.'s annual technology conference that November. "In those days, I was hardly ever asked," Isaacson explains.

Hopper—one of the extraordinarily few women involved in the earliest days of computing—is well known in the mainframe world for having programmed the first large-scale digital computer, at Harvard University in 1945, as well as for her influence on the development of the Cobol programming language.

Always in strong demand as a speaker, Hopper couldn't make the Motorola conference because her schedule was too full. "I was walking on air for two weeks," Isaacson says. "She's a maverick. I was in such awe of her. I collected pictures of her on my office wall. It was so important to me, although I doubt if she even remembers it."

Hopper, as it turns out, does remember the episode. "She seemed to be an intelligent girl; I thought we might as well give her a chance," Hopper recalls. Besides, Hopper felt Isaacson's message dovetailed nicely with her own. "Isaacson's ideas about moving toward the future were what I'd been saying for several years," Hopper maintains.

As Isaacson's reputation grew, her ambition crystallized. She had decided she "wanted an empire." Although she wanted to take advantage of her name and experience, she felt she lacked the nuts-and-bolts business savvy to start up her own company. Because David Wilson had handled most of the details of running their computer store, she didn't have much practical experience.

Then, in the course of her consulting, Isaacson met someone who had the means to lead her closer to her goal. Her biggest client, H. Ross Perot, was the head of Electronic Data Systems Corp. (EDS) in Dallas, which he had built from scratch into the country's second largest computer services company. Perot made Isaacson an offer that would teach her what she needed to know and thereby give her the courage to take the necessary risk.

He invited her to work for EDS as a sort of consultant-in-residence. Although Isaacson didn't really want to go to work exclusively for any one company, her fifth meeting with Perot removed all her objections. "He said, 'We'll give you a budget and name you a Fellow, and you can do the same thing you're doing now,' " she recalls.

Carte blanche. A potentially unnerving prospect, this opportunity to initiate and follow through on anything she desired was extremely attractive to Isaacson. In March 1978 she joined EDS.

"Ross meant what he said," she says, "but the culture didn't exist at EDS to let it happen. So from the beginning, there was pressure on me—not from Ross, but from other people—to produce something. Probably Ross counted on that, and on the fact that I can't live in an environment where I don't feel productive by other people's standards."

So she decided to start a company within EDS. As usual, however, her interest lay in a project that was ahead of its time. This time her choice spelled disaster. At EDS she set up a group called Evolution 1, which produced broadcast-quality videocassette instructional materials about small computers and was aimed at retailers, schools, and corporations. Today it's big business. In 1979 it was a complete flop.

"It was too early, and the concept wasn't quite right within the EDS structure," Isaacson says. "The business failed, although we made the money back, but I was really quite shattered by it. I felt a great sense of personal failure."

In spite of her disappointment, Isaacson had learned a lot at EDS, not only about starting and running a business, but about succeeding. "Ross Perot is fantastic," she says. "He's one of those people who think bigger thoughts than others, and once they start doing it, they can't have smaller ideas again. I call them intergalactic thinkers."

A key ingredient of that kind of "bigger" thinking is the belief that anything is possible. "Ross could have thought small and made a good living," she says. But then he wouldn't have been the daring industry hero who successfully stormed an Iranian prison in 1979 to save two of his engineers from the religious fanatics holding them.

He also would not have been the head of a company that General Motors later wooed and won (for $2.5 billion in 1984) in an effort to revolutionize the manufacture of American cars through computer technology. (Perot's outspokenness at GM made for a rocky relationship, however, and in 1986 GM bought him out for $701 million.)

Perot's brand of "really important thinking" had a profound influence on Isaacson. She geared up for her solo flight. After her failure with Evolution 1, Isaacson was particularly determined to succeed. Furthermore, she needed a large income to support her teenage sons' expensive boarding schools and she, personally, was no longer willing to sacrifice. At 38, she wanted to live well. Although she was taking an entrepreneurial risk, in a sense it really wasn't that big. Her reputation and experience were such that, if this venture didn't work out, she could always get a high-paying job in someone else's company, humbling as that may have been.

When she set up shop, she wanted to do it right. "Women have image problems when they run businesses from their homes," she says. She would have an office. Before leaving EDS, using negotiating skills learned from Perot, she carved out a money-making deal that would provide the seed money for Future Computing, yet take up only a quarter of her time over the next two years.

A "reasonably large computer manufacturer" that she's still not free to name hired her to help it decide whether or not to enter the micro business. Specifically, she advised and educated people in the company, and negotiated with software companies for her client. The client paid a quarter of the contract's value in advance—$60,000—enabling her to rent an office, hire a secretary, and buy a copier and a computer.

In January 1980 she married husband number five, Egil Juliussen, and for the first six months of their marriage, until she actually set up Future Computing, they spent every dinnertime together discussing what the company would be.

"It was more like a dream than a plan," she says now. "We studied two companies as models—Dataquest, Inc., and International Data Corp. (IDC)—which are in the business of forecasting and commercial analysis like Future Computing, but in different industry segments.

"We planned it to be that kind of company. The plan was for me to start it as a consulting business and try to get the consulting revenue up high enough so Egil could leave Texas Instruments (TI) and join me," she says. At TI, Juliussen was considered the top market forecaster. When he could join Isaacson, Future Computing was expected to change somewhat, to take full advantage of his expertise.

"The plan was to then try to start a newsletter or maybe hold a seminar to turn the company into more of a publishing company, like IDC or Dataquest," Isaacson explains. "We thought all this would take ten years."

Instead it took two. In June 1980, Isaacson started Future Computing with just her reputation and a secretary—and one comfortable deal. Less than a week later, another fortuitous alliance was forged. "An IBM salesman called me up," she recalls. He wanted Isaacson to participate in a two-day presentation to Sears, Roebuck & Co. executives designed to persuade Sears to get into the PC retailing business. Although IBM had a genius for marketing, it didn't know a thing about merchandising, but it did know it would have to sell its Personal Computer differently than it sold computer mainframes. IBM wanted to make a deal with Sears, the merchandising expert.

Isaacson was one of about ten industry gurus the IBM salesman had invited to participate, and she was not completely unknown to Sears. About three months earlier, she had given a speech on computer retailing at Ben Rosen's Rosen Forum (later to be run by Esther Dyson). At the end of her Rosen Forum speech, in what was meant to be a humorous send-off, Isaacson had lambasted Sears for its experimental display of an Atari computer. The master of merchandising had made every error possible in presenting a computer to the public, she felt.

"They had put the computer in the camera department, in the aisle, with a plastic box around it, bolted down," she recalls. "The computer was connected to a screen up above, displaying some gobbledygook you couldn't understand. There was a sign on the thing saying 'Do Not Touch. Ask a Salesperson for Assistance'—as if you could even find one.

"I showed a slide of this and then made probably my first forecast. I said, 'I'm going to forecast how many of these computers Sears is going to sell. Three—one to the chairman of the board . . .' " Isaacson didn't get a chance to finish. "Everybody just roared."

One person in the audience, though, wasn't laughing very hard. "I was sitting out in the lobby afterwards and this very tall, really big guy walked up to me and said, 'I want to introduce myself. I'm the buyer for computers for Sears.' "

While Sears had been selling brilliantly everything from pillows to plows for nearly a century, it found itself up against something that very few people understood, much less understood how to sell. But as Isaacson had so pointedly demonstrated, the personal computer was a multidimensional, interactive machine that simply couldn't be locked away from the buying public.

The Sears buyer had recognized immediately and unforgettably that Isaacson could teach the acknowledged experts a thing or two. IBM succeeded in persuading Sears, and after the seminar, Sears called Isaacson back. "I signed a one-year contract to help them create the business plan for the Sears Business Systems Centers."

By October 1980, she was working with Sears and, under a nondisclosure agreement, she learned all about IBM's planned introduction of the Personal Computer. A year later, Sears opened its first business center, on the same day IBM shipped the PC. Sears would eventually open business centers in 103 of its stores nationwide.

Isaacson had made an indelible mark on about as big a client as you can get, and the relationship would continue to bear fruit for both parties. For Sears, Future Computing became its laboratory to test the micro products it was considering selling. For Isaacson, knowledge about IBM's unreleased PC would put her a giant step ahead of almost everyone else.

Future Computing's first research report, "IBM's Billion-Dollar Baby," all about the PC, came out just two weeks after the PC was introduced, and people were starved for technical information and advice about its possible impact.

"Our timing was fantastic," Isaacson remembers. "Because I had been involved through Sears with the IBM PC for some time, I knew a lot about it. So by the time IBM announced it, the whole industry needed to know. I wouldn't have been able to do the report if I hadn't been thinking about the product already through Sears."

It was not just knowing the facts that put Future Computing in the limelight. "We took a very different stand from any of the other research companies," Isaacson explains. "We took the point of view that the product was going to be very successful. That sounds silly now, but at the time, the press and the other research companies like IDC and Dataquest and The Gartner Group took the point of view that it was a ho-hum IBM product and that it would not be successful." Even IBM was not so confident.

"It turned out that we were the only voice that was positive about the product," she says, "and today if you read that report, a very large percentage of what we predicted has come true." Naturally, the report was very popular at IBM, which bought copies by the boxful. Not only did Future Computing make a quarter of a million dollars from its first research report, but it also established its credibility, on which no price can be set.

From there, Future Computing's growth was impressive. Revenues shot up from $400,000 in 1981, the first year, to $1.3

million in 1982, to $3.8 million in 1983. From the two people who started out in 1980, Future Computing grew to seven employees by the end of 1981 (including Juliussen), then mushroomed to 60 by the end of 1982, and to 100 by the end of 1983.

At last Isaacson's propensity to do something before anyone else thought of it paid off. Future Computing was the first micro-oriented market research company in the country, and by 1981 a hunger for hard facts was making stomachs growl. Isaacson was right there, equipped to fill a need as it grew. "Egil and I thought it would be big," Isaacson says, "but we never would have guessed or planned that it would happen so fast."

Lore Harp: From Motherhood to the "8K Baby"

"I was always fairly persuasive," says Lore Harp. And it's a good thing she was, too, because she and partner Carole Ely had absolutely no leverage when they started Vector Graphic, Inc., in July 1976. As the president and vice president of an unknown entity that just barely qualified as a company, Harp and Ely simply acted bigger than they were.

One of Harp's first Vector phone calls—dialed from her kitchen—was to the western regional sales manager for a major memory chip manufacturer. He suggested they meet the next day at her office.

"We'd love to," she told him, "but we're in the middle of moving right now." Moving into the downstairs bedroom, that is. She suggested a meeting over drinks instead. The next day, exactly one hour after Harp and Ely had incorporated, they held their first meeting, at the Westlake Inn.

"He looked at Carole and me and I could just see the reaction going on in his head: 'Oh, my God, what have I gotten myself into?' " she remembers. "He was quite male-oriented—not to call him a male chauvinist—but I think the major problem was he didn't understand where this industry was going to go. He just did not see the opportunity."

They got nowhere that day, but before another 24 hours had passed, Harp and Ely had found another supplier and negotiated a $75,000 deal for 50,000 chips to plug into their memory boards. So persuasive was Harp that Vector Graphic started right out with 30-day credit terms from vendors—which was fortunate, since she and Ely had started the company with only $6,000 of their own personal money.

Harp's housewifely boredom and the growing marketplace for computers' innards had converged beautifully. Once Vector Graphic was launched, suddenly there was too much to do, with not enough time to do it and problems she had never faced before. But Harp demonstrated a keen instinct for business that apparently had just been looking for an outlet. She was a natural.

Very quickly the business became a neighborhood project. "I would get bowls out of the kitchen and put all the little components in them, and my children and Carole's would put the kits together," Harp recalls. "We also hired a lot of high school kids, part-time. It was chaotic with children, dogs, cats, and neighbors' kids."

In spite of such informality, the operation was anything but a lark. And the deadly serious dealer side of the business is where the duo really made a killing. Vector dazzled dealers with its attention and support, so that people grew to depend on them for quality treatment. "Basically we treated dealers the way we would like to be treated," Harp explains.

She assigns their approach in some way to gender. Certainly the rest of the competition, largely male, was for the most part treating dealers with indifference. "I'm sure there was something of a female innate protectiveness about wanting to take care of something we'd started," Harp says. It's no coincidence that they called their memory board—which was attached to a larger so-called motherboard—the "8K Baby."

Five days after sending out a "Dear Dealer, Meet the Vector 8K Baby" letter, they'd call up the dealers to see whether the letter had arrived and then try to make a sale. It usually worked. "Most people were flabbergasted by the attention they got and by the fact that we were women," Harp says.

Harp and Ely also had style. "We had more marketing appeal than anything around," Harp says immodestly. "We had three-color flyers. We had a well-designed logo and nice linen paper. Even the way we packaged the [memory board] kits had class.

The boxes were printed with our logo in green and white. They used to call us 'the girls in green and white.' "

Sexist connotations notwithstanding, "the girls" were taken very seriously by an industry unaccustomed to such lavish attention. Their "8K Baby" letters went out to every dealer listed in the trade ads of all the competing manufacturers. After the (usually successful) follow-up phone calls to clinch a sale, they would wait a week and call again.

It was the after-sale attention that really wowed clients. "I would ask whether they had received the board, whether they had had a chance to put it together, and whether they liked it?" Harp says. "And how many more did they want to order?" The dealers were nothing less than overwhelmed. In a world where technical details were king, Vector began rearranging priorities.

How did Harp, who had never even held a "real" job, make the transition from wife and mother to head of a growing company? In addition to her apparently innate business acumen, she simply drew on what she knew. "It was a question of nurturing the process along," she explains. "You don't send the child off on a trip without later checking to find out if he or she got there." So it was with memory boards.

Vector also made itself very visible. "We advertised," Harp says. "We had half-page and full-page ads in trade publications. We went to shows." Vector was everywhere, and always offered a helping hand. If a dealer had a problem with a board, Harp would sometimes call her husband, then working at Hughes Research Laboratories, and ask him to call the dealer back. "So we were troubleshooting over the phone right from the start."

Harp never pretended to be a technical guru, but instead made the most of her marketing talents. "Most of our competitors were very technically oriented people who saw a tremendous opportunity and wanted the satisfaction of having little computers they could play with," Harp explains, "but they really had no interest in following through, in getting the word out to the world as to why the computer is great and what it can do for the customer. We took the other road."

It paid off quickly. In December 1976, five months after incorporating, Vector Graphic moved out of the downstairs bedroom and into a 1,200-square-foot facility, still in Westlake Village, and hired its first assembler and first receptionist. "It was all such fun then," Harp recalls. One thrill was handing her next-door neighbor, the receptionist, her first Vector paycheck. "It was just great."

By January 1977 Vector had started to market a complete "turnkey" computer system: assembled, tested, ready-to-go machines. At that point it quit selling memory board kits. Business picked up fast and in July 1977, Bob Harp quit his job at Hughes and joined Vector full-time as chairman of the board and director of R&D.

The industry really began to move during 1977, with Tandy, Apple, and Commodore taking center stage. That trio went after the home market, at the time considered the hottest prospect for small computers. Harp and Ely, however, had decided to go after the small-business market. Years would pass before it would finally become obvious to everyone that business was the first significant market for computers.

How did the neophytes figure it out so early in the game? "Beats me," Harp offers. "The thing is, I looked at it not in terms of some esoteric analysis. I was looking at the real, practical aspects and trying to deduce it from that."

At the beginning, microcomputers were used by technical people and people who loved to tinker, she points out. "I was looking more at the applications rather than the tinkering. It's the difference between driving a car with the purpose of getting somewhere and playing with the engine."

Sensing correctly that she was on the verge of phenomenal success, Harp was as quick on her feet as she had been running track in Germany. One of the things that helped her to react quickly to change was the close control she kept on the business from the start. "Even though we were operating on such a small scale at the beginning, we were very organized," she explains. "We kept books and financial statements from Day 1."

Furthermore, moving quickly is simply her nature. "One of the things I can do is make very fast decisions," Harp says. "I plan a lot, make decisions, and am risk-oriented. If I make a mistake, I acknowledge it and try not to make the mistake again. But making any decision is better than no decision at all."

In the midst of fast growth, success, and expansion, Harp was still operating basically on instinct, although each day brought more experience. In 1977 she found a mentor. Vector bought disk drives from Micropolis, Inc., in Chatsworth, California, whose president is Stuart Mabon.

"Stuart and I had the same lunch, at the same place, the same time, for years," she says. Salade nicoise, quiche, and half a bottle of wine. Such is the fuel for technology.

"I could tell him about my fears, my lack of knowing certain things, and he really helped me out," she says. "I was never afraid he'd look at me and think, 'What's she *doing*?' " She respected his opinion and he respected her innate abilities, even as she revealed her inexperience.

Meanwhile, Vector was growing by leaps and bounds. By 1979 the company moved out of the 1,200-square-foot facility into a 5,000-square-foot building. A year later, still growing, Vector found a 20,000-square-foot corporate home. By 1981 rapid expansion put the firm into even bigger—and much more expensive—quarters.

"Everyone was scared," Harp remembers. Vector was already paying almost $17,000 a year for rent, and the move would more than triple that price, to $60,000 a year. But Harp thought it was a necessary jump. "I knew we were going to grow very fast." In September 1981 Vector moved into 120,000 square feet in Thousand Oaks, California.

A month later, the company went public. Vector's initial stock offering, worth $13 million, marked the beginning of a bittersweet affair with Wall Street—eager, as always, for a highflier.

Vector seemed like a sure thing. In its first five years, the company had zoomed from $400,000 in annual sales to $25 million. Furthermore, it was one of the new and exciting high-tech stocks that were again giving Wall Street something to live for. For the moment Vector Graphic was a darling of the investment community, and it looked as if it would only continue to soar. Harp was poised and ready for the big time. At that point, no one could have guessed that the highflier's engine would soon start to sputter.

Ann Piestrup: Making the Abstract Concrete

"Everybody I know who is working with computers and children is finding that our old models of what children can do are changing," Ann Piestrup wrote in 1984. "They can understand coordinates at ages three and four, and do plotting of computer graphics.

"They can visualize things in three-dimensional space with positive and negative numbers at the age of seven . . . and then perform transformations on these objects similar to what is taught in college and graduate school.

"Why? There was never before a medium that makes these abstract things concrete the way a computer does," she explained. "Computers can build a success orientation that's as good as the best that teachers can do. Children can be on the learning edge, where they are challenged but feel competent."

If the microcomputer had not evolved, Piestrup could still have used other media to attain her goal of revolutionizing children's education, including books and films, through which she had already expressed many of her theories about education. "But I was always thinking there must be something better," she says. The micro proved to be that better something: the ideal vehicle for her to do what she had set out to do.

As soon as she became aware of the existence of the personal computer, Piestrup realized that her educational theories would translate perfectly into computer software. But until that moment of discovery, Piestrup lived with a disconcerting vagueness about how to give form to her ideas. It was pure chance that led her to the micro, and it did so with dramatic timing.

While Piestrup was pregnant with her only child, her husband suffered a massive heart attack. After their daughter, Sarah, was born in March 1977, Piestrup stayed home at first to care for the baby but was "very unhappy," she remembers.

"The heart attack shifted my perspective from being the little wifey, who could stay home with a baby and bake bread and make soup, into being the principal wage earner for the family," she explains. "I thought I might need to support open-heart surgery, since Mel was very severely damaged by the heart attack."

Soon, though, she learned she had an even greater worry than hospital bills. "He was inoperable," she found. "The doctors told me he might die any day and there was no point in operating because it was so bad." But Mel Piestrup pulled through, and today he heads a small high-tech company.

The very real possibility of losing him, however, completely shifted Ann's perspective. She had to start thinking about how to guarantee her own long-term financial security. "I didn't want to be living out my retirement on what I'd put into my IRA," she says.

To start making money quickly, Piestrup took on some consulting work with RMC Research, for whom she had earlier worked for four years. "They really bent over backwards to have me there," she says. RMC not only let her bring Sarah and a babysitter into the office, but they set up a playroom for the baby.

Apart from all the turmoil in her personal life, still fixed securely in the back of Ann's mind was her overriding goal: to make a difference in education. The question was how to make it happen. It was a chance conversation that revealed her pathway to the future. When a programmer friend came visiting one evening, he talked about the latest thing in high tech, the microcomputer. Her guest's description of the micro uncovered for Piestrup the very key to the puzzle before her.

"Until then, I'd thought of computers as huge machines used primarily for statistics," she recalls. "I'd had no idea that they could produce pictures—in color, no less!—and music, or that they could be made compact and relatively inexpensive, or that people could program them to be simple enough for young children to use. But as my friend talked, I became convinced that computers could really make a difference in the way kids learn." There, at the dinner table, the seed of The Learning Company was planted.

Although she hadn't planned on beginning quite so soon, fate had decreed that the time was right to get on with it. Her sudden need for financial independence propelled her into the project that would help her realize a lifelong ambition. Ironically, her worst luck couldn't have come at a better time. As Piestrup soon found out, the business climate was invitingly ripe for the type of venture she had in mind. The creation of her own company would serve all her needs.

Nevertheless, it was a long road from her discovery of the micro and decision to start a company to actually bringing software products to the marketplace. Her first priority was to get her hands on a computer.

Through friends, she heard that the Apple Education Foundation had just been formed and was giving away computers for worthy educational projects. In March 1978 she set up shop as a sole proprietorship called Advanced Learning Technology and immediately wrote a grant proposal to the Foundation.

"I proposed something that I thought was just what they'd like to fund. I shifted my ideas a little bit," she admits. "I think it's essential when you're trying to get other people's money to find out what they're interested in. If there are guidelines, you follow the guidelines. It doesn't mean you don't do what you want, but if they want a five-page proposal, you don't write a ten-page proposal."

Her plan was to develop and market a software program, tentatively called "Above-Below, Left-Right," that would teach spatial concepts to preschoolers. "This is what the Apple Foundation said teachers were crying for," Piestrup says.

The Apple Foundation liked her ideas, but wouldn't deliver on a computer until she could find a programmer. It took Piestrup nine months to find a good programmer, but finally she did. In December 1978, the Apple Foundation sent her $1,000 in grant money and an Apple computer.

"I opened it up at Christmas time at my home," Piestrup recalls. "I remember pulling the computer out of a big white box and realizing there was more power in that computer than in the original computers that filled entire rooms."

During the nine-month hiatus, Piestrup had researched the educational software market and gratifyingly found that the field was essentially wide open, especially in terms of using the color graphics, music, and voice capabilities of the microcomputer. "There was very little in educational software at that time and, in fact, nothing that I thought was very good," she says.

Heartened, Piestrup forged ahead. Her programmer started working on the program Piestrup had proposed to the Apple Foundation, which would eventually be a Learning Company hit called "Juggles' Rainbow" utilizing the panoply of micro charms: music, graphics, and voice.

Meanwhile, Piestrup was looking for other sources of financing to carry her along. Her approach, as always, was direct. "I never see barriers to talking to the people who are making things happen," she says. "If I want to get something done, I just call people up and try to do it." Characteristically, she went right to the top. "I found my way to the Chief of Information Technology within the Department of Education," she recalls. He told her that the National Science Foundation (NSF) and the National Institutes of Education (NIE) were jointly soliciting grant proposals for computer-assisted educational projects.

Perfect. Now all she had to do was figure out how to write a government grant proposal. "I read the directions." She also used her family's grocery money to hire a word processing specialist, who typed up Piestrup's proposal for logic and geometry programs for second- and third-graders.

Piestrup also learned that she could apply for congressional funds to develop software for *Via Allegra,* the Spanish version of *Sesame Street.* "I made a huge effort to make a proposal for them," she recalls, "and waited for a long time to find out if it was funded."

The news was good. Her grant proposal was approved, and Piestrup was promised a check for $300,000 in six months. "When I heard it was funded, I hired two people, contingent on the money coming, and rented an office," Piestrup recounts. But the person in charge of education for HEW suddenly resigned, and the whole project went on hold—indefinitely. "So there I was with an office and a staff and no money." The group fell apart, but Piestrup kept at it alone.

Although her original NSF/NIE grant application had been rejected, the day after the *Via Allegra* project fell through, Piestrup found out that NSF/NIE had more money available, and that she had one weekend to whip up another proposal.

Exhausted but undaunted, she had to immediately find someone to help her. "When my friend who had helped me write it the first time said she had to move that weekend, I said, 'I'll pay the movers,' " Piestrup remembers. She was determined not to lose the opportunity that was still within her grasp.

And she didn't. Even though the proposal was written in a frenzy, it was one of nine that won generous grants—against stiff competition (including the Apple Foundation and 183 others). Piestrup was thrilled to find out that her company would be $130,000 richer within the year, enough to fund software development through the end of 1981.

One might imagine that once a person has won a large grant, he or she is on easy street. For Piestrup, it wasn't so simple. From the time she learned that she had won the NSF/NIE grant to the time she actually got the money, Piestrup spent an entire year—with no income—preparing to meet the requirements of her benefactors. Her tasks are familiar to every first-time entrepreneur.

"There were all sorts of hurdles," she recalls. "I had to write a policy manual for the company and set up an accounting system. I went to tax seminars to find out how to handle my employees' taxes, and I had to find a lawyer and an accountant to help me with all those things.

"First I wanted to find out how everything works before I got somebody else to do it. I learned how to do the taxes and decided I didn't want to do that, so I got somebody else to. But it wasn't a mystery to me so I couldn't be hoodwinked about it."

Meanwhile, Piestrup was relentless in her pursuit of the decision makers. Every morning at 6:00 A.M. California time, she phoned the NSF office in Washington to make sure things were still progressing. Having been burned once, Piestrup was determined that it would not happen again. "It was *not* going to die. They were *not* going to forget me," she says with the same intensity she felt then. "I really wanted that thing. I just did everything it took to get it."

Sometimes the obstacles seemed insurmountable. "At one point, I had three days to get a school [board] to approve doing research in their district," she recalls. "I had arranged a tentative one, but it fell through because the district wanted to control the project."

That was especially bad news because the Palo Alto, California, school districts were constantly being recruited as "guinea pigs" for the research projects of Stanford University's graduate students. Not only were the districts already in high demand for research, but Piestrup's subjects had to be gifted children.

In that seller's market, however, and in three days, Piestrup managed to find people who would help her. "The school board of the school I approached had a special meeting to discuss the issue," she remembers with gratitude. "I would have lost the grant if it hadn't been for that. People had to do a lot of work to help me."

Finally, Piestrup's doggedness, optimism, and hard work paid off. With the October 1980 arrival of $130,000 in grant money came the luxury of settling down to some serious software development work. To do that, she needed technical talent.

Piestrup recruited Dr. Teri Hoch Perl, a mathematics education expert, as Advanced Learning Technology's second full-time employee, and software development continued apace.

Networking led Piestrup to her next employee, who turned out to be key in the company's evolution. Reluctant to depend on a single source of funding, Piestrup had continually pursued other ways to get money, even while waiting for her grant to come through.

One person she talked with was Dan Fylstra, founder of VisiCorp, which marketed the first electronic spreadsheet program, VisiCalc. Having gotten his own first round of venture capital, Fylstra was considering acquiring Piestrup's "company," although at the time it was nothing more than a few ideas printed on some stationery. When Fylstra finally decided to eschew educational software and dedicate his company solely to business productivity software, Piestrup was sorely disappointed. But all was not lost.

Fylstra had also been talking with other nonbusiness software creators as potential acquisitions. One of them was Warren Robinett, author of Atari's best-selling Adventure game, who offered Fylstra a game based on a graphics utility program he'd developed for the Apple.

In those days, Mitch Kapor (then "just a kid," according to Piestrup)—later to found the phenomenally successful Lotus Development Corp.—was working for Fylstra. And Kapor made a crucial connection. He telephoned Piestrup to say that Robinett had written a very nice game program that VisiCorp couldn't use, but that Piestrup undoubtedly could. Kapor couldn't have been more right. Soon after, Warren Robinett became Advanced Learning Technology's third full-time employee, as a software engineer.

"The grant funding made it possible for me to get the very best people I could," Piestrup says. "Warren is very gifted—very gifted." Of course, she didn't know that at first glance. "To find out if he could program, I made him finish Juggles' Rainbow," she says in amused hindsight. "In about one day, he did it—zip!"

Robinett did for Piestrup something she could not do: He translated her ideas about education into the language of the computer. "He told me an idea that was better than my ideas," she recalls. "He drew these AND's, OR's, and NOT's in the air and even though I couldn't really take in the whole thing, I thought, 'That is elemental, just like the things I've thought about in math, and that's exactly what the future needs.' I was pacing with excitement at the thought. I couldn't sit still."

AND, OR, and NOT are the three basic operations of Boolean algebra, a system that allows mathematical methods to be applied to logical thought. And, in fact, Boolean theory was germane to the design of electronic computers. But Piestrup didn't know that. All she knew was that, thanks to Warren Robinett, she had stumbled onto something that was at the very heart of her ideas about educational software.

Piestrup believes that a fundamental secret of success is the ability to recognize and acknowledge a good idea. "It doesn't have to be my idea, but I feel one source of power is a sense that tells me, 'Aha! That's great. Let's do that,' " she says.

With Perl and Robinett and $130,000, the fledgling company spent the next year developing the basis for what would be three of its most successful products: Rocky's Boots, Gertrude's Secrets, and Gertrude's Puzzles. "But at the end of that time, the programs were still in rough form; they needed music and they needed joystick control," Piestrup notes. To be blunt, they needed more money.

It was October 1981. "When the NSF project ended," Piestrup recalls, "we had no money for about three months. Teri, Warren, and I went without a salary, and Teri offered to let us use her house as our office." Even Lesley Grimm, the newest employee, worked without pay her first three months.

But money, and plenty of it, was just around the corner. "Someone who'd been on the Apple Foundation Board and had gone to work at Melchor Venture Management approached me about accepting venture capital," Piestrup explains, "and I met with Jack Melchor." Melchor is one of the biggest names in high-tech venture capital, having helped finance Software Publishing Corp., Rolm Corp. [later bought by IBM], and many others.

In 1981 high-tech venture capital was at flood tide, and the experts were predicting "exponential growth" in the educational software market. In the negotiating stage, Melchor paired up Piestrup with Fred Gibbons of Software Publishing Corp., whom Melchor had financed a few months earlier.

"Fred was to evaluate our product and our company and make a recommendation to Melchor about whether to fund us," Piestrup recalls, "but he got so enamored of what we were doing that he helped us write our business plan." Naturally, Gibbons recommended that Melchor fund Piestrup's group, and Melchor did just that.

Now, venture capitalists are not purely altruistic. In offering its financial support, Melchor's company expected a return of 10 to 20 times its original investment within five years, because of what was perceived to be the dynamic nature of the educational marketplace. Furthermore, any entrepreneur who accepts venture capital must give up some control of his or her company in exchange. Although the terms are negotiable, company founders typically give up at least 40 percent of their company's stock.

Piestrup declines to reveal how much Advanced Learning Technology gave up, but she does say, "I think [Melchor] was exceedingly generous. I think he would say that, too, because at that point all we had were three little prototypes and not one commercial bone in our bodies."

Anxious lest outside influences might rob her software artists of their creative freedom, at the same time Piestrup had to face the fact that without the venture capital, there would very likely be no more company, period.

"It was either disband or get venture capital," she says. Furthermore, she was impressed with the intelligent enthusiasm Jack Melchor displayed for her ideas. "He likes to help people with a dream," Piestrup says, "and he understood what we were doing."

But her employees were dead set against it. "The three of them very much wanted to stay away from venture capital in order to keep our educational side intact," she remembers. "They wanted to move to Teri's back room and hang Baggies [in which the early and ill-financed garage entrepreneurs had packaged their software] in ComputerLand or whatever. It was really me that said, 'No, we are going for venture capital.' "

In January 1982 Advanced Learning Technology accepted an infusion of $300,000 from Melchor, contingent on its hiring a new president (which it did, with Melchor's guidance). It expanded its office space in Portola Valley and became known as The Learning Company, or TLC. It also hired the pricey Regis McKenna public relations agency. "At that point we became a real company," Piestrup says.

Becoming a "real company" meant many changes and internal adjustments. "The company had to shift from being an R&D company, which I understood really well," Piestrup explains, "to being a marketing and sales company, and with that my role shifted too, of course. I was no longer the CEO and there was a great deal of money at stake, instead of just one grant that I had all budgeted."

That turn of events proved to be difficult for Piestrup. "The hardest thing has been letting go of the direct power," she said in 1984. "For example, hiring a president and then letting him do that job, and just holding myself back from telling him what to do. I don't really want the role of president, but then, I would love to call all the shots. Letting go is not the easiest thing in the world."

Robinett, too, had some difficulty with the transition. "The difference was night and day," he told the *Palo Alto Weekly* in 1985. "During our grant stage, we did whatever we wanted. Then, with the venture capital, there was all this pressure." But the pressure yielded results. Within six months of getting the funding, TLC released six new products.

One of them was destined to become a classic—and the company's all-time best-seller. Aimed at children aged nine and up, Rocky's Boots was an immediate hit with its double role as an entertaining game and as teacher of computer circuitry and Boolean algebra, and therefore of logical thinking.

In its stage of being market-tested by children, Rocky's Boots had proved to be even more than the developers had hoped. "The game contained mathematical material that's usually not presented to students until the second year of college," Piestrup explains, "but we began to see that kids seven years old and younger had little or no trouble understanding it." That goes for adults, too. "People in college have said they never understood Boolean algebra as well," Piestrup says. The secret to its success lay in having managed to pull off the tricky feat of presenting abstract ideas and relationships in concrete images.

Not only did Rocky's Boots manage to teach the abstract through the concrete, but it did it in an enjoyable way, in keeping with TLC's underlying philosophy: that educational software should be simple, direct, fun, colorful, and unfailingly playful.

Typical of the praise lavished on the hit product was columnist Erik Sandberg-Diment's review in *The New York Times* (July 19, 1983), in which he advised that ". . . if you have an Apple and kids, not getting Rocky's Boots is like having a toaster and not buying bread." Besides selling well, Rocky's Boots won the coveted approval of the National Education Association (NEA), as well as awards from *Learning* magazine, *InfoWorld* magazine, and *Parents' Choice* magazine. Every Learning Company product, in fact, got NEA approval and several awards.

In designing TLC's software, Piestrup incorporated the successful teaching methods she had observed in her ten years as a researcher. "I was very impressed with the fact that the successful approaches with children involved many senses—eyes, ears, and hands, not just abstractions—and they let the child have a choice," she notes.

Consequently The Learning Company's products compared very favorably with the existing educational software, which consisted invariably of drill-and-practice programs that were no more exciting than a textbook. Piestrup realized that software didn't have to require the child to read, but could instead prepare a child to learn to read.

All TLC software creates a world filled with positive reinforcement, where failure is impossible and success is rewarded with the opportunity to make new discoveries. "Our software builds confidence because you can't lose," Piestrup says. "You come to the answer." Mastery leads to ever greater challenges, and the person is in control at all times, not the computer.

Piestrup credits another educational software pioneer, Joyce Hakansson, with a concept of major importance to TLC. "She taught me that a computer should never tell children they are wrong," Piestrup says. "There is feedback but it is gentle, so risk taking is encouraged." TLC's software is also strictly nonviolent, featuring little creatures that cause mischief instead of weapons, explosions, and destruction.

TLC's programs concentrate on skills often underemphasized in traditional educational curricula: logical thinking, problem solving, conceptual learning, and creativity. "Kids need different thinking skills for the computer age than they needed before," Piestrup explains.

With healthy sales, awards galore, and unanimous praise, The Learning Company quickly established a reputation disproportionate to its size. "We were perceived as being an industry leader when we still barely had any products out," Piestrup says. Soon after the release of Rocky's Boots and the other five original programs, Piestrup started getting phone calls from IBM. "We had gotten on the cover of *InfoWorld,*" Piestrup explains. "IBM read the article and said they wanted every product we had. I was really proud of that." But at the same time, she was reluctant to comply. "I was really hesitant to take on a project with IBM when we were such a small company. We were only eight people. I didn't want to take an IBM contract unless I was sure we could absolutely deliver," she adds.

"I didn't know what the IBM PC was like because I'd only worked on the Apple and I thought it was pretty risky to take on lots of money from IBM," she explains. Furthermore, internally the company was a bit unsettled, and that also bothered Piestrup. Robinett was becoming increasingly restive and it looked as if the president hired in January 1982 might be moving on.

"But I remember Melchor saying, 'Do you realize who IBM *is*? You mean they had to call you more than once?' " she laughs. Finally, it seemed folly not to go ahead with the IBM deal.

"So we were one of only two companies in California, as far as I know, that had the PCjr the year before it was released. We had a locked room for it in our offices, and we rewrote all six of our programs for the PC and the PCjr," she says. "It was a big endorsement of our company at that time."

But, soon after the contract was signed in January 1983, Robinett did leave The Learning Company, and so did the then-president. At that point Piestrup was under the gun to find a new president "who would work out." She persuaded Marcia Klein, a vice president at Regis McKenna who had handled the TLC account since 1982, to take the job.

While at Regis, Klein had been instrumental in positioning both The Learning Company and Piestrup herself in the marketplace. Klein, who had also handled the Apple Computer account at Regis, was bursting with the marketing expertise TLC needed.

"The company had been quite disorganized," Piestrup says, "and she [Klein] pulled everything together and really turned it into a company." Since it looked like the educational software market was about to explode, the company geared up for fast growth, redesigned its packages, and expanded from 10 to 30 people.

In March 1983 a second round of venture capital financing brought in $3.2 million from a group of five investors. TLC moved to new offices in Menlo Park and, instead of publishing exclusively for Apple, Atari, and Radio Shack, it started getting its goods out to the distributors and retail stores.

Through Klein, the company put its software into computer and software stores, bookstores, department stores, mass merchandisers, and toy stores and also started selling through direct mail. TLC made deals with Addison-Wesley, Simon & Schuster, and American Express. Klein signed up more than 60 distributors, including Micro D, Softsel, SoftKat, and First Software—all industry leaders of the day.

"She put the company in the black for the first time in its history," Piestrup says. "Every month she was there, we met our projections." In fact, TLC doubled its sales during the year Klein was there.

Although Klein's predecessor had negotiated the contract with IBM, it was during her tenure that The Learning Company made its mark vis-à-vis its IBM connection. When the PCjr was announced on November 1, 1983, with its 16-color graphics, animation, music and sound effects, along with it were ordained TLC's six original software packages.

The future looked wide open, for both The Learning Company and Piestrup herself. But reality would be quite different. The expected boom in educational software turned out to be more of a fizzle, and the new power behind The Learning Company—money—would maneuver Piestrup out of a job.

3
The Micro Boom

After the pioneers of the personal computer industry had set the stage, developed the basic technology, and otherwise gotten the ball rolling, then came another wave of entrepreneurs: those who saw that an industry was indeed forming and that there lay an opportunity.

In the boom years of the industry, change was the only constant and things moved very, very fast. There was plenty of uncertainty and speculation about who would come out on top, and no technical standards whatsoever. Only with the unexpected runaway success of IBM's Personal Computer, introduced in 1981, did things start to settle down—to the benefit of some and the extinction of many others.

These were the glory years of the industry. Wall Street was highly receptive to micro stock offerings, venture capitalists were getting unheard-of returns on their investments—unusually fast—and the world at large suddenly became aware of what had been happening since 1976. The future fairly shimmered with promise.

Lorraine Mecca: Hitting an Industry Nerve

As the seventies drew to a close, the pioneers of the microcomputer revolution started to feel the satisfaction of having been there first, as the rest of the world began to catch on to the excitement. But the overall structure of the young industry was still developing.

Indispensable to the manufacturers and users alike was a product distribution system, to get computers and their many accessories out to the buying public.

Unfortunately, such a vehicle existed only in frustratingly rough form, as computer-store owners found out when they tried to stock their shelves. When Lorraine Mecca decided to start a distribution company to help her husband run his computer store, she had no idea that she was hitting an industrywide nerve.

Six months pregnant, Mecca talked her cousin Perry "Mitch" Mitchell into going into business with her, even though this first pregnancy was so difficult that she had been confined to bed for three months. By six months she was mobile for only six hours a day.

Now, why would a woman in her position want to start a business? Unused to inactivity, she was "going crazy" by the end of six months. "I wanted to do something," she says. "It was all tied together. I wanted to get it all done fast." Drawing on her past experience in electronics distribution, she decided to try it herself, offering mainly Apple computers and peripherals to dealers.

To convince Mitchell to act as her combination sales representative and delivery man, Mecca had to paint a picture of moderate success, at most. A professional boat captain, Mitchell was frequently gone for months at a time, taking boats through the Panama Canal for their owners. When he was in town, he rested.

"I remember telling him, 'Don't worry, you only have to work a few days a week. Stores don't open until 10:00, so you can sleep late every day,' " she recalls. He bought her line, and in July 1979 Mecca incorporated.

She rented a warehouse and two offices in a business complex in Orange County, and she set her cousin to work doing outside sales. Meanwhile, Mecca did everything else, working around the clock. To drum up business, she got the names of as many computer stores in the country as she could, and sent mailings out to them. Her first source of names was the trade publications.

"Apple would have listings of its dealers in its magazine ads, and so would Commodore," Mecca says. Mecca would type every name and address into her computerized mailing list. "After a while we started subscribing to Yellow Pages for large metropolitan areas and we just went through all the C's."

Because she was able to negotiate credit terms with vendors who knew and trusted her from her days at Connector Distribution, while her own customers (the dealers) paid COD, Micro D was profitable from the start. Whereas many start-up companies spend months, and sometimes years, trying to creep out of the red, Micro D shone like ebony.

Just how warm its lustre was didn't become evident until the end of Micro D's first fiscal year, three months later. "It was Halloween and I was closing out the general ledger," Mecca recalls. "The general ledger we were using was strictly a cost-accounting system, so that as you write checks or receive checks, you deduct from or add to your bank account, but you never really know how much people owe you or how much you owe anybody. You only know exactly what you have in the bank, so it's deceptive."

To get an idea of what the receivables were, she kept a running total of all the invoices. "I had a huge file in my word processor of every sale, every item we sold, so I could do a search by either invoice number or store name or product and find out who was buying what.

"That last day, I printed out that file and first I added up all the numbers, and then I added up the ones that were still unpaid. And I found out that in the [first] six weeks we were open for business, we'd done over $60,000 in business," she says, still amazed.

"I'd had no idea, because the checks we'd received were so much less than that, because we shipped just about everything UPS and you don't get your money back for about three weeks. I didn't have all the money back and I wasn't even aware of what our sales were."

When she called her husband with the news, he figured that she had to be wrong and told her to add it up again. "I added it up again and it came out with exactly the same number," she says. "I called him again and said, 'Geza, we sold over $60,000!' He said, 'I'll be right over.' "

Mecca had made no mistakes in her math, and Csige decided that day to quit his computer stores as soon as possible and join Micro D. "This is our opportunity to make money," Csige told her. It was wonderfully clear that Csige and his partner weren't the only dealers having trouble getting peripheral equipment when they needed it. Mecca had struck gold.

Success, unfortunately, takes its toll. Mecca couldn't help but feel that she had grabbed an unexpectedly lively bull by the horns; she could neither let go of it nor contain it totally. Demand was high and manpower was nonexistent. In fact, the day her daughter was born, Mecca worked until 6:00 P.M., gave birth at half past midnight, and was back at work the next morning.

"When I got home, Geza had moved the computer to my bedroom and forwarded the office phones there. We were up and running the next day," she remembers. The birth took place only a week after Csige's decision to join her, but he wasn't there yet. And, baby or no baby, the work had to be done. "There was no alternative. There was nobody else to do it," she says.

By the time their daughter was two months old, Csige had left the stores for good and come to Micro D. "It was sort of scary," Mecca says, "because that meant Micro D was our sole source of income. I felt real worried, because here I was with this baby and maybe no source of income if it didn't work." Nevertheless, they took the chance, putting every single egg in one basket.

As business partners, Csige and Mecca discovered that they complemented each other nicely. "Geza is good at seeing the big picture and understanding concepts," Mecca says. "I'm very focused. I take care of the details. I'm like the line and he's the quarterback."

On two occasions, in fact, Csige's perceptions have put the company several giant steps ahead. Even before he was at Micro D full-time, around Christmas 1979, Csige became concerned that almost 90 percent of Micro D's products were manufactured by Apple Computer—but Micro D was not an authorized Apple distributor.

How did Micro D get the Apple products, then? "Every way we could," Mecca admits. Ironically, one source was retail stores. "Apple had a dealer price," Mecca explains. "If a dealer bought one Apple, it was $880. If they bought four, they were $810 each.

"So if the computer store really only needed one but wanted to make the money, they'd come to us and say, 'Look, we only need one. We'll buy four, and you give us the money for three.'

That way, they made out because they got the $810 price for one, and we could buy the three and sell them for $880—the normal price if you were buying them one at a time—and make money."

The ComputerLand chain of stores, in particular, had "an incredible advantage," Mecca recalls. "ComputerLand stores bought them for $700 each because of the way corporate [headquarters] did their buying. So a ComputerLand store was able to buy a computer and sell it [to the public] for even less than some of the other dealers were paying."

Micro D was not at all shy about taking advantage of the situation. "We went to a couple of ComputerLand stores and started buying from them," Mecca says. "We would pay them their commission fee and an incentive and buy the computers for less than the dealers could buy them [from Apple] for." Then Micro D could turn around and sell to other dealers, at a profit. "Now, all of this was not authorized activity," Mecca acknowledges, "but when there are products and there's demand, there are ways to buy them."

Micro D also took advantage of Apple's practice of closing down for two weeks at Christmas. "It took them another two weeks before they got back into production enough to ship," Mecca says. "So for the main Christmas period and right after Christmas—when people were really buying that kind of thing—there was no product available. You couldn't get it from Apple; you couldn't get it from your distributor. We knew what would happen and we were in a position to stock up, so you could get it from Micro D."

However, the party was ending for those who were "making out" on Apple's distribution methods. Apple was aware that its products were getting into the market through unauthorized channels, and was getting ready to do something about it.

"Geza knew it wouldn't last, so our objective was to go from being more than 80 percent Apple to being 20 percent Apple," Mecca says. Micro D began an effort to distribute a preponderance of Apple-oriented goods manufactured not by Apple itself, but by other, so-called third-party, vendors.

Fortunately, just as Micro D had opened its doors for business, the third-party products had started proliferating, including computers, peripherals, and software. The blockbuster VisiCalc spreadsheet software was brand new, and it caused a surge in demand for Apple products and add-ons. Micro D concentrated on getting those products and made an especially big push into Hayes modems, which would become the de facto industry standard.

Early in 1980, Apple did what Csige had foreseen a couple of months earlier. Without warning, Apple canceled all its outside distributors, deciding to act as its own distributor. Although that gave Apple much more control over what went where, it also put a lot of distributors out of business.

Micro D, however, was in fine shape. "By the time it happened we'd switched over to mostly third-party vendors, so we were the only distributor with a developed channel for add-on Apple products," Mecca explains.

In its first full year, Micro D brought in $3.6 million in sales. By the end of its second year, 1981, Micro D had more than tripled its business to $12.4 million, enough to warrant opening a second warehouse, in Dallas. Sales in 1982 more than doubled to $25.3 million—and Mecca was on top of the world.

"1982 was great," she says. "We were growing, we had a new building, I was pregnant with my second baby, then we started opening new warehouses around the country, expanding geographically. That was tremendous." That November they opened another warehouse, near Baltimore.

In 1982, a miracle happened on Wall Street. One of the biggest bull markets in history had started in August, enabling many micro companies to go public and raise huge amounts of money from buyers giddy with high-tech fever. It was a rare and exciting opportunity for companies—especially technology firms—to raise some cash. During the entire time since World War II, comparable conditions had existed only briefly in the late 1960s.

Micro D needed cash to continue its fast growth. "We were leveraged 8 to 1," Mecca says, meaning that for every $1 of net worth Micro D had, it had borrowed $8 from the bank. By the spring of 1983, Mecca's and Csige's thoughts had turned toward the possibility of going public.

Once again Csige's intuition came into play, and this time it brought the company its greatest gain. The stock market was hot and wild, but it surely couldn't last forever. If Micro D wanted to take advantage of the current situation, it would have to act fast. Csige was convinced that the high-tech "killings" in the stock market would end, very specifically, by that July 15.

How is Csige so precise in his predictions? "I rely much more on a feel for things, as opposed to a lot of thinking about things," Csige says. "I just feel things—I mean I feel things a year in advance if I'm really involved in something.

"Plus, I think I'm always scared," Csige laughs. "When things get really good, then I get scared and I begin to look around for things that could go wrong. And when things begin to boil, then I *really* get scared and I want to be in a more protective mode.

"In 1983, we'd gone through a lot of different approaches to get financing, and I was afraid we weren't going to get any. With the hot market in computer technology, I really began to push for things—to try to get it done before something unpredictable would happen."

On the basis of Csige's uncanny track record, "We pushed something fierce to do the legwork before [July 15]," Mecca recalls. That meant writing a prospectus in two weeks instead of the usual six, and getting the Securities and Exchange Commission (SEC) to respond to it in four weeks instead of the usual eight.

How did they get a prospectus—a formulaic, detailed financial document about which the SEC is very picky—written in two weeks? "We locked all the principals in the company in a conference room and no one was allowed to leave," Mecca explains, in all seriousness. "Normally, it's hard to get the key officials together in one place for more than eight hours."

And how did they get the prospectus through the SEC so quickly? "Prayer," Mecca says. In truth, it was simply very well written, done the way the SEC likes to see it done. As Ann Piestrup has observed on the subject of applying for anything: If there's a formula, follow it.

Going public was by far the greatest challenge the company had faced up to that point. "The time pressures were incredible," Mecca says. Naiveté added its own tribulations. "It was a brand-new learning experience. No one on the staff had gone through it before."

The entire process began around May 15, the prospectus was submitted to the SEC on June 7, and Micro D went public on July 12, 1983. When Mecca woke up on July 13, she was worth approximately $55 million. Her 3.4 million shares (51 percent) of Micro D stock had commanded an initial offering price of $16 per share. Besides gaining the paper wealth, she personally cashed in $4 million worth of her own stock that day. "I couldn't believe it," Mecca marvels. "When I filled out the deposit slip, there weren't enough spaces for all the zeros—either for me or for the company."

Csige's instincts were almost frightening in their accuracy. The very day before Micro D went public, the high-tech market started to fall. The boom was over. Micro D, however, got top dollar for its offering, bringing in $25 million for the company that day and instantly gaining a big advantage over the competition.

Jacqueline Morby: First on the Scene

The excitement surrounding the micro industry was just about to break when Jacqueline Morby found her way into that enclave. By 1980 several factors had combined to put Morby into a very valuable position.

For one thing, political changes had suddenly made high-tech investments very attractive to venture capitalists. A decade earlier, before high tech was hot, the capital gains tax stood at 25 percent. That was a nice, comfortable rate for venture capitalists, because it meant that they didn't have to pay much tax on their profits. But by the mid-seventies, the tax was upped to give Uncle Sam 48 cents of every dollar of investors' profits. Naturally, they stopped investing so much. Since their willingness to invest was in direct proportion to how much tax they had to pay on each dollar of profit turned, most waited for better weather.

Suddenly, in 1978, the clouds broke, thanks largely to the efforts of the American Electronics Association, which was instrumental in getting the capital gains tax again lowered—to 28 percent. This meant that success was again affordable, and the money people wasted no time. Whereas in 1977 venture capital firms had committed $39 million to invest in new businesses, the very next year that figure skyrocketed to $570 million—almost 15 times as much.

In 1980 the capital gains tax was lowered even further, to 20 percent, and by 1982 another $1.7 billion would be poured into new businesses, many of them in high tech. By then, of course, the venture capitalists were virtually on the prowl, trying to ferret out the potentially big winners before anyone else did. In 1983, at the zenith of high-tech mania, venture commitments would reach $4.5 billion.

Naturally, besides making available billions of investment dollars, the situation also created a need for more people able to make the investment decisions. In 1978, the year the money would start to fly, Jacqueline Morby graduated from Simmons Graduate Management School and joined the world of venture capital full-time.

From her first day at TA Associates in Boston, she was on her own. "You don't get a lot of help or coddling here," she says. "You have to be your own person and a self-starter. We're a very entrepreneurial organization. Everyone's out doing his or her own thing.

"[Managing partners] Peter Brooke and Kevin Landry were very supportive, but there wasn't time for them to help me in terms of training, although they would give help if anyone needed it," she says. "It wasn't just me—no one got training here."

As it was, Morby didn't really need training. A lot of her personal success comes from her intuition. "Part of our work is having people trust you," she says. "You have to judge and understand people. I'd say it's 30 to 40 percent of our job."

Some credit also goes to her experiences in South America. "Down there, I was dealing with uncertainty all the time," Morby notes. "I was negotiating my way around in another language and there was always unfamiliar territory, both physically and socially. I think it was good training."

With keen insight, she soon identified the then-neglected area of mainframe software as potentially lucrative. "It seemed to me then that hardware was going to become more of a commodity," she explains, "and software would be where the value existed in computer systems." That happened to be a fundamental truth that was not yet obvious, even to most people in the computer industry.

Morby believes that she reached that watershed conclusion "by accident." Her close examination of the thriving mainframe hardware industry uncovered the mainframe software industry living very much in its shadow. At that time most venture capitalists weren't paying any attention at all to software.

Once discovered, however, it could not be ignored. Morby intensified her investigation. "I visited a lot of mainframe software companies and saw how profitable they were," Morby says. She studied the market predictions and saw that mainframe software markets were growing at 40 percent compounded a year, a very rapid growth rate for any industry.

Along the way, of course, she gained an excellent understanding of what software really was. Morby discerned an opportunity for TA that was still undiscovered by the crowd, and acted on it.

It was not an easy road. Morby made what are known as cold calls on about 100 companies in 1978 to 1979, and at least 30 of those were mainframe software companies. Many didn't need venture capital; some had never heard of it. It fell to Morby to educate the uneducated, evaluate her prospective investments, and, if they looked promising, try to persuade them to accept venture capital in return for bargain-basement-priced stock in the company.

When it works right, the system can be an exhilarating win-win situation. If a venture capitalist buys, say, 5 million shares of a new company at 25 cents a share, the company receives $1.25 million on the barrel, to use as it sees fit. Then if the company later goes public at, say, $10 a share, the venture capitalist rakes in $50 million overnight—40 times what it invested.

Just as a movie is culled from thousands of hours of filming, Morby's scores of company visits resulted in just three mainframe software investments: McCormack & Dodge Corp. (Needham Heights, Massachusetts); Capex Corp. (Phoenix); and Artificial Intelligence Corp. (Waltham, Massachusetts). McCormack & Dodge and Capex were both later sold, giving TA its payback, and Morby has a seat on the board of directors of Artificial Intelligence Corp.

Having gained entrance into the mainframe software arena, Morby began to hear rumblings about microcomputer software and figured, "There must be something interesting here." Not only had she discovered venture capital itself just before its resurgence on the financial scene, but her timing again was exquisite in pinpointing micro software as a potentially explosive market.

Many otherwise sophisticated people simply didn't understand software at that time, but Morby did, and that was her edge. While most investors shied away from it, Morby forged ahead. "I realized there were [software] products that could be packaged, requiring little modification, that were therefore standardized products and not risky in themselves," she explains.

It remained for her to track down actual micro software companies to invest in. Just as locating the mainframe companies had been a Herculean task, so was sorting out the micro companies. The micro industry was still so new that even the eventual superstars didn't necessarily stand out as such.

To help put it all in perspective, Morby devoured industry magazines, looking for ads placed by likely prospects, and walked the floors of countless trade shows. "I'd visit all the booths at the trade shows," she says, "the most tiring work of all." Tiring indeed, with tens of thousands of people swarming over acres of floor space, jostling one another, with dozens often jockeying to see the same thing at once.

All part of the quest to invest. After whittling her potential client companies down to four, Morby made cold calls on each of them to narrow the field even further. She zeroed in on Digital Research, Inc., of Pacific Grove, California.

"DRI was a very exciting company, very innovative," she says. "In my first interview with [DRI President] Gary Kildall, I saw that he had an amazing marketing understanding of the direction of microcomputer software. I also felt he would be easy to work with." Morby was sure she had a winner.

But Kildall was not easily won. "It was probably the most difficult investment I've made," Morby says. "Gary wasn't sure he wanted any venture capital, and it took about six months to convince him he did. It seemed like forever—uncertainty is the hardest thing."

For Kildall, the offer finally made sense, and not just for the money. "With Digital Research, the whole purpose of having us invest was to get a management team for the company," Morby explains. DRI agreed to terms that the company has kept confidential.

One thing that's no secret, however, is Kildall's respect for Morby. "I first met her in 1980, when she was just getting involved in micros," he recalls. "She understood a lot of things in a very short period of time, especially for someone with a nontechnical viewpoint."

From DRI, Morby's hard work and intuition led her to three more micro software investments: Sierra On-Line and Spinnaker Software Co., on whose boards of directors she sits, and Softsel Computer Products, Inc. In all, she invested $8 million in the micro software industry for TA Associates. In 1981, TA acknowledged her vision and hard work with a vice presidency. Morby's efforts were rewarded in less tangible ways as well. "Nothing is more exciting than to find a company that's a terrific investment," Morby says. "It's like discovering gold."

While Morby knew exactly what she was doing, her early investments in micro software did not always earn the approval of her colleagues. "Spinnaker was a controversial investment around here because the principals weren't from operating backgrounds," she recalls. They were two sharp Harvard Business School graduates, working in high-tech-oriented Boston consulting firms, who were pitching educational software.

"If we hadn't been so well-versed in microcomputer software, we would have said, 'You're crazy, go away,' " Morby says. As it was, the two Harvard graduates almost turned Morby away. One of them dropped in at TA's office on a fact-finding mission, hoping to see the manager of the office. Instead, the manager's secretary told him, "Jacqui Morby will see you." Morby then suggested lunch. "I didn't want to have lunch with her," admits Bill Bowman, Spinnaker's cofounder. What Bowman didn't realize was that the manager he wanted to see was actually junior to Morby. "I didn't know who [Jacqui Morby] was—a secretary or what," Bowman recalls. "I had never heard of her. But a consultant never misses an opportunity to B.S." Over coffee, Morby astonished Bowman by asking, "Why don't you and Dave work up something we can finance?" He and Dave [Seuss, his partner] did, and Morby liked what she saw. In May 1982 Spinnaker got its first infusion of venture capital—$800,000 from TA Associates.

"They were really, truly excellent marketing people," she explains. "They didn't especially know the software market as well as we did, but they had an expertise that nobody in the software business had and we felt we could introduce them to the right people." And another company was born.

"If we hadn't taken them on, who knows if they would have been financed by other people?" she asks. Others saw it as something of a long shot, but Morby's belief in her own judgment was quickly justified. "Spinnaker was unbelievably successful," she says. "In four months they had products out in the marketplace and they were beating the projections all along the way."

Although Morby's pursuit of micro software investments can be seen as daring in terms of timing, her decisions were based on hard facts transported from the mainframe environment, as well as her firsthand observation of the micro industry. She understood software, and that knowledge took away much of the risk that rightfully panicked others.

Instinct played no little part either. Quick judgments are part of the investment game, in both the high- and low-tech worlds. "I can usually tell in the first 15 minutes of meeting someone whether we want to finance them or not," she says.

How can she tell? "You just know," she says. "You meet them, you might even like them, but the market's too crowded or the product's not unique enough. If you really know an area like I do, you can quickly determine if the management team understands what it's doing. If it's an area you don't know much about and you're too busy, you'll probably just reject it."

Of course, only the future will tell how successful Morby's investments really were. The industry shakeout and slump of 1985 to 1986 have added up only to a disquieting uncertainty. Failure is an ever-present possibility—and therein lies the most difficult part of Morby's job.

"When your companies don't do well, it's very upsetting," she says. "It's not fun to lose money. It's embarrassing for you and for the firm, and it's difficult because you feel responsible: The investors put their trust in you. But ultimately you do, sooner or later.

"There have been investments where I've wondered if I made a mistake, but I don't know yet," Morby says. "It's hard to tell. It takes a while." One investment opportunity that she rejected, however, gave her many a second thought.

"Adam Osborne was a reference of Gary Kildall when I made the DRI investment," Morby recalls. "So when I called Adam, he said, 'Hey, I'm putting together a company called Brandywine Computers, so I'll send you the business plan.' For a long time I looked at Brandywine but I didn't [invest in] it."

Brandywine Computers turned into Osborne Computer Co., a flashy high roller whose performance was spectacular for a time. And every milestone of Osborne's increased Morby's wistfulness. "I regretted it for a long, long, long time," she admits.

But Osborne stunned the entire industry when it went bankrupt in September 1983, only five months after abruptly pulling out of its scheduled initial public offering. Osborne Computer turned out to be the failure that marked the beginning of the decline of the industry. "Now I don't regret it anymore," Morby notes, "because I would have lost my money. But it looked awfully good for a long time."

Typically, venture capitalists can count on 40 percent of their investments showing a total or partial loss. Another 30 percent are expected to be among what financiers call "the living dead"—companies whose performance gives the entrepreneur an annuity but never gets the venture capitalist liquidity.

Only 30 percent of a venture capitalist's investments will be bona fide winners, and of those, only 3 percent will be superstars, giving back at least ten times what was invested. But even though uncertainty far outweighs triumph for venture capitalists, these sky divers of the financial world just love to take risks.

Every year, TA Associates makes 30 to 40 investments in all areas of technology—and occasionally in other areas of business—and rejects out of hand about 1,000 business plans that come over the transom. Morby and other first-wave micro venture capitalists, of course, moved out of the micro arena long ago, and on to such other areas of technological interest as telecommunications, data communications, semiconductors, and networking systems. "The microcomputer industry is no longer an interesting area for investments," Morby says.

Her reasons delineate perfectly the current state of the industry. "The market's changed dramatically and is now dominated by one company, IBM, so the micro area is not a new market anymore," Morby explains. "Suddenly it's an industry of big companies."

But it was fun while it lasted. "Seldom in the history of venture capital investing has there been an industry where companies could grow so large so quickly," Morby notes. "I don't think there will be similar instances in the future where growth is so rapid and there's such a boon for investors."

Janelle Bedke: "The Power of Simplicity"

When Fred Gibbons recruited Janelle Bedke for his start-up company, she hesitated long enough that Hewlett-Packard can forever feel flattered, then went for it. "It was a matter of knowing what I needed to do," she says, "namely, to get myself into an environment where my efforts were tied to the result."

Not only that, but—like Gibbons—Bedke saw clearly the need for software that was useful *and* easy to use, in keeping with the personal computer's democratic appeal. "I was taken by the excitement of starting this company and by its potential," she says. "I like achieving and I love doing things."

She's also not averse to taking a gamble. Of Software Publishing Corp.'s (SPC's) three cofounders, Bedke bore the brunt of the risk at first by working full-time to lay the groundwork for the new company while her two partners kept their HP jobs and gave nights and weekends to SPC.

That first year, Bedke wrote the software manual for the company's first product and developed the marketing brochure. She also worked with the ad agency and the package designer, saw to it that disk labels were manufactured and delivered, and acted as liaison with Apple Computer, on whose popular Apple II micro the firm's product line would first run.

The philosophy behind Software Publishing's pfs: (for personal filing system) line of software is that it will do what most people want most of the time, without complicated extra features that would only rarely be used. Not only does it stick to the basics, but it is extremely easy to use, even for someone who has no experience with a computer. The pfs: line is modular, meaning that each type of application package is bought separately, but can be mixed and matched with any other pfs: applications. Data files created for one application can be used by any other pfs: application; no retyping of data is necessary. One of SPC's past advertising mottos, which still expresses the company's philosophy, was "The Power of Simplicity."

Although Bedke was the first of the three to actually devote 16-hour days to the project, her cofounders were just as totally committed to the venture. John Page, a 12-year HP veteran and database-management software expert, worked at HP full-time that year, while spending hundreds of "spare" hours writing the software that would soon become known as pfs:File, SPC's first product.

Fred Gibbons, a 5-year HP employee who was then a marketing manager, conceived of SPC in March 1979, orchestrated the core group of Bedke and Page, and poured about $50,000 of his own money into the expenses that first year. Besides cash, Gibbons also gave many of his nights and weekends to Software Publishing that year. "He was very active in setting the strategy and working with me on marketing questions and so forth," Bedke says.

In September 1980, pfs:File was finished and announced, and the orders started rolling in. "For the next six months I packed boxes and answered the phone," Bedke recalls. "If I couldn't sleep at night, I'd get up at 3:00 A.M. and pack boxes until I felt sleepy again."

In January 1981 Gibbons quit his job at HP and joined Bedke full-time as president. The following month Page also bid adieu to HP and assumed the duties of engineering manager for SPC. Now they were all out on the same limb.

By April, things started happening fast—not all of them good. First of all, Bedke had a run-in with the police. "There were no businesses in Atherton [California] and there weren't supposed to be any businesses in Atherton," she recalls. "But every day the UPS truck would pull up in front of my house until the neighbors got suspicious and finally complained."

The local police chief called her in. "It was a little traumatic at the time because I got this official-looking letter," she recalls. "But in truth, I just made an appointment and went to see him, explained the situation, and everything was all right. We were thinking of getting an office anyway at that point because we were really outgrowing my house," she notes. "We had hired additional people and they were getting in my way." Within two months, SPC had moved into an office and Bedke had her house back.

April had also brought a much more pleasant incident. SPC received an infusion of venture capital, to the tune of a quarter of a million dollars, from Jack Melchor, future benefactor of The Learning Company. "The best time to raise money is when you don't need it," Bedke says. "When we first went for some money, we had a proven track record. We had been doing business for six months and were beginning to turn a profit, versus going to a venture capitalist with only an idea." By the time Software Publishing sought financing, it was an easy sell.

In going after venture capital, SPC did not struggle with the same conflict of money versus control as The Learning Company would nine months later. SPC planned from the start to go public eventually, which by definition meant that its ownership would be diluted. In planning to sell its stock to the public, SPC was looking forward to garnering what are generally considered to be the real benefits of being a player on Wall Street: higher visibility, prestige, and credibility.

So for Software Publishing, giving up some control in 1981 for an injection of venture capital was not at all worrisome. It could only propel the company toward its stated goal. "The venture capital money was to ramp up growth," Bedke says. "We could have gone along with three people, but we wanted to blast it out."

Blast it out they did. They increased their advertising and hired more people to help with marketing and software development. In June 1981 they shipped their second product, pfs:Report, meant to be a companion package for pfs:File. Pfs:Report allowed the user to analyze the data stored by pfs:File—it created various reports using those data and provided calculations, such as totals and averages.

Every product was a hit. Sales for the 11 months ending September 30, 1981, were $718,000. The following May, the firm attracted another $1 million in venture capital, from four different financiers, for more expansion.

"We wanted to increase our investments in engineering and advertising," Bedke explains. By September 30, 1982, sales had more than quintupled over the previous year's, to $4 million. One thing had become certain: There definitely was a place on the shelf for easy-to-use software.

IBM Enters the Fray

While scores of upstart companies were hustling to set up shop in the mid-70s, IBM—staid, entrenched, and traditional—stood by in silence. Mainframes were its business and for the longest time it showed no inclination to think small. Still, the company was not quite as aloof as it seemed. While publicly it feigned disinterest, privately IBM had set at least a few wheels in motion.

As early as 1976, IBM had placed prototype terminals and microcomputers in homes experimentally, to see how and how often people would use them. In addition, it set marketing and engineering teams to work studying the commercial potential of the microcomputer market. In spite of such early moves, the mainframe king was still "just looking."

By the end of the seventies, IBM was looking back on a decade during which it had lost significant market share. Whereas 60 percent of the large-computer market belonged to IBM in 1970, by 1979 its claim had slipped to 40 percent. Although IBM still held the lion's share, it had been laboring those ten years under an enervating antitrust suit brought by the Department of Justice in January 1969.

That farewell gesture from the Johnson Administration, filed on the president's last day in office, would keep IBM's (and the government's) lawyers busy in a Manhattan courtroom week after week, year after year, for more than a decade. Temporarily subdued and forced to defend its every action, corporate IBM retracted its competitive claws to the point of mere playfulness.

As the seventies slipped away, however, the percentages made it painfully obvious that something would have to be done, lawsuit or no lawsuit. No longer could IBM play dead and still remain alive. Acutely aware of the danger of further inaction, in 1979 IBM's top brass made a quiet commitment to "explore" new high-growth markets (such as the personal computer) as well as new distribution channels (such as independent retailers).

At the same time, many of IBM's technologists were being inspired by the contagious excitement on the other side of those Big Blue walls. For reasons that had nothing to do with market share, many were dreaming (but not quite expecting) that the giant would give them a chance to get in on what they knew was a revolution.

IBM soon enough saw that this was the high-growth market it was looking for and, finally, that the time was right to act. By mid-1980, IBM's then-chairman Frank T. Cary and then-president John R. Opel were of one mind: that IBM should go ahead with the development of a microcomputer.

Because the emotional and technological risks had already been taken by others, for the most part, the fattest cat on the block could now curl up with an invention that already purred.

Cary and Opel agreed to waste no time, but to put together a development team immediately and push it to its limits. Starting at ground zero, they wanted to see a viable product within one year. Once they had made this decision, they had to find someone to take on the awesome responsibility of overseeing the project.

The late Philip D. (Don) Estridge, then a respected but relatively obscure small-business-systems engineer, volunteered for that challenge as quickly as many others would have run the other way. As director of the new enterprise, Estridge would be responsible for everything: the development, programming, manufacture, sales, servicing, and distribution of what was to become IBM's most popular product.

By 1979 Estridge had already served IBM well for 20 years. His rock-solid technical background included IBM work for the U.S. space program in the 1960s, engineering and programming for IBM's Federal Systems Division, and similar efforts for its smaller business systems. Entrepreneurial by nature, Estridge was happy to assume complete responsibility, and his take-charge approach proved essential to the project's success.

In going ahead with the development of a microcomputer, IBM broke all its own rules. In a drastic departure from IBM theory and tradition, the Cary/Opel team created an independent business unit (IBU), headed by Estridge, to operate like a small, independent company within the larger one.

The gesture instantaneously cut a wide swath through the miles of red tape and many levels of authority that normally hold development progress to a fast crawl in any huge corporation. The IBU, Cary said after his retirement, was "IBM's answer to the question, 'How do you make an elephant tap-dance?' "

IBM essentially acted as a venture capitalist for the IBU, Estridge explained to *Business Week* in 1983. "It gave us management guidance, money, and allowed us to operate on our own," he said.

Beginning in July 1980, a 12-man core development team in Boca Raton, Florida, worked 70- to 80-hour weeks with the type of joyful fervor that had characterized the early industry. For them, the freedom and excitement of the project made the hard work feel good.

Such a spirit of independence within IBM was unheard of, although the company would eventually create about a dozen more of the IBUs. And there were no regrets. Once the word got out to the rest of IBM that Boca was looking for more help on the personal computer, the full potential of the project became resoundingly apparent.

Estridge's group was authorized to go from 12 people to 150 by the end of 1980. A trip to IBM's facility in Boulder, Colorado, to interview prospective transfers brought out a crowd of 200 people, when only 20 or 30 were expected to show up. By the end of the day, 500 calls had come in. That unsuspected enthusiasm in the ranks mimicked perfectly the explosion of interest that had been so invisibly pervasive in the outside world.

Fully staffed with the most free-wheeling and probably most enthusiastic group within IBM, the Entry Systems Business Unit was on its way. In 12 months, as planned, the engineers had come up with a reliable and powerful—if not ground-breaking—business microcomputer, which was publicly unveiled in August 1981.

And in a stroke of genius, IBM had years earlier copyrighted the widely used—and formerly generic—term "Personal Computer," with which it christened the new addition. Suddenly, the phrase everyone had been casually tossing around for half a decade meant only one thing: IBM.

At the time, it was not at all clear that IBM would eclipse, or even pose a threat to, the existing players. In those days there were already about 150 competitors in the microcomputer field, although Apple Computer and Tandy Corp. (maker of Radio Shack computers) were leading the way with a very comfortable 23 percent and 16 percent of the market, respectively. Supremely confident, Apple ran a full-page ad in *The Wall Street Journal* that said, with some condescension, "Welcome, IBM. Seriously."

The head of the number three personal computer maker at the time—Commodore International Ltd., which then had a 10 percent share—also publicly welcomed IBM into the fray as a needed legitimizer of the still fairly ragtag industry. Such generosity of spirit expressed a sense of security that would prove false indeed. For IBM had done something that would not only legitimize the industry but would take it by storm, something that surprised those who liked to believe the giant could copy but not innovate.

Although the industry standard in 1980 was a microcomputer built around an 8-bit microprocessor, IBM upped the ante to 16 bits, permitting the PC to work faster (by processing many more bits [basic units] of information at a time) and to handle longer and more complex software programs.

The IBM PC also offered users sharper screen images, a more sophisticated keyboard than most machines on the market, self-testing on startup, and expandability (for a price) that would allow a user to store the equivalent of 160 single-spaced typewritten pages in memory (ten times the norm).

From the start, IBM contracted with VisiCorp to have VisiCalc—the original spreadsheet program—available for the PC, as well as (from other vendors) accounting, word processing, and communications software, with one game package thrown in. The combination of higher speed, more power, more memory capacity, and workhorse software meant that serious business users finally had a machine adequate to their needs—and, in many cases, it came from the same outfit that made their corporate mainframes.

IBM's pervasiveness worked greatly in its favor. To many people, particularly the less technically sophisticated, "IBM" and "computer" were (and still are) synonymous. IBM's reputation alone proved to be a powerful seller.

Although many industry pundits and competitors expressed doubt that the PC would ever really go anywhere, Portia Isaacson's Future Computing was among the very few to predict stunning success for the PC. True to Isaacson's belief, the IBM PC would become the standard in an industry without standards.

The Wall Street Journal, too, was uncanny in its projection—printed the day after the PC's unveiling—that IBM would take the industry lead within two years. In truth, it took precisely 28 months. The Personal Computer caught on with a fury, much to the surprise of even IBM.

Joyce Wrenn: Making the Elephant Dance

While Don Estridge's team was working quietly but feverishly in Boca Raton, Joyce Wrenn—then director of information systems in IBM's General Products Division in San Jose—was becoming more and more captivated by the ever thicker atmosphere in California. "You couldn't live in Silicon Valley during that era without being aware of microcomputers," she says.

Contrary to the reactions of many in the mainframe world, Wrenn immediately sensed that the micro phenomenon was much more than a passing fancy. "I found it terribly exciting to have computing power at one's own fingertips," she remembers. "When I first entered the industry back in 1959, I essentially had a whole computer at my fingertips, but it wasn't practical to have that whole computer very often because you had to share it with other people.

"The thought that you could have so much computing power on your desktop and use it yourself, along with having color—the possibilities to me were just extremely exciting." So inspired was she that Wrenn independently developed a proposal for IBM to get into the micro software business.

She had no idea IBM was already on its way. Because IBM is so huge, she explains, "unless you have a need to know about a given development, you wouldn't hear about it. Because of the work I was doing in San Jose, working with mainframes and terminals, there would never be a reason for me to find out about [the Personal Computer]."

On her own, however, she had reached many of the same conclusions the Boca people had. "At that point there were mostly games and very little educational software," she recalls, "and it didn't take a lot of conjecture to see, with the power of the micro, what could be put on it."

In discussing her ideas about microcomputers with various IBMers, conversation after conversation pointed toward Boca Raton. Many of Wrenn's thoughts about the software that IBM should offer its customers were very similar to Estridge's, and her years of software development gave her an authority rarely matched. The natural consequence was for Wrenn to join the Florida team. Three months after the first PC was shipped, she moved 3,000 miles to become the director of software publishing for Entry Systems, in January 1982.

The move was not a casual one. "Every time you go into another position there's some risk involved," she notes. "For me it was leaving California, where I lived and had a support system, to come across the country to Boca Raton and getting into a whole new area of the business in IBM. But then, without risk it isn't as much fun."

As it happened, the month she assumed her new title was the same month the Justice Department decided its 13-year-old antitrust suit against IBM—dubbed "the Antitrust Division's Vietnam"—was "without merit" and summarily dropped it. With the PC already launched, there were no longer any impediments to going full speed ahead.

And that's exactly what happened, because the IBM Personal Computer was a tremendous and unexpected success. When the PC broke away from the pack, Boca went wild. "It was delightful because there was such a challenge," Wrenn says, "and it was such an explosive environment, in terms of changes and the rapidity of change—you know, every day."

While delightful, it was also incredibly hectic. "One of the biggest challenges was just staying abreast and trying to get ahead of a very rapidly changing environment," she notes. "IBM was growing us because we needed more people to do the work," she says, "and I can remember the chart that showed waves of manufacturing to try and meet the demand.

"While we had that going on, we were working on introducing the PC XT, which was the follow-on to the PC," she says. "Then we were introducing these products around the world, which meant having the basic systems material translated into five languages, and I was working on that. At the same time, we were beginning to branch out into many application areas and we were assimilating more people and trying to get them on board in keeping with where we were heading. I mean, we were just *really* busy.

"My now-husband was amazed that the parking lot at the IBM building was always full on Saturdays and Sundays. I worked part of every weekend the whole time I was there, and usually until 7:00 every night."

The Entry Systems Division managed to keep Wrenn far busier than she'd ever been. "In other jobs at IBM I've always been able to find enough time to do some work in addition to the job I was hired to do," she explained at the time. "That has not been true here.

"The environment we're in is so dynamic and there has been so much to do and so many challenges and opportunities that, for the first time in my career, I have not really had time to take on other activities. Instead, there was always more work than I could get done in a given day, so I had to prioritize and always think in terms of, 'What part do you just throw off the end of the desk?' and I learned that early."

Having opened the door to software developers of all kinds all over the country—including free-lancers working out of their living rooms, IBMers writing software on the side, and third-party software companies—Wrenn and her staff were responsible for screening, evaluating, and accepting or rejecting all submissions.

Wrenn's purview embraced the whole spectrum of potential IBM software: educational and entertainment, productivity, and such vertical markets as accounting software.

As would any other software publisher, Wrenn's group evaluated each package submitted according to criteria that ultimately tried to measure the commercial potential of the product: Is it unique? Does it meet a need? Is it easy to use? Is it well documented? Is it user-friendly? Does it have sufficient "help" screens?

Does it provide rich enough functions to really solve the user's problem? Or—on the downside—is it the 25th product in its category?

Software from an outside source that was deemed desirable would be obtained on a royalty basis. Once a software package was chosen, Wrenn and her staff worked with the author to hone it to IBM's style, standards of performance, and ease of use.

With "several hundred" people reporting to her (IBM maintains a stubborn vagueness about such statistics) in several different U.S. locations, Wrenn directed the evaluation of many hundreds of submitted software packages, accepting and producing more than 150 as official IBM products.

Wrenn essentially had the last word on which software products IBM chose to sell for the PC under its own label, although Don Estridge had the power of veto, and exercised it once or twice. ("No one at IBM except [Chairman John] Akers has final say on anything," Wrenn notes.)

Meanwhile, besides dealing with the enormous and sudden demand, IBM had to completely change the way it had always sold its computers and its software. The company had long had a complex private distribution system for its large systems, but now it had to switch gears and start thinking "retail." These small computers and their software would have to be sold in stores, not during tête-à-tête sales calls with corporate data processing managers.

Wrenn had to push hard to make IBM's old-line managers understand what they were up against out on the street. "I ran into a lot of opposition initially," she recalls, "but I could see that we *had* to have high visibility, we *had* to get it in front of the dealers, and the only way we'd accomplish that would be to actually use different approaches. The standard IBM approaches just wouldn't work.

"But I could see that within IBM it had never been done before. Essentially, we were putting software out in a retail store on consignment: They'd pay for it after it was sold. I championed that, and worked very hard to make that happen."

Needless to say, the IBM imprimatur made lots of people rich. Those who impressed the giant often carved out lucrative agreements that let them compete against the world with IBM's name behind them—Software Publishing Corp. and The Learning Company among them. But even without an actual IBM royalties contract, many independent third-party software and hardware developers made a killing in the PC-oriented marketplace. And IBM more than welcomed third-party efforts.

A perfect example of such a mutually rewarding independent effort was Lotus Development Corp.'s 1-2-3 integrated software package. Just as the VisiCalc spreadsheet program had given many thousands of people a reason to buy an Apple computer in the seventies, Lotus 1-2-3 simultaneously spurred IBM PC sales and rode the wave of the PC's success. In the six months after the January 1983 introduction of its first product, Lotus raked in $12 million in sales.

But even the contract winners couldn't relax. Because a contract with IBM can frequently double or triple the sales of a small company in a single year, those companies must constantly consider the possibility that IBM can just as easily cancel orders and thereby cut profits.

"Just because you sell [IBM] one product doesn't mean you'll ever sell them another product again," noted a software company founder who personally made millions from a single IBM deal.

IBM itself watched out for the dangers it posed to the little guys. "We tried not to be the majority of any small company's income," Wrenn says. "We would worry if we became their sole contract, because it just wasn't wise. And if we did something at some point that would put a small vendor in jeopardy, we really got raked over the coals. Even though IBM is very competitive, we were not out to hurt anyone in the industry, so to speak."

But even without direct dealings with the giant, no one in the industry can escape the pervasiveness of IBM. There's even an acronym for what IBM inspires—FUD, for "fear, uncertainty, and doubt."

People in the industry talk about "the FUD factor," recalling perhaps the dread felt by many before every IBM announcement. When the industry gets wind of a new product from IBM, rumors fly and hearts pound. The irony is that the company that can most afford all the publicity it needs . . . doesn't really need it. It's news even when the giant sneezes.

"Everybody now is to some extent at the mercy of IBM," Lotus founder Mitch Kapor told *The Wall Street Journal* in December 1983. "When the elephant dances, the grasshoppers have to be very careful."

Although the very word "shakeout" still makes many former and current industry figures shudder, for Wrenn and IBM the opposite is true. Everyone else's bad dream was their success story.

While the top three micro hardware vendors' market shares shrank steadily starting in 1982, IBM sold more and more PCs every year. It's not surprising that far more software was written for the IBM PC than for any other computer. By 1986 an estimated 100,000 programs had been written to run under the IBM PC's operating system.

Many software developers quickly limited their software development to IBM, dropping their previous other clients because of the perceived risk. In an uncertain world, one thing was sure: IBM wasn't going under tomorrow.

And what does it feel like to be an integral part of such a powerful entity? "I think that we have a responsibility, if you will," Wrenn said at IBM. "We are aware that what we do is going to be observed. Therefore, if we say we are heading in a particular direction or we are looking at a particular standard or set of guidelines, I always am aware that what we do may in fact impact other folks. So I think we have some additional responsibility there. We try to always do things very responsibly with that in mind."

As for the legendary power of IBM over everyone else in the industry, "I think that's overplayed a good bit," Wrenn says. "I think, particularly in our whole approach to the PC, where we have an open-system architecture and want and need third-party software companies to produce their software for our hardware, I think we have gone out of our way to try to make that possible and to encourage third parties—and will continue to."

Furthermore, the sword of IBM undeniably cuts both ways. The glint that chills the hearts of the competition can easily defend chosen third parties from the perils of the marketplace.

"Many times a software author is interested in writing a product but not in doing all the other things necessary to get it to market, in terms of producing the documentation, having it manufactured, marketing it, and advertising it," Wrenn explains. In such a case, where the author's product offers a good fit with IBM's product, IBM can afford to take over those expensive and time-consuming functions, and in some cases a product will get to market that otherwise never would have.

As difficult and time-consuming as her job was, Wrenn gave it a "10" compared with the rest. "The job I have now, I must say, is the most challenging, the most demanding, and (I guess I can honestly say) the most fun of all the ones I've had at IBM, and I think I've had some very good ones," she said in mid-1984.

It was also the most highly visible job she'd ever had at IBM. Instead of being essentially buried from the outside world in the folds of IBM's bureaucracy, Wrenn was in charge of what became a very public entity. "I was speaking with the press and making a lot of public statements and representing IBM on a very broad front," she explains. "I had really not done that before, and I found it difficult initially—but then it got much easier.

"Fortunately I don't think I flubbed up at all, but I kept a relatively low profile. It was a time when other people would reveal their strategies and approaches and so forth . . . and that just isn't the way IBM has ever operated.

"So those of us from IBM would appear quite reticent." Was it hard for Wrenn to maintain the IBM silence? "Yes. You'd like to be able to share exactly where you are, what's happening and so forth, but typically you didn't."

The dynamism, the importance, and the excitement of the Entry Systems environment proved very satisfying to Wrenn. "That, and the fact that it was always a great challenge," she adds. "But it's the challenge, it's the ability to make a contribution as a person, that means you're growing. And that's fun.

"What more could you ask for from a job?" she wonders. "To get paid for it and to have a nice lifestyle in addition to that is super, but to spend every day doing something that is fun is just great."

At the same time, the un-Blue world will be secretly pleased to hear that IBMers are also subject to earthly frustrations. "That's not to say there aren't days when it's terrible," she acknowledged at the time, "and you say, 'Why did I go to that meeting?' or 'Why did this happen?' There are those days, too."

Therese Myers: Adversity Builds Strength

Before Quarterdeck Office Systems started developing its Desq product, there was no such thing as an "operating environment." As briefly described earlier, operating environments—also known as integrating or windowing software—are an extra layer of programming that let personal computer users run several software packages from different vendors simultaneously and easily switch data among them. In the case of Desq, users can make up their own set of commands so that every connected software package has identical ones. That eliminates having to remember the obscure strings of symbols and letters written into most software.

Before operating environments came along, there were two options for the user who wanted to quickly exchange data among individual application packages, but each had limitations. "Modular" packages were single-application packages from the same vendor (such as Software Publishing Corp.) that could share their data, and "integrated" software packages (like Lotus 1–2–3) allowed the sharing of data among several applications contained in one big package. If a user had neither modular nor integrated software, but still wanted to use the same data with several different programs, he or she had to do a lot of retyping and was constantly sliding floppy disks in and out of the computer.

Modular software allowed users to put together any combination of programs they wanted, but it tended to be at the low end of the power spectrum. On the other hand, buyers of complex integrated software were locked into the designers' perceptions of which functions should be melded together—no more, no fewer. There was no opportunity to pick and choose the exact combination of functions one wanted, and users frequently had to pay for at least one application they hardly ever used.

Buyers of integrated packages were thrilled just to have the ability to move data between or among the applications they did use. For that reason and in spite of its drawbacks, by 1983 integration was generally regarded as the wave of the future. Unfortunately, intergrated software is typically so complex that, for example, Lotus 1–2–3 has singlehandedly sent thousands of users scurrying to attend week-long seminars to figure out how to make it useful.

It was this nest of problems that Quarterdeck sought to eliminate. While the rest of the world was going bananas over integrated software, this company turned the concept of integration inside out. Quarterdeck's idea was to let users indulge their old habits while gaining more versatility at the keyboard. "We said, 'We'll take on the burden of being smart—of making all these programs run together, because people have lots of files written for different software and they've already developed work habits using that software,' " Terry Myers explains.

In the words of one admirer, Quarterdeck came on the scene as nothing less than the Great Liberator. "Terry Myers represents the freedom of the Western mind," says Stanton Kaye, a filmmaker who has done promotional work for Quarterdeck.

"The most diversity and pliability are available through her system," he says. "It's a matter of democracy here: democratic free enterprise versus state capitalism." While that may be something of an overstatement, it's true that Quarterdeck's concept can be regarded as an attempt at liberation.

Of course, not everyone saw it that way, especially the legions of integrated-software proponents. Quarterdeck set sail squarely in the face of the prevailing wisdom. But total dedication to the company was the hallmark of the Quarterdeck crew as it set about creating this new kind of software. Unity of purpose being half the battle in a development environment, Quarterdeck was well equipped.

Also invaluable was Myers's natural ability to put herself in a nontechnical person's shoes. As she told *Fortune* magazine in 1984, "I hate machines. I can't really operate them. I'm the one who says, 'I can't make this work,' and my colleagues go back and make it easier for me."

That naiveté is, paradoxically, the source of her sophistication. She is skilled at avoiding the frequent developers' mistake of assuming that the user knows as much as they do. Myers's instincts tell her which features work and which don't, what might annoy or please a computer user, and what might be dispensed with altogether.

"I'm a user of computers but not really adept," she admits, "so I like things to be obvious. Part of my contribution is to make things as obvious as possible to the nontechnical person."

In developing what would become Desq, technical wizard Gary Pope—still working out of a garage—wrote his own artificial-intelligence-like development language, which he called Simple. Started in September 1981, Simple was finished by the following April, at which time he started sculpting it into the product Desq.

"Simple was really a productivity tool that let us try something and immediately see how it felt, how it looked, and what the characteristics were," Myers explains. Without such an "intelligent" language to work with, Quarterdeck's efforts would have been much more laborious.

With Simple in hand, the developers spent a grueling six months writing the intricate code for Desq. But November 1982 brought some startling and unwelcome news. With Quarterdeck still more than a year away from having a finished product, a chillingly similar software product was displayed at the micro industry's major trade show, the semiannual Computer Dealers Exposition, or Comdex.

The well-established and respected VisiCorp had announced its VisiOn windowing software. Even though Quarterdeck was hard at work on what was essentially a better product, VisiCorp in a moment had stolen Desq's thunder. For most of the technical community, the concept of windowing or integrating was new in 1982, and VisiCorp was the first to tout it publicly.

"I called Gary and said, 'It looks just like us,' " Myers recalls. The blow to Quarterdeck was severe, since the world now began its wait for windowing software from a proven hard-hitter, while Quarterdeck was still deep down in the minor leagues.

"The VisiOn announcement caused us some problems in my charter," Myers explains. "We purposely had acquired just enough money to show the feasibility of our product. After the VisiOn announcement, the only way we were going to get the second round of financing, which we needed to even have a beta test site, was to sign two hardware vendors as OEMs [original equipment manufacturers, who would sell Desq bundled with their own hardware].

"So in the winter of '82 I'd get up in the morning and call all the hardware guys, but nobody'd ever call me back," she recalls. California sunshine notwithstanding, those were dark days for Quarterdeck. "We were about running out of money and we didn't have any response at all from the hardware guys such as DEC or Wang so we decided to go to Comdex Spring in April with the main purpose of getting hardware vendors."

Their approach was direct. "We Mailgrammed every microcomputer hardware vendor in the United States and told them we were going to be at the show [with Desq]," she says. Then the best possible thing happened. "We were the hit of the show." Breathing sighs of relief, Quarterdeck's developers relentlessly continued composing Desq, estimating that it would be completely done by November 1983, seven months away.

Meanwhile, the wheels turned slowly in the process of actually signing up OEMs. "Nothing happens fast," Myers says. It would take six months to get firm commitments, but they would be worth the wait. They would, in fact, constitute Quarterdeck's greatest victory to that moment: a triumph of timing.

On November 9, 1983, Quarterdeck managed to sign up as OEMs two of the biggest players in the hardware game—Digital Equipment Corp. and NCR Corp.—both of whom were longtime IBM rivals in the large-computer domain who had migrated downward to the micro scene. And the double play came just in the nick of time. November 9th also happened to be the very day before MS-DOS creator Microsoft Corp. would announce its own windowing software product (called Windows). Windows would prove to be among the most anxiously awaited (but latest to arrive) micro products ever announced, from a company that had already been blessed by the hand of IBM.

Microsoft would not have to wait six months for commitments; the OEMs couldn't sign themselves up fast enough. Based on Microsoft's reputation alone, 26 hardware vendors flocked to the dotted line. Although Quarterdeck's lucky timing on the DEC and NCR deals rivaled Micro D's perfect timing in going public, the announcement of Windows marked the beginning of a very trying period for Quarterdeck.

As with some of the greatest scientific discoveries in history (including the computer), technology has a way of producing independent yet similar developments simultaneously. Although such coincidences serve to reinforce the validity of one's work, gratitude for the flattery of imitation quickly gives way to much fiercer emotions. Duplication of efforts spells only trouble in the marketplace. For Quarterdeck, what had been wide-open territory was filling up with some formidable competition.

Nevertheless, Quarterdeck had landed the crucial prerequisites for a second round of venture financing—its first two OEM deals—and the next month, a veritable fortune flooded Quarterdeck's bank account. In December 1983, a whopping $5.6 million came through the door, from Quarterdeck's three original financiers as well as four others. At least Myers no longer had to worry about making the payroll for a while.

With pockets reassuringly full, things might not have been too bad if Quarterdeck had been able to come out with the full-fledged Desq that winter (1983–1984), as planned. As it was, the hardest challenge yet lay quietly in wait, ready to pounce.

Product in hand, Quarterdeck set about testing Desq with as many existing MS-DOS programs as possible. Programming being the creative endeavor that it is, however, not all the software on the market was constructed in uniform ways. The result was that Quarterdeck had to modify and remodify Desq endlessly to accommodate every MS-DOS program it wanted on its "100 percent compatible" list.

The fine-tuning phase would take up the next six months. "Desq was a nightmare in some ways," Myers says. "Much of the software out there bypassed standard DOS programming conventions in the interests of speed and performance, so it needed changes. And every time, we had to figure out how its programmers had bypassed conventions. It was a trial-and-error process."

By contrast, when IBM later attempted to achieve compatibility for its similar product, Topview, it simply handed out free copies of Topview to all the independent software developers and asked them to test it with their own products. "*We* said, 'Oh, God, we've got to test all these products! Let's get all the hit products in and see if they work.' We did it all ourselves. It's a difference in clout," Myers understates. When IBM discovered software that didn't work with Topview, it deemed it "misbehaved."

Quarterdeck didn't have that luxury. Instead, for the next six months, 11 developers and testers sequestered themselves in cramped offices one block from Santa Monica's sparkling Pacific, working six days a week, keeping at it until 2:00 A.M. at least every other night. The pressure was on full force.

Worse still, complications arose with every new release of MS-DOS software packages. "Version 1.0 of something worked but when Version 1.1 came out it didn't work," Myers recalls. "We were smart enough to fix it so that both versions worked." Still, such modifications are not made overnight. Every change required took them further past their deadline.

But there were bright spots even during this discouraging period. During 1983 alone, Myers turned down four offers from companies that wanted to buy Quarterdeck. All four suitors would have kept Quarterdeck's top management in place but wanted to relocate the company. Myers was tempted, but after careful consideration, she said no. "The company's ours. That's what makes it exciting."

And yet, the stumbling blocks were piling up. The competition was very tough and Quarterdeck's product was behind schedule. In the end, it all boiled down to a single challenge: getting people to understand the differences between Desq and the perceived competition.

Only Desq allowed someone to keep using his or her favorite MS-DOS software packages from different vendors, while allowing up to nine applications to be displayed at the same time on one screen. At the time, the preannounced but nonexistent competition was "tightly coupled," a limitation that meant it could integrate only its own application packages or other vendors' specially rewritten versions.

But no matter how much better one's idea may be, it's hard to sell a concept without a product in hand. For half a year after the Microsoft Windows announcement, Desq would exist only in prototype, not in quantity. Neither VisiOn nor Windows existed in quantity, either, of course, but their developers could rest on their legendary reputations, a point of some bitterness for Myers.

"[VisiCorp President] Dan Fylstra caused all that hardship—a year and a half of hard work—because of his preannouncement," she laments. As it turned out, VisiOn never really caught on because of its high price, poor marketing, and the need for a then-sophisticated and expensive computer system to run it on. Finally, VisiCorp sold VisiOn to Control Data Corp., which released a revamped version of the software in early 1986. By that time, though, it was virtually ignored.

Meanwhile, for Quarterdeck a most frustrating chapter was finally closed. By May 1984, Quarterdeck was ready to show the world what it had been talking about for the last two years. Desq finally went out the door and the kudos finally came in.

In June "The Seybold Report" newsletter deemed Desq "limitless in its potential" and called its documentation "the best." A July review in *InfoWorld* magazine called the software "big, powerful, effective, and complex." A writer for *Business Software* magazine's September issue said he would "recommend [Desq] highly." The October *IBM PC Update* called Desq "a delight." All in all, Desq again felt like a hit.

But originality, enviable as it is, can be its own punishment. The major stumbling block in promoting Desq was the fact that it was an entirely new concept. "People didn't know why they wanted it," Myers explains.

"We thought Apple's Lisa computer [based on windowing technology] would do the concept selling for us, but [the Lisa] failed. Then we thought VisiCorp's VisiOn would do it, but VisiOn was tightly coupled. So we were left to do the educating."

Headed straight for what they knew would be a wall of indifference, they rode the brakes. "We opted for slow sales at the beginning," Myers explains. "Our goal in the first few months was to target only about 250 corporations and selected dealers because of the amount of education involved. Quarterdeck focused its energies on potential customers in *Fortune* 500 companies in engineering, aerospace, and other technical areas. "We couldn't reeducate people on a broad advertising basis, so we decided we'd pick the best accounts and sell to them."

By the end of the summer, Desq sales were still sluggish and Quarterdeck was totally unprepared for the old one-two that awaited it in Dallas. On August 14, 1984, Myers and Pope sat right up front as IBM unveiled what it called its "strategic software product," an operating environment called Topview that at first glance was the spitting image of Desq.

"I sat there thinking, 'This is so awful,' " Myers remembers. "I asked myself, 'How could we have picked the one product that would be IBM's strategic product?' Gary and I never envisioned that when we started the company. You never go into business thinking like that." Not only that, but Topview was priced at $149, to Desq's $399.

In a day-long presentation, IBM tried to combat the same ignorance Quarterdeck had long been battling about the nature of integrating software. "IBM spent two out of eight hours talking about giving up old habits," Myers recalls. Again, the feeling of validation was small solace to this David facing that Goliath, which could afford to do as much educating as it felt necessary.

Initially dismayed, Myers soon channeled her mental energy into the satisfaction that Desq was a more powerful product than Topview. The immediate challenge was in waiting for Topview's shipping date early in 1985, so Quarterdeck could demonstrate one-on-one the differences between the two.

Esther Dyson: Making Sense of it All

"I'm tremendously intellectually curious and I like to know what's going on," Esther Dyson says. "I love this business, I like understanding it, I like the recognition and the feeling that I'm contributing to people's understanding of the business."

As editor of the *RELease 1.0* newsletter, Dyson can be sure she's helping to elucidate an industry that has frequently had many people puzzled. Her professional opinions benefit from her business background (as a writer for *Forbes*), her financial experience (as a Wall Street analyst), and her sincere love for the industry.

By the time the IBM Personal Computer had begun to change everything in the micro industry, Dyson was a longtime observer of high tech. "I fell in love with software [as a securities analyst] at New Court [Securities Corp.] before the personal computer industry existed," she explains. "In fact, I think that's a valuable perspective I bring to the PC industry: I do understand there was something before PCs. That's how I got involved with it."

Esther Dyson, by all standards successful in the noisy competitiveness of Wall Street in the early eighties, found her attention claimed more and more by a different kind of phenomenon. Microcomputers had recently snatched center stage on the trading floor, and they were holding a fascination for Dyson that extended beyond mere dollars and cents.

Besides, she was getting bored with Wall Street. "I don't get enormous pleasure from telling 18 different people, 18 different times, why some company's earnings weren't as good as they were supposed to be," she has said. "I'd rather find it out once and then move on to something else."

Eventually she found a way to do just that. While still on Wall Street, Dyson espied something increasingly compelling just a few blocks away. Over on Park Avenue toiled Ben Rosen, perpetuating his career as a semiconductor industry seer through the pages of his *Rosen Electronics Letter.*

Rosen, educated as an electrical engineer, had started tracking the semiconductor industry during the seventies as a vice president and senior electronics analyst at the investment firm of Morgan Stanley & Co. He organized his perceptions into a monthly newsletter so popular that after ten years he felt he could carry it alone, and in 1980 he set up shop as Rosen Research, Inc. His instincts, as usual, proved correct. The *Letter* was a smashing success, with its amazingly accurate prognostications about the semiconductor industry.

He also initiated the first strictly micro-related conference, in 1977. The Rosen Forum was soon attracting the biggest names in the industry, both as speakers and as attendees. As an industry guru, Rosen quickly built up a following that was large and loyal.

So accurate were his predictions that he soon found his way into another area where foresight is key (and much more lucrative): venture capital. Along with Dallas semiconductor entrepreneur L. J. Sevin, Rosen started a venture fund in 1981.

True to form, Sevin Rosen Management Co. hand-picked and financed, among others, what would become two of the most successful companies in the micro business: Lotus Development Corp. and Compaq Computer Corp. And Rosen found himself just where he wanted to be.

During 1981 Rosen had asked Dyson, "in a casual sort of way," to go work for him, "and I had just as casually turned it down," she recalls. "Then, a year later, I decided, 'Boy, that's exactly what I'd like to do. I wonder if he's still looking?' For about a month, I sort of hoped he would call me. Then I said, 'Well, this is silly, Esther, you're a grown-up businessperson. Talk to him yourself.' "

Daunting as the figure of Ben Rosen may have seemed to the 30-year-old Dyson, she approached him at a conference in June of 1982 and reopened the discussion. It turned out to be a rather short negotiation. On July 4, they decided she would join him at the newsletter. "I had intended to pick up a bonus, take a month or two off, and join him in October," she remembers.

Instead, by July 14 they had decided she would come aboard in a couple of weeks. She started, in typical Esther Dyson fashion, on a Saturday. She was taking a 35 percent pay cut from her Wall Street salary, but that didn't bother her. As Dyson notes, "That says a lot about Wall Street."

By August 1982, Dyson was editor and sole writer of the newsletter. Those envious of her inheritance couldn't deny that she had discovered and independently pursued an area that fascinated her, had given up a lucrative "sure thing" career on Wall Street to do it, and was following a very tough act.

"My challenge in taking over the newsletter was establishing myself," she explains, "just as my challenge in going to Wall Street was in switching from being a journalist to being in the financial world."

Inevitably there were comparisons made between founder Rosen and upstart Dyson. Many perceived her as more of a "reporter" than the sage prognosticator that Rosen had been, and it's true that Dyson's approach has been to help make sense out of the present rather than predicting the future. Furthermore, she lost some admirers (and a few hundred subscribers) with her gradual move away from semiconductors to embrace the personal computer industry as a whole.

Still, she endured, and managed to keep at least 1,500 subscribers at $395 a head. Less than a year after taking over the reins of the *Rosen Electronics Letter,* Dyson made a move that displayed tremendous confidence in her own capabilities: She bought Rosen out completely.

Rosen, who had decided to become a venture capitalist full-time, had been talking with a few big potential buyers for the newsletter, with Dyson's knowledge. "I just didn't really like the idea of working for any of them," she says. "It suddenly seemed so obvious that I should buy it—kind of like the way it is with people who are living together and they decide to get married."

Besides, she laughs, "every girl should have her own company." How much did she pay for it? "Ben gave me a very good deal, a wonderful bargain," is all she will say. Rosen wasn't being totally altruistic, however. "He really didn't have much choice," Dyson explains. "Without him or me there wasn't much to sell except a good name."

Did it scare Dyson to take on such a responsibility after only a few months on the job? "Not really," she says, "because, again, it has parallels with getting married. I mean, sure, it's momentous and all that, but it was the only thing to do.

"Let me put it this way," she continues. "It seemed less scary than doing anything else, like getting a new job or selling out to [a big company]. It just seemed inevitable, and I'd been running this thing for some time, so the mechanics didn't seem terribly scary. And I'd watched Ben and, much as I admire Ben, he's not magical. If he owned it, I could, too."

For the next nine months, she continued to operate as Rosen Research, Inc., until March 1984, when she changed the company's name to EDventure Holdings, Inc. (the "ED" for Dyson's initials) and renamed the newsletter *RELease 1.0*—partly in honor of its former name (again, an acronym, "REL") and partly in honor of the software industry.

"Like release 1.0 of a software product," she wrote in the issue announcing the name change, "it is as up-to-date and complete as possible . . . but always subject to revision as future events change the shape of the industry." She also displayed her impish sense of humor with this headline: "Rosen Research Runs Out of Stationery, Changes Name."

Besides giving her a favorable financial deal, Rosen has helped Dyson in more intangible ways. "He's been very generous in a way that only someone who's going on to something else can afford to be, not just financially but by introducing me to people."

A most generous gift, indeed, since knowing people and companies is the name of Dyson's game. "There's probably no one in the business who knows as many people and companies as intimately as I do," she says. And she has a travel schedule to prove it: Dyson is only in her office about half the time, and on the road the rest.

She not only visits companies on their own turf, but she also covers the trade shows where companies congregate. Being at the center gives Dyson a broad perspective that lets her make things happen. "I like to make resources work together," she says. "If I know a guy who's looking for somebody and somebody who's looking for that kind of job, I'll put them together."

Although she denies being a workaholic, Dyson allots only the minimum amount of time for strictly personal fun. After years of taking no vacations whatsoever, Dyson has started making room for an annual week of skiing. Otherwise, "Work—that's it," is her answer to what's most important in her life.

Her major sacrifice to the work-god has been time. "I don't have time to go to the theatre," she complains. Giving so much of oneself to the job necessarily means there's little left for anything else. "It's been very easy because I've basically not had a personal life," she admits. In point of fact, Dyson has enjoyed a nearly total integration of her personal and professional lives.

"Most of my friends know what a disk drive is," she notes. While others may want nothing better than to leave the office at the office, for Dyson the personal/professional synthesis has been a major blessing. "Most people aren't that lucky," she feels.

Single-mindedness and long hours notwithstanding, luck is something she feels she has had plenty of. "I would never attribute my success to innate ability, although I do work hard and all that, but I've also been very fortunate and terribly lucky." It's true that she was in the right place at the right time to acquire Rosen Research, but she also put herself there by being interested and qualified.

With her willingness to dedicate herself totally to her work, she found the road surprisingly smooth. "This sounds really weird, but nothing per se has been tremendously difficult," she said after two years at the helm. "There's been no huge obstacle I've ever faced except for human frailty and not enough time."

Human frailty and time—Dyson fights both willfully with remarkable endurance. Deceptively fragile in appearance, she can look positively weary by 4:30 in the afternoon of a day that has been filled with nonstop meetings. But it's no wonder; she has just welcomed back the sight that first greets her every morning: 4:30 on the alarm clock. That's when she gets up every workday, rain or shine, for a mile-and-a-half swim that "keeps me from losing my temper more than I do," as she puts it.

She uses her hour-long swim as a chance to think, sometimes about personal matters but more often about the newsletter. "I take my notebook with me and I often jump out of the pool and write down things I think of while swimming," she says.

From the pool, she plunges directly into her workday, frequently beginning with a breakfast meeting (often paid for by the other person), typically at one of the fanciest restaurants in New York. Back in her elegant offices on Park Avenue, she will spend the day receiving vendor after vendor, all hoping she will see the brilliance of their work.

A typical lunch (again frequently at a willing vendor's expense) is downstairs in her building's "cafeteria"—which happens to be The Four Seasons restaurant, where the luncheon tab easily runs to $70 per person. "I pay for a fair amount, too," she insists.

Whatever breakfast or lunch may cost in New York, it's worth it to a vendor showing a hush-hush, yet-to-be-released product that may eventually get a favorable mention in her newsletter. "I get treated very well," Dyson acknowledges, but she makes it clear that she can't be bought.

Objectivity is her byword and Dyson doesn't pull any punches. During a generally impressive product demonstration, she'll interject any and all criticisms that come to mind without regard for sensitive egos—just as she will interject a "That's nice" when she thinks it's warranted.

If she's not impressed at all by a product or an idea, she makes it quite clear, even if she doesn't come right out and say so. As one "spurned" vendor has been heard to complain, "She's typical of the 'So what?' attitude."

Though she has been called cynical, it doesn't come naturally to her. "I can go listen to people all day, and they'll tell me interesting things and I'll believe everything everyone tells me, like a nice girl," she explains. " 'You're going to do $100 million next year? Of course!' " she mocks herself. "But then when I go and write it, I say, 'Come on, you've got to be kidding!' [Writing the newsletter] keeps my thinking rigorous."

Even if she's totally unimpressed by a product or a company, she generally keeps negative observations out of print. "If you say a company is wonderful and it isn't, nobody's really going to get hurt," she says, "but if you say a company is lousy and it isn't, somebody may be hurt. Mostly I keep quiet if I don't think a product's very good. You don't take a company nobody's heard of and tell people they shouldn't hear about it—why bother?"

Her greatest loyalty is to her readers and to the truth. "I'm kind of light-hearted and I don't take myself very seriously," she explains, "so I have to remember that when I say something, people do pay attention."

The secret of her success, she says, is in listening: finding the people from whom she can learn and paying close attention to them. "Doing what I do, you have the whole world eager to teach you," she says. Her ongoing education gives her the perspective she needs to portray the industry in broad strokes for her readers.

"She's probably one of the quickest studies in a demo I've ever seen," says one software developer. "She's one step ahead," says another. The fact that she usually grasps immediately the larger significance of whatever she's seeing is one of her greatest strengths.

Besides her braininess, she's also admired for her reporter's skills in ferreting out little-known but potentially important companies before most of the industry has even heard of them. It's her prodigious footwork that leads her to the real stories in the industry. She goes everywhere, talks to virtually everyone, and listens very carefully. Although she's deluged with public relations representatives trying to set up interviews with her for their clients, she would rather be several lengths ahead of that game. "I want to find a company before it has a PR guy," she says.

She is regularly quoted in *The Wall Street Journal, The New York Times, Business Week, Fortune,* and various trade journals.

She also frequently appears on cable television's Financial News Network and on several business television programs. She even appeared on *Good Morning, America!* when IBM's PCjr was introduced.

Subscribers now pay $495 a year for 15 or so issues of her newsletter, and several hundred industry superstars pay more than $1,000 each to attend the annual Personal Computer Forum. Although these experts can't really learn very much from one another as speakers, the real value of the event lies in "pressing the flesh" and the quiet but relentless deal making that goes on behind the scenes. The Personal Computer Forum is considered the premiere gathering of industry big shots, and few can afford to miss it.

Is Dyson basking in the power she's amassed? "No. It's a little strange," she says. "I'm just one person. I try and have good, solid opinions and do a good job. What I obviously do enjoy is the fact that I can talk to almost anybody I want. People by and large return my phone calls, and I have the respect of most of the people I respect."

Dyson is uncomfortable with vendors who go overboard to court her favor. "Sometimes people create a really big fuss and I know the newsletter's important, but I *am* still just one person," she emphasizes. "I can't make or break a product and I really don't try to do that. What I try to do is figure out whether it's going to make it or break it.

"I do believe that knowledge is power, so it's been tremendously satisfying to be right at the heart," she adds. The ability not to have to take sides and being privy to lots of people's secrets, and to be trusted with them and to thereby really know what's going on, is tremendously satisfying. I'm there at the creation."

4
Winds of Change

The year 1985 was one of shattered dreams for many in the personal computer industry. For various reasons, the demand for personal computers went way down—and with it, the fortunes of countless companies that had planned for yet another boom year.

Everyone in the industry felt the effects of the slump—even IBM—and assuredly these ten women. Along with the extraordinary changes in the industry itself, there were some drastic changes in the professional lives of five of the women, who left the businesses for which they are best known to move on to other things. Although their reasons were diverse, their timing was coincidental, both with one another and with many industry changes overall.

Lore Harp: Crash of a Highflyer

"Seeing the deterioration of Vector Graphic was my greatest disappointment in business," says its former chairman, president, and CEO, Lore Harp. "And yet, on the other hand, it was not so much a disappointment as it was a frustration—seeing something get wasted, and really due to my not having enough control in the company by ownership to be able to do the kinds of things I really wanted to do."

Harp had reason to be disappointed, along with an entire industry that had watched an apparent "sure thing" in the flashy high-tech arena blast off into space, only to disintegrate before its very eyes. Vector's demise was all the more painful because it had been in the industry from the beginning and had done so many things right.

Not only had Vector written the book on dealer service, devised ingenious new marketing strategies, and gone after the lucrative business market when everyone else was mired in the home computer mentality, but it also made some brilliant technical moves early on.

Thanks to Bob Harp, Vector made some basic technological choices that would prove wise indeed. The first was building its computers around a cheap and readily available "motherboard" (the floor of the computer into which internal components and memory chips can be plugged). Bob Harp chose the so-called S-100 motherboard—popular at the time with hobbyists and later to become the industry standard—giving Vector an early jump on much of the competition. With an eye toward simplicity, he designed an accessible, easy-to-use machine that quickly and steadily took the company to the heights of success.

By the time Vector was a year old, it had gone from selling relatively low-priced memory boards to selling entire microcomputer systems for between $4,000 and $25,000. For the next four years its growth was phenomenal.

In 1978 Vector had $2 million in sales, five times its first year's. The very next year, sales tripled to $6 million, then doubled the following year, to $12 million.

During 1980 Vector also attracted $750,000 in venture capital that it didn't even need, while politely declining additional offers. In 1981, the year it went public, sales again more than doubled, to $25 million. It seemed Vector Graphic could do no wrong.

Certainly its customers thought so. In a 1981 survey of 8-bit personal computer business users, conducted by Datapro Research Corp., Vector Graphic came out ahead of industry heavyweights Apple, Commodore, and Radio Shack in terms of user satisfaction.

While Bob Harp was designing blockbuster Vector products, Lore Harp displayed an astonishing natural ability to run the business end of things. (She also armed herself with an MBA from

Pepperdine University in 1980.) In the face of skyrocketing sales, an employee roster that mushroomed to 500 by 1981, and the prospect of becoming a public company, Lore Harp never let the numbers scare her.

Instead she let knowledge be her power. She kept extraordinarily close track of every dollar, both incoming and outgoing, by signing all the checks, personally approving all invoices for payment, and signing off on every shipment worth more than $10,000. She also kept close watch on the 20 most expensive items in inventory so that they wouldn't gather dust. Quite simply, she knew her math. In areas of management where she was lacking, she brought in experts from such established computer firms as Burroughs, Pertec, and Honeywell.

In keeping with Vector's close relationships with its dealers, Harp set up a dealer training center at the firm's headquarters, complete with lecture hall and a hands-on computer room where people could learn Vector's systems. Managed by Vector cofounder Carole Ely, the training program included a four-day technical course as well as indoctrination into what Vector called its "master method of selling."

Such intimate knowledge about a vendor's products—coupled with Vector's continuing high level of service to dealers—made for an extremely loyal base through which Vector distributed its goods. That loyal dealer base would prove to be one of Vector's greatest strengths. By 1981, the company had nearly 100 Vector-only dealers out of its total of 420.

Vector also made sure it had high visibility at the consumer end. There was nothing shy about Vector Graphic. It did lots of advertising, it was present at all the trade shows, and it was generally regarded as a glittering example of the infinite promise of high tech. Lore Harp's face appeared on the covers of *Inc.* and *The Executive* magazines, and the *Harvard Business Review* ran a nine-page interview with her, complete with a two-page photo spread.

The second half of 1981 marked a watershed for both Vector Graphic and the micro industry as a whole. The high-flying company announced in late August that it planned to go public that fall, inspiring eager anticipation on Wall Street. Harp wanted to raise capital for expansion and to gain the more abstract advantage of greater credibility that public companies frequently achieve. Internally, she thought the company needed the discipline that close scrutiny from outsiders demands.

August 1981 was also the month IBM unveiled its Personal Computer, although to a decidedly less enthusiastic reception than Vector had enjoyed for its news. October would see Vector's $13 million initial public offering (IPO)—a respectable showing in a then-sluggish market—and IBM's humble shipment of its first PC. On the very day IBM shipped its PC, Sears Roebuck opened the first of its Business Systems Centers, through which it had arranged to sell both IBM and Vector Graphic products, among others. While the industry may have had misgivings about the latest efforts of IBM and Sears, it never suffered a moment's doubt about Vector's continuing success.

But, ironically, from the month Vector made its triumphant entrance in the stock market and IBM brought out its PC to barely polite applause, their fortunes careened off in opposite directions.

For IBM, a dubious entry into an increasingly crowded field would unexpectedly lead to total market domination in just over two years. For Vector, the next two years would bring a stinging turnaround in its fortunes: quarter after quarter of losses, a stockholders' lawsuit, management shakeups, employee layoffs, and excruciating disappointment all around.

Most of its problems could be traced directly to the runaway success of the IBM PC. Vector Graphic simply failed to keep up with what soon became the de facto industry standard. The company was much too late in introducing a 16-bit computer that could run under IBM's chosen MS-DOS operating system. Furthermore, when Vector finally did develop a combination 8-bit/16-bit machine, it wasn't 100 percent IBM-compatible.

For Vector, the bad news started coming as inexorably as the good news had. Only in hindsight was it clear that the successes of 1981 masked a cruel truth—that Vector's breathtaking view from the mountaintop featured a mighty steep drop down the other side.

Although Lore and Bob Harp had proved to be a winning combination of technical and managerial genius for Vector Graphic, their personal characteristics were not so complementary. By the winter of 1981, the Harps' stormy 14-year marriage was officially over.

The divorce didn't surprise anyone who had seen the Harps in action. In spite of their individual successes within the company, they simply could not stand as a united front because of the hair-trigger tensions that lurked just beneath the civility.

Industry gossip has it that the Harps' acrimony was disruptive to the running of the company, but Lore Harp vehemently denies that. "I don't know why people think the divorce is related to Vector," she says. "The divorce is totally unrelated to anything that happened at Vector Graphic."

She will even go a step further to defend her point. "Bob Harp and I should have never been married in the first place," she says. "As a matter of fact, Vector probably happened because we already had a bad marriage, so I could really focus my energies on other activities."

And what about the stories that blame marital discord for Vector's downfall? "I don't think that is the case at all," she insists. "I think that what killed the company was a lot of politics."

It's true that the Harps' impending breakup was literally public knowledge, having been disclosed in the SEC prospectus, and that it did not scare away investors. That, as well as the fact that Vector went public during a sluggish market that had started in November 1980, is a point of pride for Lore Harp.

"Having taken the company public during a time when market conditions were really crumbling," she says, "in addition to the fact that Bob Harp and I were in the midst of a divorce—and yet having been able to convince people of the viability of the company—I think was an accomplishment."

Unfortunately, that viability soon proved questionable. In March 1982, only five months after Vector went public, Bob Harp resigned as chairman and vice president of R&D, "for personal reasons," and started one of the first IBM-compatible microcomputer companies: Corona Data Systems, Inc., now known as Cordata. Although the divorce atmosphere may not have caused as much company trouble as the gossipmongers would like to believe, there's no denying that Vector lost its technical cornerstone when it lost Bob Harp. The spring that he left was a tumultuous one for Vector Graphic. His departure was followed by several others, resulting in drastic changes in the company's top management. Meanwhile, Lore Harp was getting ready to move on to other things. "I had planned to leave Vector in October 1982," she explains. "I brought in a president [Fred Snow] in June—everything was done according to schedule."

Harp continued as CEO and was elected chairman of the board in June. Also in June, Bob Wickham resigned as vice president of marketing to start his own company, following his marriage to Carole Ely.

For Vector, 1982 was really the beginning of the end, both by design and by surprise. By design, two of the original figures in the company—Lore and Bob Harp—were getting ready to move on to other ventures. By surprise, Vector began to go downhill fast.

Lore Harp's plan was to remarry in July 1982 and then go on a ten-week honeymoon, after which she would return to Vector briefly to wind down her association for good. Just before the wedding, however, Vector reported some disappointing news.

Although sales for the quarter ending April 2, 1982, were higher than the same period a year earlier, Vector's profits had dropped. By June, Vector's slowdown had continued and the company announced that for the fiscal year ending in June 1982, earnings would be flat (no increase over the previous year). An added disappointment was the discovery of a $600,000 inventory loss, suspected to be a theft.

The company attributed the drop in sales to an economic recession that had started in late 1981, a month after Vector had gone public. Vector felt that small businesses—representing one of its major markets—were delaying new purchases until the overall business climate started to improve.

Truly the recession was hurting everyone. Dealers were having a tough time financing their inventories, with the cost of borrowing money then as high as 25 percent. Vector was well aware of the dealers' dilemma and did not look the other way.

"We think it's more important to support dealers in times of trouble," Harp had told a trade newspaper in 1981, "because the dealers will remember which suppliers helped them out in the hard times and will be more loyal to them and do a better job for them in the future."

And she meant it. By 1982 Vector had signed an inventory financing agreement with Westinghouse Credit Corp. that allowed dealers to pay for inventory on consignment, instead of on delivery to the dealer. That meant they could afford to stock more Vector Graphic systems in their stores.

Another pact, with U.S. Leasing Corp., eased the burden for dealers by allowing them to lease instead of sell Vector systems to customers. Whatever other problems Vector may have had, dealer relations was never one of them.

In spite of the troublesome signs Vector showed during the first half of 1982, Lore Harp went ahead with her plans. On June 30, she and husband-to-be Patrick J. McGovern (owner of International Data Group) started a venture capital fund with $10 million of their personal money. "When I came back [from my honeymoon] in September, I just wanted to spend another six weeks or so [at Vector] to make sure everything was running smoothly, which it wasn't. So I stayed and tried to make sure that things would actually happen."

The next year would be an exercise in frustration for Harp. "To make a long story short, the situation did not work out, [because of] all sorts of circumstances. If [Vector's board of directors] had followed my advice, the company would have been in much better shape," she believes.

Harp's vision was to develop a leading-edge machine that could support several different operating systems and would feature, among other things, built-in telecommunications networking and video communications. "If all that had actually been maintained, I—to my dying day—believe that the company would not have gone down the tubes," Harp says.

"But Vector had a board of directors that was not—how should I put this kindly?—not capable of really seeing what was needed in the industry," she says. "I don't think they were making decisions that were in the best interests of the company."

Someone was certainly making some wrong choices. Ultimately Vector's biggest mistake was remaining so long with the CP/M operating system in what turned out to be an MS-DOS world. IBM's decision to make Microsoft Corp.'s MS-DOS the heart of its Personal Computer would be the downfall of the CP/M universe.

Those companies too stubborn or too shortsighted to follow IBM's lead all too often found themselves closing their doors. The only major holdout from IBM compatibility that even survived was Apple Computer (with its own proprietary operating system), which had a formidable five-year headstart in the industry. In spite of a large installed base and almost fanatical customer loyalty, Apple still had to swallow dropping to number two.

When IBM really started moving ahead, Vector and countless other early entrants found their goods being pushed off the shelves of computer stores in favor of the "Establishment" machine. By 1982, the IBM PC was well on its way to becoming the market leader. By April of 1983, Vector had shown significant losses for three of the previous four quarters. Something had to be done. A few days into the month, the firm laid off 100 people and cut the pay of its directors and officers.

Another serious blow soon followed. Even though IBM PCs were in short supply, IBM suddenly cut the price of the PC by 20 percent and introduced a more powerful new model, the PC XT. That predatory action precipitated an industrywide round of price-cutting that hurt profits at a number of companies, Vector included.

By the end of April 1983, not quite a year after assuming Vector's presidency, Fred Snow resigned, and Harp again took on the job of company president. At the same time, Vector's vice president of finance also left the company. Meanwhile, the thousands of people who had put their money down for shares of Vector Graphic were becoming more disenchanted with each passing fiscal quarter. In July 1983, one of them did something about it.

Arthur Schwartz, who had bought 100 shares of Vector in November 1981, filed a class-action suit against the company in Los Angeles Superior Court, charging negligence, fraud, and violation of state and federal securities laws. The suit charged that certain former and current directors and officers of the company misrepresented the facts in connection with Vector's IPO, and that they made misstatements in the ten months after the offering.

One can hardly blame Schwartz for his displeasure, considering for example that Vector reported a $2.9 million loss for 1983 compared with a profit of $2.4 million the year before. The matter wouldn't be settled until 1986, when the nine former directors of Vector Graphic named in the suit agreed to pay $2.5 million to Schwartz and the class plaintiffs.

Naturally, Vector wasn't the only company in trouble. The flamboyant Osborne Computer Co. sent shock waves through the industry when it filed for bankruptcy in September 1983—amid a barrage of lawsuits—only five months after it abruptly canceled its IPO.

Analysts couldn't help but scout the underbrush for the next casualty, and there were plenty of the walking wounded to choose from. Of the 150 microcomputer companies in existence at the time, only about 30 would survive. Once a company was perceived as a risk, consumers became wary of buying from a firm that might not be around to service their purchases.

Even within Vector, some felt it was time to get out while the going was good. In the wake of the October 1983 announcement of another quarterly loss—of $701,000—three directors resigned "for personal and business reasons." One of them was cofounder Carole Ely.

At the same time, Vector was reordering its marketing strategy. In an effort to pinpoint areas of more certain success, Vector decided to focus its efforts on the agricultural and legal markets, where there was a need for Vector's products and room for a new entrant. With an optimism born of desperation, Vector ran full-page newspaper ads—half paid for by employees and suppliers—insisting that the company "has earned and will continue to occupy a position of significance in the microcomputer industry."

But the numbers said otherwise. For the quarter ended January 3, 1984, Vector would report a $1.8 million loss, compared with year-earlier quarterly earnings of $107,000. It was the company's fourth consecutive quarterly loss in what would be an unbroken string of losses over the next two years. Vector would never again post a gain.

Finally Harp had had enough. "When it started to appear that they were not going to follow what I had laid out, I literally walked out of the office on December 15, 1983, and didn't come back," she says. "I essentially left the company in protest, which is not really public knowledge. I was thoroughly disgusted, to say the least. I didn't officially resign until April of 1984, until a new president was brought in, but I actually was there only in name."

Vector's losses continued apace. In June 1984, the company laid off 20 percent of its remaining workforce and soon after reported a $7.6 million loss for the year. At that point, its auditor, Arthur Andersen & Co., warned that the company might be unable to continue as a "going concern." Chairman Jean Deleage let it be known Vector was open to a merger or acquisition possibility.

Looking out for themselves, employees started quitting before they could be laid off and in October 1984 Vector cut another 100 people from those remaining. The losses continued to mount, quarter after quarter, by the millions of dollars. In November 1985 Vector let go 12 more people, which by then constituted a third of its workforce.

With poignant timing, two days before Christmas 1985, Vector finally filed for protection from its creditors under Chapter 11 of the Federal Bankruptcy Code. Two months later it announced the suspension of all manufacturing operations, but said it would offer support and spare parts for existing systems, and would continue to seek a merger with another company.

The merger never came. In February 1987 Vector Graphic officially breathed its last breath. All hope was gone. It discontinued all operations and started liquidating its meager assets to pay creditors.

"Vector never cut it in the MS-DOS market," was the succinct analysis of one industry observer. "Vector never changed with the times."

The Slump and the Shakeout: Transforming the Micro Landscape

Toward the end of 1983, as Vector Graphic had become painfully aware, IBM had the micro market race just about won. With 25 percent of all sales, IBM was neck and neck with Apple Computer and steadily pulling ahead. Many companies were hearing, as Vector was, the ominous pounding of the hooves that would eventually trample them completely.

As the maturing micro industry became ever more competitive, its formerly casual business climate became much less forgiving of mistakes. It must be said: Only the strongest survived. Many of those who had helped shape the early industry, like Vector Graphic, later stumbled and finally fell, for reasons almost always related to IBM. Thus was and is the power of IBM.

For years the greatest success story of the industry, Apple Computer saw its share of office computer sales sliced in half over the course of two years, from 1982 to 1984. For a company that in 1982 still led the pack, at 22 percent of the market to IBM's 18 percent, placing a strong second was small consolation. Apple had more than met its match. No one else in the hardware game even stood a chance.

The early boom was over, and with it went all the crazy, seat-of-the-pants management schemes that were no longer remotely adequate. Those who had learned about business as they went—and there were many—were no match for a giant company that had started out in 1914 with an electromechanical tabulating machine and had introduced its first computer back in 1952.

One segment of the industry that was better protected from the disappointments heaped on everyone else was the market for products compatible with the IBM PC. Because IBM had broken with tradition and made its PC's technical specifications available to the outside world, imitators naturally followed. (If a company wants to ride on somebody's coattails, it might as well grab a tux.)

Bob Harp was among the first to see the opportunity and act on it with Corona Data Systems (now Cordata), the company he started after leaving Vector Graphic. The makers of compatibles started out offering what were called transportables, smaller versions of the PC that were meant to be portable. Although they typically weighed a bulky 30 pounds or more, the machines could actually be taken out of the office by businesspeople, even carried on airplanes. Furthermore, they ran IBM software, and they cost considerably less than an actual IBM PC.

A stellar example of the so-called IBM clone market is Houston-based Compaq Computer Corp. Started in 1982 by three former Texas Instruments employees and with an influx of venture capital from Ben Rosen, Compaq shipped its first product in January 1983.

When IBM slashed the price of its PC by 20 percent three months later, Compaq and the other clone makers really cleaned up. Demand for the PC was six times what IBM could build, and the compatible makers rang up huge sales by filling the void for retailers desperate to meet the demand.

Compaq did spectacularly well. The Compaq computer soon earned a reputation for being well made, reliable, and cost-efficient—and that judgment translated into dollars. In January 1984, Compaq reported the best first-year performance of *any* company in the history of American business, with sales of $111 million.

The surge in demand for PC-compatibles had done wonders for all the clone makers. IBM, realizing that in a sense it had created its own worst enemy, was thorough in its offensive. The industry front-runner didn't limit its competitive strategy to new products and lower prices. It also managed to put the kibosh on a few clone makers in courts of law.

Corona Data Systems was the target of one such suit, having done too good a job of making its machines IBM-compatible. There are varying degrees of compatibility in the clone computers, as anyone who has tried unsuccessfully to run Lotus 1-2-3 on a less compatible unit will forlornly attest.

Users may have been pleased with the Corona's high degree of compatibility, but IBM wasn't. In February 1984 IBM sued Corona, claiming that its design of a particular internal software layer infringed on an IBM copyright for the PC.

Corona, without admitting that it had copied IBM's software, immediately agreed to destroy existing copies of its own program and develop another one that did not infringe. Corona was fortunate enough to bounce back fairly quickly from the setback.

High-flying Eagle Computer, Inc., of Garden Grove, California, wasn't so lucky. In February 1984 Eagle lost a copyright infringement suit brought by IBM, in what proved to be a critical blow. After an out-of-court settlement, Eagle didn't ship a single product for two months—and that was its undoing. For its fourth quarter 1984, Eagle posted a $15 million loss. By 1986 its staff had dwindled to 60 people from a high of 330, and it didn't have the money to market its newest product, a 32-bit "supercomputer."

During the last week in July 1986, Eagle had no choice but to liquidate.

It was abundantly clear that all the clone makers had to keep close watch on IBM's every move, so that they could mirror it, or better it, or somehow circumvent it. But although IBM was the agent by which the dreaded industry shakeout finally occurred, soon enough even IBM would be feeling the pinch—because of circumstances beyond anyone's control.

In the stock market, the huge rally that had begun in August 1982 started to fizzle out in July 1983 (as Micro D's Geza Csige had so astutely sensed). Personal computer stocks had led the rally and personal computer stocks led the decline. In terms of actual microcomputer sales, 1983 and 1984 continued to be explosive selling years for the companies that were still around, but by 1985, even the survivors were feeling threatened. Demand slowed alarmingly compared with past sales figures, and those who had anticipated growth at the same phenomenal rates of the previous few years (regularly 40 percent to 50 percent) were unprepared for this new, decidedly unglamorous vision of high tech.

For the entire year 1985, sales of personal computers "skidded dramatically" after their long stretch of rapid growth, *The Wall Street Journal* reported. Personal computer sales for the first 11 months of 1985 fell 13 percent from the year-earlier period, according to Infocorp, a market research firm in Cupertino, California.

What had gone so suddenly wrong in 1985? One theory blamed a lull between significant products, suggesting that users were waiting for IBM's rumored "PC2" to come out. (It never did.) Others pointed to the increasing centralization of corporate buying patterns, as well as a drop in 1985 capital spending.

Then there was a relentlessly strong U.S. dollar, which put a damper on foreign sales. Another disturbing possibility was buyer disappointment with past products that didn't perform as promised.

While all those factors may have played a part in the industry slide, one observer saw the situation in more simplistic terms. "Last year saw an explosion in personal computer sales," a business reporter wrote in September 1985. "This year, businesses are trying to figure out what to do with all those personal computers."

In truth, users may well have known just what to do with all those personal computers. The fact is many users had simply reached their saturation points with the current technology. The buyers had bought and bought—and bought just about all they needed for the time being.

In June 1985 Dun & Bradstreet Corp. released the results of a survey it had taken of 5,000 companies in the United States, companies of all sizes and statistically representative of the full range of businesses in the nation. The survey showed a sixfold increase during the previous two years in the number of personal computers used in U.S. businesses—more than twice the expected rise.

That kind of explosive growth naturally leads to maturity, and with maturity comes a loss of innocence. "It's a slump relative to expectations, but it isn't a slump relative to every other industry that exists in the world," Gideon Gartner, president and cofounder of The Gartner Group, told *InfoWorld* in August 1985.

"If you look at the total demand for personal computers, it's pretty damn good. The reason it looks shabby is because 1984 was way above trend line," Gartner observed. "1985 is a good year." In terms of dollar volume, the industry that grew an astounding 56 percent in 1984 still expanded a very respectable 23 percent in 1985.

Respectable growth or not, vendors had (understandably) fallen into the trap of basing their production on past demand. Consequently most ended up with too much product and not enough customers. Though it had long been held that a shakeout was inevitable, when the sales slump came on top of it, the unhappy outcome was that even more players would have to leave the game. And they did—in droves. The "golden boy" industry finally had to face the reality of the cyclical nature of business, from which it had felt itself marvelously exempt.

Compaq, however, managed to start on top and stay on top. Why? Compaq was brilliant in its analysis of future demand. Even though the business computer market had grown 100 percent from the first quarter of 1983 to the first quarter of 1984, Compaq accurately predicted that in the following year, ending the first quarter of 1985, growth would be half that much—and the company acted accordingly.

As a consequence, while most of the industry was nervously biting its nails during the slowdown, Compaq pulled in its greatest successes. In the generally disappointing fourth quarter of 1985, Compaq set record highs in both sales (up 39 percent) and profits (up 47 percent). In 1985 Compaq became the youngest company in history to join the ranks of the *Fortune* 500, with $504 million in sales. Compaq's performance was astounding in a year analysts called "the worst ever" for the micro industry.

But Compaq was a stunning anomaly in an otherwise bleak picture. Besides bulging inventories resulting from overly optimistic expectations, the surviving hardware manufacturers had to contend with aggressive competition from yet another source: Asia.

Japan and South Korea were particularly prolific in generating a stream of reliable, low-cost, IBM-compatible microcomputers that were sold under both U.S. and foreign brand names. By January 1986 analysts estimated that the Asian element had captured at least 20 percent of the American market, which apparently had matured into sophisticated bargain hunters. During 1986 it became possible for the first time to buy a personal computer for less than $1,000.

The U.S. and Asian clone makers alike put the squeeze on IBM itself, with their high quality and low prices. Although IBM remained one of the country's most profitable companies, its overall 1986 earnings were down 27 percent from the year earlier—the company's worst showing since 1982. Part of the blame fell on the PC line, whose 1986 sales were flat compared with the year earlier.

Dropping microcomputer prices put dealers in a bind as well as manufacturers, since their profit margins shrank along with their price tags. When margins are cut in a period of slow demand, dealers can't make up the difference through volume selling. A lot of them had to quit the business, too. Whereas the number of computer retailers quadrupled between 1980 and 1984—to a high of 4,400 stores—industry pressures had closed the doors of more than 1,300 of them by the end of 1986.

During 1986 the industry started feeling the long-term effects of maturity: more mergers, more consolidation, and a higher percentage of start-ups failing. Long gone were the days when

$500 and a good idea were enough to launch a multimillion-dollar business.

* * * * *

Since 1985 was a time of uncertainty, tumult, and change for the micro industry as a whole, it's not surprising that 1985 also brought all those things (in differing degrees) to most of the women in this book. By the end of 1985, five of the women had left the ventures for which they are best known, either to join other enterprises or to start their own new ones.

Lore Harp, who had left Vector Graphic in December 1983 to become a venture capitalist, found that she missed the involvement of managing a company. So in August of 1985, she started a new one, in the decidedly un–Silicon Valley market of feminine hygiene products.

In March 1985 Ann Piestrup left The Learning Company and got involved in other innovative high-tech projects for education. In May 1985 Joyce Wrenn left IBM and moved to San Francisco to work for the Bank of America in its systems area.

In July 1985 Lorraine Mecca and Geza Csige left Micro D, as they had long planned, and a year later were setting up a charter fishing operation in Hawaii. In August 1985 Portia Isaacson left Future Computing and by October had started three new high-tech ventures at the same time.

Ann Piestrup: Uprooted

The micro entrepreneurs of Silicon Valley had long been sheltered from economic storms of any kind, but in 1985 many suddenly found themselves at the complete mercy of forces beyond their control. Ann Piestrup, who had overcome many obstacles to bring to the public her ideas about learning, finally had to admit that she had reached an insurmountable barrier.

In the face of the general slump and a very weak home computer market, Piestrup's impressive personal attributes weren't enough to guarantee her own security. In the last week of February

1985, an interim president of The Learning Company—who apparently had been brought in by the board of directors to wield a very heavy axe—fired Piestrup from her own company. Two days later she had handed in her keys and walked out the door.

The resourcefulness, enthusiasm, and single-mindedness that had taken Piestrup through the difficult early years and made The Learning Company what it was were apparently of little practical value once the company was "real," once it had moved into a high-stakes league and had grown large enough to sustain itself without its founder's direct hand.

As she watched her company's name added to the list of wounded on the micro battlefield, Piestrup found herself in a position all too familiar to many entrepreneurs. Having started successful companies on the strength of a dream, many discover abruptly that they've outlived their own corporate usefulness—at least in the eyes of the financiers, whose main concern is necessarily the bottom line.

The most celebrated example of the phenomenon is the story of Steve Jobs, the wunderkind founder of Apple Computer who, along with Steve Wozniak, took his dream from a garage workbench to the *Fortune* 500 in seven years.

After hiring no-nonsense John Sculley away from PepsiCo, Inc., to better manage Apple in light of IBM's increasing market share, Jobs eventually found himself forced out of the company that he had come to identify with to an extraordinary degree.

As many as 50 percent to 60 percent of all companies backed by venture capital reportedly go through significant management changes before they reach maturity. Of course, that knowledge is small consolation to the company founder who's just been told to leave an enterprise that would never have existed at all if it hadn't been for her.

Piestrup can address the emotional impact of the events in her own case. "It's very painful and it was done quite coldly," she said soon afterward. Only later could she be more philosophical. "This often happens with entrepreneurs, when it gets to a stage where their original fire is more in the way than a help."

But what happened at The Learning Company to force such a drastic move? After her company received its second-round $3.2 million in venture capital in 1983, Piestrup was written up in

Fortune, Business Week, Time, Scientific American, Working Woman, The New York Times, The London Times, and more.

She appeared on national television, including two appearances on *The Phil Donahue Show.* She gave talks to thousands of teachers around the country, did teacher training in several states, keynoted computer conferences, and wrote magazine articles—all while continuing to design software.

Convinced that The Learning Company's products were unsurpassed on the market, she deflected several buyout offers. "We were the best and I didn't want to be associated with other people's products," she says, while admitting that this attitude "might have been bad for the company." For the moment, however, she and the entire industry were riding high.

But the phenomenal success of the micro industry was feeding on itself. Basing their projections on the quantifiable market boom that took off in 1982, most observers predicted continuing explosiveness in the foreseeable future. Early in 1983 *Business Week* put the growth of the home computer market at more than 100 percent a year—a figure that didn't seem at all unreasonable to most.

But 1984 was the year of reckoning for educational software. While business micros took the lion's share of the market, sales of home computers fell way below projections. Many schools were financially strapped, and the software market in general was growing increasingly tight. Educational software was a business for idealists, not realists, some said. The shakeout had begun in earnest. "Everyone around us was dropping like flies," The Learning Co.'s Teri Perl told a reporter.

The root problems for the educational market were disturbingly circular. Only 10 percent of U.S. households owned computers in 1984, even though half the households in the country included children. People could not justify paying the high prices of both hardware and software to buy something they were not even sure they needed.

At the same time, software development costs were so high that a small company like Piestrup's could not afford to bring its packages down to an affordable price. A price tag of $10 would almost have guaranteed success, but even TLC's prices, which were moderate, ranged from $30 to $50. With increasing demand could come lower prices—for both hardware and software—but demand wasn't likely to increase noticeably until prices dropped.

Money was not the only issue. "I think one reason the market is not healthy at this time is that there are some terrible programs on the market," Piestrup said in 1984. "They're not at all worth the money and parents don't have a way of finding out what is worthwhile.

"It's hard, from reading reviews and package copy, to distinguish the good software from the not-good software," she noted, "so they buy what they hear about in advertisements. And companies with big advertising budgets don't necessarily spend as much to make good software."

The Learning Company felt it boiled down to a waiting game, in some respects—waiting for inferior products to be forced off the market and waiting for computers to become cheaper, easier to use, and more powerful. For all that to happen, Piestrup estimated that the wait could possibly last the decade, and she had every intention of seeing it through.

The year 1984 was difficult for The Learning Company in another way too. After only a year as president, sudden and serious health problems forced Marcia Klein to leave the company, much to Piestrup's sorrow. "She's wonderful. We were really close partners," Piestrup says. "It was hard for me when she left."

So, for the third time in two years, TLC had to find a new president. Melchor's team came to the rescue, and helped recruit someone with a very nuts-and-bolts approach. Piestrup was pleased and impressed with the business savvy of this new president—that is, until she found out what he had in mind for her.

"They decided to break even at all costs," she explains. "They basically stopped developing products for about a year, and my main [contribution] in the creative side and also the PR side wasn't as valuable anymore. So in a way it made some sense for the company to get rid of me."

The actual firing was a formidable blow to Piestrup, who feels it was done with neither finesse nor sensitivity. "Afterward, it took about a week of just being devastated," she admits.

But there's no doubt that somebody up there likes Ann Piestrup, because the very day after relinquishing her position, she left it all behind for a week in Germany, at the invitation of the

Aspen Institute in Berlin. She was among 20 international guests who were fêted, chauffeured, and generally pampered.

"I sort of stayed in shock during that time and just went to this other wonderful world," she says. "Then when I came back I said, 'Oh my God, I'm unemployed!' I'd never been in that position before."

Her salary, which was unusually modest to begin with, had dried up practically overnight. Because The Learning Company had chosen not to buy back any of her stock in the company, she had to immediately start thinking about how to bring in some cash. Suddenly she found herself in a position distressingly similar to the one that had inspired her to start The Learning Company in the first place.

Still feeling wounded, "I just put out my feelers a tiny bit," she recalls. "I told just a couple people—and within hours people started calling from major hardware companies." At the time she thought that working for a hardware company might be a good move, because she'd have major funding and wouldn't have to "fight for it tooth and nail."

Even though she had just spent six years at the helm, Piestrup felt she could easily ally herself with another group. "I don't feel like just immediately starting another company," she said then, "particularly one that competes in that market. My heart is still really with The Learning Company and I'd like to support it."

All the same, her departure gave her a new sense of freedom and adventure. "Getting away gave me a little perspective," she says, "and it gave me a chance to think about what I'd really like to do in a way that I wouldn't have, because I was too loyal to the venture capitalists to consider leaving. Now I'm very excited about what else I can do."

She finished her speaking commitments for The Learning Company while immediately getting involved in several futuristic software and educational projects. Since the president who fired her was at TLC for only three months, she developed a good relationship with his successor and occasionally does consulting work for her former firm.

As for The Learning Company, 1985 marked its entry into the teenage market. "That's who buys software," Piestrup said shortly after her departure. "Electronic Arts targets the teenage boy and does much better [financially] than [TLC does]."

Although The Learning Company wasn't giving up on the 3 to 13 age bracket, that segment was glutted with products and TLC felt its survival depended on diversification. The company's first teenage offering was the critically acclaimed Robot Odyssey, which made the Softsel Hot List in only a week. "We sold every copy we published," Piestrup said.

When Piestrup left, The Learning Company was profitable, had a couple million dollars in the bank, had revenues two and a half times those of a year earlier, but still existed in an unstable marketplace.

However, it also had a new president who had taken his former company from $2 million in sales to $200 million in just a few years. "He's excellent and he's there for the long term," Piestrup says. "He's willing to grow it and he has the insight to do it."

Joyce Wrenn: Sailing Into a Storm

After more than two decades at one company, does the company become entwined with one's very sense of self? Not if you're like Joyce Wrenn. "I guess I wouldn't say IBM is [part of my identity] as such," she said in 1984. "Clearly, working for IBM and being in the IBM culture for 23 years I'm sure have influenced me, but I don't tend to think of myself solely as an IBMer. That is one *part* of my life.

"My career with IBM is of course important to me for a lot of reasons, but I never, ever lost my own sense of identity in that process," she continued. "And there's a saying at IBM—'One person can make the difference'—and I really do believe that. So you tend to feel that you as an individual can make a difference, and you retain your own identity."

What about the stories about legions of identical IBMers, forced into a mold of someone else's making and living according to strict rules of behavior and discipline? "I have had a great deal of freedom and flexibility, and I think that it's perhaps greatly misunderstood externally," Wrenn feels. "I think people tend to think of us as a blue-suited army, and that is by no means true. If people went to some of our programming laboratories, they would see most people in blue jeans and beards and so forth, and being very comfortable.

"The people who are calling on customers—you want to dress in the way your customers are dressed. They're businesspeople so you tend to wear business attire," she adds. "I've never been asked in any way whatsoever to compromise my own integrity or identity, or my own ideals. In fact, the company has been very supportive; it's been a very good company in that regard."

Fulfilled as Wrenn was at IBM for more than 20 years, she also remained independent enough to consider other alternatives. In December 1984, about to turn 49, she estimated she'd probably spend another 11 years at IBM, although not necessarily at the Entry Systems Division. "I guess I'd say I'm very flexible," she concluded at the time.

Within months, it became obvious just how flexible she was when she left IBM for good, in May of 1985. Back she went to her old California haunts, but to an entirely new professional milieu. Wrenn became senior vice president in charge of data and applications management at Bank of America Corp. in San Francisco. She had gone from the second-largest company in the world to the second-largest banking company in the United States.

"Although I wasn't looking for an opportunity, they [BankAmerica] called me," she explains, "and the more I thought about it, I thought, 'Gee, that sounds like a really interesting opportunity.' And I eventually wanted to come back to California, although it was a little earlier than I had planned."

She also had begun to realize that her upward path at IBM wouldn't have allowed her to return to California at all. "I'd always realized my time at Boca was limited because I was already at a director level and there aren't that many positions in software at that level," she says. "The only upward mobility would have been in the New York area, where IBM is based. The fact that the bank was in San Francisco was really appealing."

At BankAmerica, Wrenn would report to the celebrated Max Hopper, an executive vice president and the head of its computer operations, who had made his mark in the early 1970s by developing the first and foremost automated airline reservations system in the country, for American Airlines.

At BankAmerica, Wrenn would assume the data administration function for the corporation and be responsible for application tools and technology, including software testing and development technology. "So it was going back to some of the work I had done before I went to Boca," she explains.

At the same time, she was entering a totally different and very complex industry. "I can apply my managerial experience and my technical background," she said soon after starting the job, "but I have a lot to learn in terms of the financial services business."

But a little disorientation didn't faze Wrenn. Despite having aligned herself with a notoriously paternalistic company for 24 years, Wrenn is still basically adventurous. "I enjoy getting into something that is not all that well structured, and trying to find the right opportunity in that structure, and going after it," she says. She had certainly proved that in Boca Raton.

Not everything at BankAmerica was strange, after all. Very familiar was the bank's largely IBM computer installation, as well as a number of ex-IBMers who had migrated there before her.

Does Wrenn have any regrets about leaving IBM? "Not really," she said shortly after joining the bank. "I enjoyed my career with IBM. It's a fine company and I still have many friends there and communicate with them. But it was an interesting time in my life to consider a new opportunity, after three years in Boca. It was a big decision, clearly—but once it was made, I tend to look forward. So I didn't have any down times; I was not depressed in any way afterwards. In fact, I went from one job to the other with no break.

"And of course I love to stay close to actual users of the software and I have that opportunity here [at BankAmerica]," she added. "It's a chance to learn a whole new business, and if you look at deregulation in terms of where the financial services business may go, it holds a lot of interesting possibilities. And I was very impressed with the people I met here at the bank."

Wrenn would soon change her upbeat tune, however, when it became apparent that BankAmerica was in serious financial trouble. "I came on board in May [1985], and that quarter was the first time the bank reported a serious loss," she later explained. "When I accepted the job, there had only been one bit of negative publicity, and that was a real estate problem or poor investment out of the L.A. office."

It turned out to be just the tip of a very distressing iceberg. Earnings at BankAmerica had been declining for several years, mostly because of bad loans, but the worst was yet to come. For the fourth quarter of 1985, Bank of America showed a $178 million loss, bringing the loss for the year to $337 million. For the first time in 50 years, the bank suspended dividends.

And that wasn't all. On the very day in January 1986 that the bank reported its fourth-quarter loss, the Treasury Department levied a record $4.75 million civil fine against it for alleged illegal money laundering. The bank denied any criminal activity.

Wrenn was terribly dismayed by this turn of events. After all, she had left the world's most profitable industrial company, only to find herself in a rat's nest of uncertainty. "It's a bit of a stressful environment," she admitted.

She was further jarred when Max Hopper resigned from BankAmerica to return to American Airlines, just six months after Wrenn had come to work with him. "I had established excellent rapport with him," she says. "Whenever you lose your immediate manager, it's a bit disconcerting."

Hopper made a point of telling the press that his departure had nothing to do with the bank's financial problems and that he was not "deserting" the bank. He insisted that he had "a high degree of loyalty and faith in the bank."

Still, Hopper's resignation was one of a spate of departures of key executives and middle managers during 1985. Bank officials downplayed what appeared to be desertions by pointing to the bank's ongoing efforts to streamline its 86,000-person workforce in light of its financial troubles.

But Wrenn is no fool. She kept her eyes open, and by the time another year had passed she was back with Hopper, this time at American Airlines—ready to learn yet another industry.

Lorraine Mecca: Take the Money and Run

By August of 1985, Lorraine Mecca had joined that tiny percentage of the populace that can say at the age of 36, "I'm retired." Which is not to say that she doesn't have plenty up her sleeve for the future, but as for Micro D, Inc., Mecca created it, grew it, took it public, and then placed it gently in capable hands—just as she had planned to do from the beginning.

"When I started Micro D, I had a five-year plan," she explains. "The idea was to work as hard as I could for five years, ignore the kids, the house, the family—everything except the business—and see if that kind of effort would make a difference. And it did, it made a tremendous difference."

The bottom-line difference was that she walked away with several million dollars in her pocket as opposed to a Chapter 11 filing. Of course, 18-hour days and seven-day weeks don't guarantee everyone success and financial security. Plenty of micro entrepreneurs worked long and hard, only to succumb to myriad market pressures.

In some ways, Mecca was just plain lucky. Her timing was superb—in starting the company and, especially, in taking it public just hours after the high tech market had peaked. If Micro D hadn't gone public when it did, in July 1983, its fast growth would have come to a screeching halt.

Although 1981 sales of $12 million had more than doubled to $25 million in 1982, so had costs risen. Micro D had opened two more warehouses, and the number of employees had more than quadrupled between 1981 and 1982, from 21 to 92.

Even an infusion of $1.5 million in venture capital from Adler & Co. in April 1983 couldn't pay all the bills. To perpetuate its success, Micro D not only had to keep expanding, but also had to keep its own computerized operations up to date, and the financial well was almost dry. "We could not borrow any more money," Mecca says. "Even though we had more potential for growth, the bank was getting real nervous."

In going public, Micro D leapfrogged the competition by raising $25 million for operations in a single day. The success of the offering allowed the firm to open a fourth warehouse in Chicago a month later—August 1983—and to repay the bank its $6 million.

Another $1.5 million went toward installing a new and bigger computer system for keeping all the branches on-line with headquarters. The millions remaining gave Micro D a lovely cushion against the unknown. That was most fortunate, because the unknown was speeding toward Micro D and the rest of the industry with a satchel full of unpleasant surprises.

But for the time being, Micro D's growth continued rapidly. Sales for 1983 almost tripled from the year before, to $70 million, and the number of employees more than doubled that year, to 197. In March 1984, Micro D's fifth warehouse came alive, in San Francisco.

Mecca and Csige, meanwhile, were coming to the end of their planned five-year stint. "And we were exhausted," Mecca says. After Micro D's initial public offering, at the height of the company's growth, they started looking for an executive team to take over. "We had a good substructure of vice presidents," Mecca recalls, "but none of them was really the person we were grooming to take over."

In October 1983, they hired Richard Lionetti away from rival Softsel Computer Products, Inc., and made him executive vice president, with the hope that they could eventually entrust Micro D to him. In May 1984 Lionetti was named president of Micro D, and Mecca lessened her day-to-day involvement in company operations, as planned.

But even with its healthy cash reserves and impressive track record, Micro D started to feel the crunch in 1984, just like almost everybody else. The breakneck growth of the previous few years had started to slow down, putting the squeeze on vendors, retailers, and distributors—few of whom expected it.

Even though 1984 was a record-breaking sales year for Micro D, with $114 million, the company's profits were up only 24 percent, as opposed to a 183 percent increase the year before. In 1984 Micro D was only "marginally profitable," as Mecca put it.

As IBM's increasing market presence and a slowing rate of growth forced the rest of the industry to become ever more competitive, prices started falling and, with them, profit margins.

That held true for everyone's profit margins: vendors', distributors', and retailers'. Everyone got squeezed.

The intense competition among retailers (resulting in price cuts that netted them lower profits) meant that a number of retailers simply couldn't bring in enough money to pay Micro D what they owed. Furthermore, the emerging trend away from walk-in retail sales and toward direct corporate sales began to cut both retailers and distributors out of the loop. Hundreds of retailers closed their doors for good in 1984 and 1985. And many vendors began paring down the number of distributors they used.

As distributors vied for market share, their prices (and profits) went down as well, and they started offering further (expensive) incentives to retailers. Until November 1984, for example, retailers had to pay their own shipping costs for Micro D's merchandise, but the realities of the marketplace changed that. Micro D decided it would pick up the tab.

The entire industry started examining longtime business associates with a very critical eye. Distributors suddenly had to weigh each vendor's financial stability. "We have to protect ourselves now," Mecca said. "We have to make sure vendors can afford to advertise their product and create user demand."

Unpopular products became a very expensive problem. Micro D too frequently could not return vendors' unsold merchandise because the vendor had no faster-selling merchandise to exchange for it, or even because the vendor had gone out of business.

The general market slowdown translated into weak demand for certain products, particularly educational and entertainment software—which, unfortunately for Micro D, comprised a substantial percentage of its inventory. The situation forced Micro D into one of its most painful experiences.

In the fourth quarter of 1984, Micro D took a write-down of $2.5 million in inventory and receivables. The announcement that much of its business was essentially worthless was made at an American Electronics Association conference in late October.

Since the meeting is regarded as a forum for getting good news about a company out to the analysts, it was that much harder for Micro D to deliver the bad news. In such a situation, companies sometimes try to bury a bombshell until it's officially announced, but Micro D decided to take it on the chin.

"We could have gone to the conference and pretended everything was hunky-dory," Mecca says, "or we could stand in front of 500 analysts and tell the truth—which we did." Was it really that hard? "It was one of the worst days of my life," she says.

Strangely enough, she says, the general response was, "Is that all?" With the overall state of the industry and Micro D's (and everyone else's) steadily shrinking stock value, the analysts were ready for anything.

After four years of unrestrained optimism and fast expansion, Micro D and many others had to reverse their outlooks and their operations. "We have to get leaner each month," Mecca said a week after announcing the write-down. "1985 will be a hard year. We'll be cutting out everything that's not absolutely essential and some things we now consider essential.

"That means getting people up to fourth gear the minute they walk in the door," she explained. "We have to go full-bore the whole time—no relaxing. We have to be the absolute best: We have to buy right, pick right, pack right, ship right, and collect money fast. There's no margin for error; it's our profit margin."

She couldn't have been more right. Nearly everyone in the industry suffered in 1985. Micro D itself reported its first loss ever that year, of $3.1 million on $119.8 million in sales.

Things were rough for Micro D right from the first flip of the 1985 calendar. In January Richard Lionetti resigned from the company. So out the window went Mecca's and Csige's pretty retirement plan. "There was no way we could leave then," Mecca says. "The company was going in the wrong direction." And Mecca was back at the helm full-time.

Rethinking their strategy in light of the new spirit of consolidation in the industry, the duo began mulling over the idea of merging with another distributor. Micro D was not alone in its thinking. Early in the year, it was approached by First Software Corp., another fast-growing micro distributor based in Lawrence, Massachusetts, about that very possibility. "We were very receptive," Mecca says. Such a merger would automatically create the biggest hardware and software distributor in the country.

"The thing that was so attractive was that [First Software] had a management team, a very strong president, very strong CEO, and strong chairman," Mecca explains. First Software, for its part, had reached a point where it needed more capital to maintain growth. Its options were to go public (in an unfriendly stock climate), get another round of venture funding (not so readily available at that time), or combine with someone cash-rich.

"It was the perfect tie-in," Mecca thought. "We would consummate the merger, Geza and I would bow out gracefully, and the new management team would take over." Negotiations went ahead.

Months passed, with the lawyers and accountants trying to fit the two parts together gracefully. But the rules of accounting had the final say, and in the end they said, "It can't be done." Unless the merger could be treated as a "pooling of interests"—an exchange of stock, not cash—neither party could afford it.

"The government has lots and lots of regulations about that because [pooling of interests] is a nontaxable transaction," Mecca explains. Unfortunately, the structure of the agreement between Micro D and First Software was found to violate some of the pooling rules. At the end of July 1985, in the very final stages of negotiations, Micro D announced that the deal was off. Micro D lost not only its perfect match, but also the $130,000 spent trying to effect it.

As soon as it was clear that the merger was not to be, Mecca and Csige started talking to Linwood "Chip" Lacy, Jr., who had been general manager of Micro D in 1982, but was subsequently lured away by his former employer.

Micro D had been "trying to get him to come back to the company for quite a long time," Mecca says. This time, she and Csige succeeded. In a single day, they called off the First Software deal, handed in their resignations, and appointed Lacy chairman and CEO. Micro D had suddenly made the transition from an entrepreneurial to a professionally managed company.

To help with their separation from the company, Mecca and Csige took up temporary residence in Honolulu. "It stopped us from going into the office every day, which I would have done," Mecca explains.

Even though leaving was what they had always planned to do, it was not done cavalierly. "It's real hard," Mecca said during a visit to California that October. "I still have to keep myself from going in while we're here just for a little while."

And she would have had every right to do just that, since she still held 51 percent of the company's stock. Even after selling 63,000 shares in November for tax purposes, she still technically had control.

"But I'm not exercising it," she explained in December, after returning from Hawaii. "I'm not on the board, I'm not an officer of the company, I'm not there every day. Although I could go in and say, 'I want to own the new board,' I'm not doing that. But I have that power."

After the New Year, however, she sold her remaining stake to Ingram Distribution Group of Nashville, Tennessee, instantly adding $6.6 million to her personal fortune. Ingram, one of the largest distributors of books and videocassettes in the country, then owned a controlling 50.3 percent of Micro D.

Ingram already owned Ingram Software, Inc., a Micro D competitor that distributes primarily microcomputer software. In June 1986 Ingram paid $300,000 to venture capitalist Frederick Adler and associates to buy an option to raise Ingram's stake in Micro D to 60.7 percent.

While Mecca and Csige got away free and clear, the company they left behind was a bit unsettled by the failed merger and by their departure. By the end of the third quarter of 1985, Micro D was losing money and market share, and employee morale was at an all-time low.

The new management team moved quickly to set new sales goals and to introduce more high-end products into its lineup. The strategy worked immediately, producing fourth-quarter sales 42 percent higher than the same period the year before, and boosting workers' confidence considerably.

But Mecca's January sale of her shares to a primary competitor brought morale back down a notch, as employees started wondering how secure their jobs would be. Cost control remained a theme into 1986, and Micro D forged ahead into a marketplace that didn't look as if it would be getting friendlier anytime soon.

In May 1986, however, Micro D signed an agreement that made it an authorized distributor of selected products for the more than 600 ComputerLand franchised stores in the United States and Canada. Lacy called it "a major business opportunity" for Micro D.

First Software, on the other hand, fared much worse. On April 19, 1986, First Software filed for protection from its creditors under Chapter 11 of the Federal Bankruptcy Code.

As for Mecca and Csige, they took some time off to regroup. "I don't think I'll stay retired more than a few months," Mecca said soon after leaving Micro D, "but I need the break just to wipe out the old slate and let some ideas come in that aren't totally computer-related—because there's a lot else happening out there."

Portia Isaacson: "This Business Has Me!"

"What Future Computing has done that is not public knowledge—particularly in our early days—is more important than what is [public knowledge]," claims Portia Isaacson. "Although I can't discuss it, I have worked with nearly every major computer manufacturer that has come into the retail channel, and I've influenced each one's whole approach to that channel." Most of those deals, however, are still covered by the nondisclosure agreements that are de rigueur in the industry.

Isaacson's and Future Computing's involvements with manufacturers have called for hammering out serious details, such as the terms and conditions of a vendor's market-entry plan, identifying which and how many stores a product should be in, and developing product rollout strategies.

"That's how we're inside the industry at the bargaining table," Isaacson explained while at Future Computing. While other industry analysts—like Esther Dyson, for example—may be privileged to see new products before they are officially introduced, they're not generally in on the decision to produce them.

The fast growth of Future Computing in its first four years mirrored, and in fact was intertwined with, the growth of the personal computer industry itself. The fact that some of the biggest names in the minicomputer and mainframe businesses came calling on Isaacson for advice about their micro plans gave her enormous influence in helping shape the micro industry.

Besides such close associations, Future Computing also served as an information clearinghouse for both new and established companies, pinpointing industry trends and potential future markets through its dozens of newsletters and reports published each year.

Future Computing was one of the very few sources of hard facts and figures in existence, since it had shrewdly established a network of 1,000 representative computer and specialty stores that faithfully reported their actual sales figures each month. While most market research firms relied only on vendors or distributors for unit sales information—which was often inflated to make everyone look good—Future Computing's sales data were inarguable.

Its long-range projections, on the other hand, sometimes were not. Although Future Computing built its reputation on early and accurate insight into the potential impact of the IBM PC, the firm later came to be known for predictions that often turned out to be too optimistic.

Future Computing projected in 1983, for example, that the educational software market would grow more than 70 percent per year and reach nearly $1 billion by 1987. The Learning Company, among others, would quickly tell you that's not quite how it worked out.

Then again, some projections have been too pessimistic. In 1983 Future Computing estimated the market for the programming language Pascal to be about 40,000 packages. In the following two years a single company, Borland International, sold 300,000 copies of its Turbo Pascal software, surprising even itself.

In the fast-moving personal computer world, fortune telling is by definition very risky business. During 1982 alone, Future Computing had to change its long-term forecast for the home computer three times because of new developments in that market. But mistakes or not, Future Computing in many ways led the personal computer industry by the hand into its maturity. Not only was Isaacson's timing perfect in offering the guidance the industry needed, but her own personality and charisma practically guaranteed that her venture would flourish.

"You've seen a speaker who, through whatever technique, holds the audience right here, and has the awareness to sense when they're shifting away and does something dramatic to get them back," she says. "And you've listened for two hours and thought it was ten minutes." Dispensing with false modesty, as usual, Isaacson puts herself squarely in that category. "On a public forum, I'm a very powerful, dynamic, opinionated speaker," she claims, and few would deny it. "No one leaves the room when I'm talking, and I can take anybody on. I'm trained extensively in debate, which is a form of combat, and I'm very good at it."

In the less public debates of business negotiations, too, Isaacson long ago figured out how to be irresistible. Later, when seminars started springing up to teach that very thing, she attended one to find out more about herself.

"I took a course called 'Persuasion by Hypnosis,' which sounds real sensational," she says, "but it's not. People who take the course are primarily attorneys and salespeople—people who, in short periods of time, have to move a group to action or get a commitment, who have to be very persuasive in a group setting.

"The course was about controlling the group, in a way, and how to use what are called 'waking hypnosis techniques,' " she says. "I had, in fact, used them and didn't know it, before I took the course." She was even using them back in her Stratford, Oklahoma, high school debates. "Even then I could hold an audience like you wouldn't believe," she says.

Without these particular attributes in its founder—as well as Isaacson's already established relationships in the computer community—it's questionable whether Future Computing would ever have gotten off the ground. She was the company's prime attraction and major product from the first day.

With Isaacson at the helm, the company not only got off the ground but rocketed straight up. The micro industry's boom in the early eighties propelled Future Computing's own expansion, and within two years it had gone from strictly consulting to a product-oriented company.

At its height, Future Computing had more than 300 clients paying $15,000 to $50,000 a year for its reports, newsletters, and consulting services. Besides IBM and Sears, Future Computing's clients have included Apple Computer, Digital Equipment, AT&T, Xerox, Kodak, Gillette, RCA, and *Time* magazine.

Future Computing also hosted more than a dozen seminars a year—costing up to $895 a day per person—at which industry luminaries, including the other nine women here, regularly addressed audiences of scientists, engineers, company presidents, and marketing experts. Seminars offered in-depth analyses of many different topics within the categories of hardware, software, retailing, and new technologies.

Any business that boosts its income more than 900 percent in its first two years has to move extremely fast. And Future Computing did. "We had a new organization chart every day," Isaacson says, "and I spent probably most of my time at Future Computing, and definitely most of my emotional energy, on the people. That meant building the organization—and unbuilding it—having to shuffle people around, always dealing with people's egos, emotions, and insecurities."

The company had to scramble in other ways, too. "Because we'd grown so fast with no outside funding, there was never a payday I knew I would make in the first three years of the company," she reveals. "But we made every one and, in fact, we never stretched our suppliers.

"But, in order to make each one, I had to stay absolutely right on top of the cash flow every day, juggling the company's products and collection activity and marketing and expenses in all sorts of ways," she explains. "That's a responsibility that gets harder and harder as the company gets larger."

Future Computing's astounding growth brought changes not only in the company's functions, but also in Isaacson's functions within the company. By the time her then-husband, Egil Juliussen, had been with Future Computing for a year, its rapid growth meant that someone had to assume responsibility for the firm's overall functioning.

"Egil had no desire to manage," Isaacson says, "so I had to and wanted to manage the company, while juggling the client work. I had to [make the] transition from being the company's primary product to being the general manager of the company."

Fitting together the puzzle pieces of a rapidly growing organization is drastically different from being a visionary and consulting with bigwigs about the shape and future of an industry. Nevertheless, Isaacson committed herself totally to the job of general manager. It turned out to be the hardest thing she had ever done.

"Being a general manager is a balancing act," she explains. "To any general manager report, in some way, product development, marketing, planning, finance, personnel, sales, building facilities, computer systems—everything about the company falls on [the general manager's] back ultimately.

"So if you've done a good job, you've tried to hire strong managers in all areas that report to you," she says, "but you never have a perfect aim. So day after day, hour after hour, you have these 15-minute meeting schedules, and it's problem after problem after problem, because that's all they bring you—they can handle all the easy stuff."

Every single day, Isaacson handled the seemingly endless problems that a general manager must, and she did a fine job, as evidenced by Future Computing's success, but her own perfectionism seriously eroded her sense of accomplishment. "I'm very insecure while many of these activities are going on," she admitted while running Future Computing. "I know I don't have the knowledge base it would take to make the best decision in the situation." Inevitably she would berate herself for falling short of perfect. "At the end of a day I go home feeling really inadequate," she said.

"General managers who have come to feel success at their job have learned how to be happy with the balance: the fact that at the end of the day they picked the right 20 problems to handle, they handled them all in some way—they moved them forward—and on the net, they got 'adequates,' " she says.

But Isaacson is not capable of being happy with the balance. She wants to be a superstar at all times. "All of my life I've migrated quickly to things I really excelled at, and if I wasn't good at something, I just dumped it," she explains. "I need to feel like I'm winning all the time, that I'm doing it well. When I started Future Computing, I was doing consulting, doing business strategics, analyzing and explaining the industry to people, and so on, and I was really good at that, and still am."

But as her role in the company evolved from consultant to general manager, so rose her level of stress, and the mental anguish took a physical toll. She started experiencing extreme pain in her back, which sent her to a chiropractor and a massage therapist. She also put on 40 pounds in three years.

"I've asked myself why Future Computing would affect me more adversely [in terms of stress] than all this other stuff I've been through, you know? Future Computing is nothing compared to going to the grocery store with three babies all under two years old," she laughs.

Isaacson has concluded that the source of her stress is a feeling of lack of control. "People say, 'Gee, Portia, it must be really neat to have your own business,' and I say to them, 'I don't think you understand. This [expletive] business has *me!*' I mean 24 hours a day, seven days a week, this business has me," she said at the time.

"Particularly because of all this growth," she said, "there's never enough support at my level, because I've always just hired people who've been there only three weeks, and they cause me more trouble, not less. And I have to be accessible 24 hours day, seven days a week—it's an incredible feeling of being captive and being out of control. It means being in response-only mode: You only handle problems when they rise to the surface, rather than saying, 'Okay, this is what I'm going to do with my day.' It isn't my day at all! It's *their* day."

The very nature of Future Computing feeds into that syndrome. "We're not ever in control," she says. "We have to respond to client needs in real time, and if IBM announces something, we shut the whole company down. We have to stop what we were doing and do something different.

"Since I've understood the [stress] problem, I've been through all sorts of ways to manage it, but fundamentally, I haven't been able to," she said. "I've been able to hold my own, but not make a lot of progress."

In late 1983, however, Isaacson started to see a glimmer at the end of that long, dark tunnel. Future Computing was approached by three potential buyers at about the same time. "If we had picked three companies we wanted to talk to, the three that came to us were the three," Isaacson says.

One of the suitors seemed particularly compatible. After nine months of getting to know Future Computing, the huge New York–based publishing company McGraw-Hill finally said it was ready to talk turkey. "We took their first offer," Isaacson says. "It was just right."

In July 1984 McGraw-Hill bought Future Computing from Isaacson and Juliussen for a reported $8 million in cash, plus additional payouts based on future profits. Coincidentally, the announcement came the very day after General Motors announced plans to buy the company of Isaacson's mentor, Ross Perot.

McGraw-Hill was a dream come true for Future Computing. "What we needed, really, was not so much money, as resources to build on," Isaacson explains. For one thing, Isaacson and Juliussen felt that Future Computing had outgrown their management expertise. And McGraw-Hill had plenty more to offer, as well. "We needed good relationships with things like [McGraw-Hill's] *Byte* magazine and Datapro [its market research firm] and its other information networks, and those you can't get through just money; you have to have a company that already has them and can share them. And McGraw-Hill has them in spades."

Future Computing became a part of a new McGraw-Hill company that included all its computer and communications businesses. "McGraw-Hill has the largest information business in the computer communications industry when they put all these together into one reporting structure," Isaacson said then. "It's a pretty exciting thing to be part of."

Nevertheless, Isaacson was waving goodbye to the entrepreneurial Future Computing. "It's exactly like when a child goes off to college," she says. "It's just exactly that feeling, because it's something you want to happen—because for the company to mature, grow, exist forever, continue to develop, it needs to happen. At the same time, you are giving something up as it grows and matures. It's not really positive, but there are some feelings of 'Gee, I miss the kid.' "

What she pointedly felt had disappeared was the feeling of risk. "That's largely positive, by the way," she reassures. "When we miss something, we miss when it was 15 or 30 people. That was when it was the most fun.

"It was entrepreneurial, flexible; you could be in a different business every week. There didn't have to be a management structure, you didn't have to have policies, you didn't even have to stay in business. If I ever get homesick, it's for that."

Isaacson felt several direct benefits of the McGraw-Hill deal almost immediately. "The McGraw-Hill situation helps me some, in that it takes a little of the emergency feeling away because of cash flow," she said a few months after the purchase. It also took a little of the emergency feeling away in terms of her management of the company. "The responsibility was more awesome when a decision I made might put the company under, which is not true now that it's owned by McGraw-Hill, so some of the terrifying responsibility has been removed."

Soon all of the terrifying responsibility would be removed. After ten years of nurturing the personal computer industry along, Isaacson had to admit she was "getting just a little bit bored with it." In August 1985 Isaacson left Future Computing and soon after started three new ventures of her own. "It's really fun to be doing something new again," she said shortly thereafter.

Her timing, again, was just right. The micro industry slump—which saw reduced demand for many hardware and software products—had extended to information about those products and their marketplace. Shrinking profit margins all around meant there was less money to spend on Future Computing's newsletters, reports, and seminars.

At the end of April 1986, McGraw-Hill announced that it would eliminate 58 of Future Computing's 79 staff members and would consolidate those remaining into its Datapro Research Corp. division in Delran, New Jersey. Although Future Computing would "retain its name and identity," according to a McGraw-Hill spokesman, the firm would move away from market research in favor of product analysis.

McGraw-Hill was quick to comment that it didn't consider Future Computing a failed acquisition, since the deal had expanded its own services to include personal computers. McGraw-Hill felt that the change in Future Computing's emphasis would make the firm a "natural fit" with Datapro.

In May 1986 Juliussen also left the company to pursue other ventures. The heyday of Future Computing was now past.

5

Still in the Game

As the personal computer industry enters its second decade, many of the earlier players have dropped away in favor of other endeavors. Others are an integral part of a maturing industry, and expect to remain so over the long haul—or at least for the foreseeable future.

While in one sense the industry has stabilized, emerging technologies will always provide change, excitement, and challenges for those yet in the fray. And, although it's a lot harder to jump into the game than it used to be, there's still room for newcomers with talent, energy, and enthusiasm.

Janelle Bedke: Catching Up with the Times

The economic climate wasn't the only thing that disrupted the micro industry in the mid-1980s. Business computer users had grown gradually more sophisticated, increasing the demand for high-performance software. Software Publishing Corp. (SPC) was doing so well with its lower-end, easy-to-use application software, however, that it hardly had time to notice the gradual changes occurring in corporate America.

SPC, in fact, did almost too well for its own good. The rising tide of its success obscured some treacherous shoals below. From first-year 1981 sales of $732,000 as a two-product company, Software Publishing zoomed up to $4 million in sales for 1982 (by which time it had a third product), then more than doubled that performance in 1983 (during which it announced its fourth product) by raking in $10 million.

In 1984—a year of fierce industry competition—SPC introduced three new products and again more than doubled its sales from the previous year, to $26 million. "While other companies are going into Chapter 11 and laying people off, we've never had a better time," Bedke said late in 1984.

"We've certainly not seen any dips. We're one of the few companies that's hiring people and, in fact, we've picked up good people from others' layoffs." By the end of 1984, SPC had 115 employees and planned to hire 70 more in the coming year.

So far, so good. Certainly SPC had done many things right during its first four years. In the summer of 1982, for example, Software Publishing forged a somewhat risky alliance with IBM that, fortunately, proved to be mutually beneficial.

The agreement called for IBM to sell Software Publishing's pfs: line, slightly modified, under IBM's own name, as the IBM Assistant Series. While the deal would give SPC valuable distribution channels through IBM's direct sales force and an instant entree into IBM Product Centers, it would also take the high-recognition pfs: name off the product.

The dangers of the agreement for SPC included potential confusion over the competing brand names and the possibility of retailers dropping the pfs: line if sales fell off sharply. Software Publishing could have, in essence, ended up competing with itself. "It was a hard decision to give up the pfs: brand," Bedke recalls.

Finally, though, SPC decided to go along with it, since IBM was likely to develop such a category of software with or without SPC's cooperation. Going head-to-head against IBM is something no small software vendor wants to do, and few could survive doing. SPC would be one of the first companies to have IBM endorse and sell its software.

Software Publishing's decision was right on the money. Both product lines sold well and, as Bedke says of the Assistant Series, "Everyone in the industry knows it's ours." Besides being lucrative—ultimately totalling 10 percent of SPC's revenues—the deal gave SPC the boost in reputation that a pact with IBM automatically bestows.

It's true that SPC frequently looks over its shoulder to make sure IBM is at a safe distance, but then so does everyone else. "You never know," Bedke says. "We think we have a great relationship with IBM, but they could change their mind and compete with us.

"You're never comfortable in this industry—it's like a roller coaster sometimes." Then Bedke adds a phrase from what must be the entrepreneur's secret handbook: "But part of the excitement is the unknown."

Software Publishing has always tried to remain flexible by exercising strict financial control, acting from a position of stability, and offering a broad base of products. From the beginning, the company has kept a tight fist around its pennies.

Operating budgets for revenues and expenses have been managed month to month, with variances closely monitored. Furthermore, SPC has not favored even its founders with plush offices or other expensive displays of prestige. It has promoted a decidedly democratic air within the company, with executives and nonexecutives alike working out of modest cubicles labeled only with each person's name—no titles.

No one in the company has a personal secretary, but everyone has a personal computer. "We use the technology" in place of clerical workers, Bedke says. "I don't need a secretary. I handle my own correspondence, I arrange my own travel plans. We have a phone mail system for interoffice communications." Only after four years in business did Software Publishing hire its first mail delivery person.

President Fred Gibbons readily admits to being "a fanatic" when it comes to saving money. The organization, then, remains the "lean and mean" structure that Gibbons, Bedke, and Page set out to build.

Why did Software Publishing thrive while others were choking? A major factor in its success was the founders' concept of SPC as primarily a marketing company supported by a strong R&D capability. It's a description that could also be applied to IBM. The micro industry is notorious for not knowing how to market its products, no matter how good they may be, and it's the few talented marketers that have shot to the very top (IBM and Lotus, for example).

Software Publishing was the first micro software firm to establish an internal engineering team. The firm also embraced the Procter & Gamble–type "brand" concept of software, with the continuity of its pfs: line. In addition, just as pioneer Vector Graphic did, SPC has cultivated a loyal dealer base. "It's key," Bedke says.

But SPC's methodical development of a solid foundation has had its drawbacks. "One of my biggest frustrations early on was to watch other companies seemingly pass us by with higher sales," Bedke recalls. "They'd make a big splash and get more press, only to auger in months later.

"Most companies are one-product companies," she says. "We were there for the long term and I knew we were better, but they'd skyrocket and plummet. I wouldn't change the way we run the company, but I want credit because these people deserve it."

"These people" are the unusually loyal employees SPC has brought into the fold. The company has an extremely low turnover rate of about 4 percent in a business notorious for its revolving-door syndrome. "We always hired excellent, outstanding people," Bedke says. "We built the company under them."

As it happens, about half of Software Publishing's employees are female. "Not on purpose," Bedke explains. "We recruited for the positions and the best candidates happened to be women." Two of the three vice presidents are women, as well as eight of the nine managers in marketing and administration.

With these inner and outer strengths, the company made impressive headway with products that consistently made the industry's Top Ten best-seller lists. By 1983, SPC was riding high. Sales had more than doubled every year since the company began, and the firm's reputation for quality and stability was solid.

Since mid-1982 the stock market had been courting high-tech companies. Early in 1983 SPC was being vigorously solicited by several investment banking firms and entered into tentative negotiations with one. It was determined that an offering of 1 million shares could probably be expected to fetch $15 to $19 a share. Bedke thought the time was right and the company could lose momentum if it failed to move ahead aggressively.

The 1982 cadre of SPC's venture capitalists also looked very favorably on a deal that would let them cash in double what they had invested and still let them keep most of their stock. Because of the high value placed on the company at that time, the offering would have still left the three founders with a total of more than 43 percent ownership in their company.

Everything looked good on paper, but the company would have had to move very fast in order to catch the high tech investment wave before it crashed. Fred Gibbons held back. He worried about the ways in which being a public company might change the corporate atmosphere; he worried about possibly short-circuiting his managers' careers by having to bring in older, more experienced executives; he worried about the additional and time-consuming responsibilities that fall to any public company and that in this instance would fall to him personally.

One of Gibbons's hesitations, as expressed in a list of pros and cons he wrote (that appeared in a Harvard Business School case study), hinged on the volatility of the micro industry.

"I do not have much confidence about the visibility of future earnings more than 12 months out in our industry," Gibbons wrote. "If we should have trouble with our earnings growth, it might be very convenient to have a lot of extra cash on hand.

"But if we should have earnings problems, I certainly won't relish facing public stockholders who purchased their stock with the expectations of a pattern of earnings growth that would justify a [price/earnings] multiple of 55–70 times."

Bedke felt just the opposite. Recognizing that other companies had grown even faster than SPC, she was convinced that the firm shouldn't back away from this opportunity to reinforce its image as an industry leader. But Gibbons's reluctance won out, at least temporarily. SPC did not go public in 1983.

By late 1984 it was obvious that the highly charged atmosphere of the mid-1983 stock market was long past, and yet the company then decided to take the plunge. Why then? "Things had changed," Bedke explains. "We felt a lot stronger as a management team. We had more experience under our belt."

The stock market certainly wasn't as receptive to high-tech offerings as it had been 16 months earlier, but during that interval both the market and the micro industry had stabilized to a certain extent. "In 1983, IBM had been [in the industry] just a short period of time and there was a lot of question about what was going to happen with IBM and Apple," Bedke recalls. "By 1984 we felt that had settled out and we had a clear picture of where the industry was heading. We felt the time was right."

A week before the actual offering, Bedke discussed her views. "We have a moral obligation to go public," she said. "It will give us outside money and increase the value of the stock held by our employees. Besides, *The Wall Street Journal* says it won't talk to us until we're public.

"It's like an insurance policy," she continued. "We don't need the cash today, but in the next year there'll be lots of opportunities and we want to be in a position of financial strength to take advantage of them. We don't want to miss out on them."

But what about investors' new skepticism about high tech? "The investment community has nothing bad to say about Software Publishing or pfs:, but they have bad things to say about the industry," Bedke acknowledged while awaiting SEC approval. "I have guarded optimism," she said. "They have a bad taste in their mouths about the industry. They've been hurt. The industry is healthy, growing, strong. We have to demonstrate that."

Because of the relatively depressed market into which Software Publishing went public on November 15, 1984, its initial offering brought in only $7 a share for the 1.7 million shares it offered. Anyone in Bedke's position would be hard put not to feel at least a twinge of "I told you so," but Bedke is gracious, and a fierce optimist, too.

"I think we left money on the table by not going out in 1983," she admits, "but the flip side of that is investor satisfaction. It's always been important for us that any customer be satisfied, and we view an investor as a customer in our company.

"It's not a good long-term relationship when the first thing that happens is that a stock goes out at a high price and then drops off," she adds. "We're in it for the long term and our investors are getting a good deal by having had us wait. So I think in the big picture, it really didn't make much difference whether we went out in '83 or '84."

Gibbons had no regrets either. "That was definitely the right decision," he says. "If you take the big picture, yes, the stock would have been higher back then and, yes, the company and the selling shareholders would have made more money, but whoever bought it in the public market would have lost a lot of money."

Although SPC had made a strong showing in 1984 (with a 160 percent increase in sales) while many others weakened, its star began to fade somewhat late in 1985, the year that rocked the industry at large. Software Publishing—stable, dependable, and admired—watched its revenues slip steadily all during 1985, except for a slight surge in the summer. For the year, though, the company still had a respectable 42 percent growth rate in sales, from $26 million to $37 million, and a 48 percent increase in profits.

SPC had absorbed some extra expenses, as well—doubling its R&D funding from the year earlier, and acquiring during the summer a smaller software company, Harvard Software, Inc., for stock valued at between $3 million and $4 million.

But the first fiscal quarter of 1986, ended December 31, 1985, was really bad news. Net income had plummeted 76 percent from the same period a year earlier, from $2.5 million to $617,000. Sales for the first quarter of 1986 were little more than half what they had been for the first quarter of 1985—$6.9 million compared with $12.5 million.

The firm attributed the dramatic decline to a poor Christmas season and, more importantly, to a market shift away from walk-in retail sales and toward outside corporate sales.

To outside observers, 1985 looked pretty bad for Software Publishing, but for the insiders, it was a year of new beginnings and a little bad luck. Besides the costs of an acquisition and heavy R&D spending, the ill health of the industry in general had to take some of the blame for Software Publishing's downturn.

Furthermore, SPC's moderately priced products just couldn't bring in the bucks. By the end of 1985, SPC had actually sold more programs than any of its competition—about 2 million copies as compared with Lotus's 1.6 million—but revenues were modest compared with those from high-priced software. SPC's 1985 haul was $37 million versus Lotus's $225 million. (Pfs: software was priced from $125 to $140, compared with Lotus 1-2-3's price of $495.)

Software Publishing's worst problem, however, was its sluggishness in responding to the growing sophistication of the user community. With more and more users demanding software to match the greater speed and versatility of the latest micro hardware, Software Publishing was losing its following to software makers who addressed that need.

"Software Publishing's cardinal sin was in failing to make its products obsolete by introducing more powerful programs," said one competitor in 1985. But SPC was well aware of the gap and had already taken steps to expand its software line upward.

By acquiring Harvard Software, Inc., SPC gained two excellent high-end products—the $395 Harvard Project Manager and the $495 Harvard Total Project Manager packages, the best-sellers in their category. For 400,000 shares of stock, SPC had acquired the profitable company, its respected name, and its successful high-end products.

Shortly after its acquisition of Harvard Software, SPC moved yet further away from the low end of things by selling its then two-year-old mail-order catalog division, PowerUp, to a new firm staffed largely by former SPC employees. Channelmark Corp. continued to use the PowerUp name, selling its line of low-cost accessory software products to corporations and institutions.

As IBM's influence grew in the micro industry, Software Publishing's commitment to the industry leader deepened accordingly, so that by 1985, 90 percent of SPC's resources were invested in the development of IBM and compatible products, and only 10 percent in Apple, specifically the Apple II. "It's a far cry from 100 percent Apple, which is how we started out," Bedke notes.

By the end of 1985, it was obvious that Software Publishing had redefined itself and was looking forward hopefully in several new directions. Unfortunately, the bottom line hadn't yet caught up with SPC's hopes for the future. Software Publishing had to announce to the world that first-quarter 1986 earnings would be substantially lower than anyone had expected.

As if that weren't enough, fate sprang a nasty surprise. On the Sunday before Christmas 1985, company president Fred Gibbons, only 36 and apparently in the best of health, suffered a stroke while skiing. Because the stroke temporarily robbed Gibbons of most of his motor control on his left side, he was forced to turn his duties completely over to Bedke for a time.

Although the incident was "a real shocker," according to Bedke, Gibbons made swift progress and was back in the office for five-hour days by the middle of January, walking with the aid of a leg brace and undergoing daily physical therapy. But bad news travels fast, especially when you're a public company. If Bedke had been looking forward to talking to *The Wall Street Journal* before SPC went public, she learned the hard way that the conversation could take some unexpected turns.

On January 27, 1986, the *Journal* ran a story under the headline, "Software Publishing Lashed by Setbacks." The article discussed SPC's falling earnings, Gibbons' then-recent accident, and the admittedly increasing competition the firm faced.

The facts of the story were true, Bedke acknowledges ("Numbers don't lie," she says), but seeing her company's problems and weaknesses exposed to the *Journal*'s millions of readers was something like finding out on the 6:00 news that one's son has been arrested.

"When I first read it, I was shocked and very disappointed," she says. Filled with enthusiasm for a stable of new products slated to hit the streets later in 1986, Bedke had to endure the frustration of looking bad when she actually felt good. But such is the price of being a major player.

The company had released no major new products in 1985, but it had big plans for 1986. In January SPC introduced a $395 graphics program called Harvard Presentation Graphics. The package was a key step into SPC's high-end future.

By the end of 1986, the company had released half a dozen high-end packages, had gotten excellent reviews on all of them, and was looking forward to being at the top of the heap again.

Therese Myers: The Underdog Bites Back

While 1985 was nothing but trouble for most of the personal computer industry, ironically it brought a great deal of satisfaction to Quarterdeck Office Systems, the longtime underdog to industry leaders Microsoft, VisiCorp, and IBM.

Even though Quarterdeck's business suffered as much as any other company's from the industry slowdown that year, at the same time its Desq software came into its own as, one by one, its competitors' products hit the store shelves.

After the shock of August 14, 1984, when Myers witnessed the unveiling of IBM's strikingly similar Topview operating environment, Quarterdeck immediately laid off 20 low-level employees (nearly half its total) and consulted Arthur D. Little, Inc., for a prognosis.

Arthur D. Little rightly predicted that the industry would go through a period of evaluating Desq against Topview (once it finally appeared), as well as against Microsoft's Windows, slated to come out later in 1985. ADL recommended that Quarterdeck abandon the idea of trying to sign up individual dealers and instead go after distributors "as soon as possible," Myers recalls.

On the basis of that advice, "we had a complete and sudden change in our distribution strategy," she says. Quarterdeck had never dealt with distributors before, and it went about acquiring them in a very methodical way. Quarterdeck initially struck an exclusive three-month deal with Micro D, for reasons of control, education, and preference.

"[The distributors] are all different; they all have different strengths," Myers explained at the time. "I just like Mecca. I think Micro D is a very professional organization and I think they have a customer base we need."

Micro D—selling hardware, hard disks, and memory boards, among other things—had just the kind of dealer-clients Quarterdeck was interested in attracting. Since Desq worked best with a hard disk, for example, dealers that sold hard disks would possibly be more successful selling Desq than dealers that didn't. Furthermore, those dealers would be able to engineer such promotional schemes as bundling Desq with a hard-disk system.

"We wanted to pick one distributor that we'd deal with first, figure out how you train a distributor, how your sales force works with a distributor, how you support a distributor, and then go to the next one," Myers said. "So we said, 'Well, let's pick the one we like.' "

Micro D turned out to be a good choice for Quarterdeck. A mailing to 3,500 of Micro D's key IBM dealers yielded a healthy number of dealers for Desq, and Quarterdeck quickly learned the ropes of vendor-distributor relations.

When the exclusive contract with Micro D expired on November 1, 1984, Quarterdeck broadened its roster to include national distributors Softsel, Softeam, and First Software, as well as several regional firms.

It would be three months before IBM's Topview would actually make its appearance—a period during which Quarterdeck's hands were tied in terms of proving its superiority. It couldn't do much competing until there was something with which to compete.

But early in February 1985, there was rejoicing in Santa Monica when Topview was finally released. Proud as IBM was of its product, Quarterdeck was even more proud of Desq, which it felt was the hands-down winner between the two.

The critics seemed to agree. " 'Topview' Debut Stirs Little Interest Among Major Software Vendors" read the front-page headline in *PC Week* magazine two weeks after Topview came out. "Curiously," the article noted, "Topview's most enthusiastic support is from the makers of such competing products as Desq, [Digital Research, Inc.'s] Concurrent PC-DOS, [Microsoft Corp.'s] Windows and lesser-known products such as [Application Executive Corp.'s] APX Core."

With the ever-present irony facing those who compete with IBM, its rivals hoped that the success of Topview would validate the philosophy behind their own products while simultaneously showing them off to competitive advantage. At the same time, rivals hoped to ride on the coattails of IBM's success by adjusting their windowing software to accept programs written specifically for Topview. They would be "Topview-compatible," which meant that they would become a viable alternative to IBM.

Immediately after the Topview announcement in August 1984, in fact, Quarterdeck had started working on a streamlined version of Desq that would be completely Topview-compatible. Desqview would be for more casual computer users, not the power users of Desq. It would also be easier to use than Desq, yet more versatile.

Although Desq had been able to display up to nine programs simultaneously, and data could easily be swapped among them, only one program was ever actually running at once. The rest were waiting in the background to be brought forward into the "active" window. They could be in the middle of processing something, but they were frozen in time.

With Desqview, as with Topview, all programs were active all the time—a feature known as "multitasking" or "concurrency." That meant that a user could, for example, print out a file or recalculate a spreadsheet in the background while writing a report in thc foreground. Concurrency also meant that a user never had to wait for the computer to finish a menial task before he or she could get back to work.

Desqview shipped in May 1985 with an attractive $99 price tag. At the same time, Quarterdeck dropped Desq's price to $199 from the original $399. IBM's Topview remained priced at $149.

IBM, meanwhile, true to its commitment to Topview as its strategic software product, started pushing Topview more aggressively than it had ever pushed a software product before. In May 1985 IBM caused a stir by offering free copies of Topview and two other software packages (one being Software Publishing's Assistant Series) to buyers of its PC XT computer.

The 90-day promotion caused dismay among the competition, who considered it predatory, and Janelle Bedke of Software Publishing went on record as being unhappy because the offer could be seen to diminish the perceived value of her company's Assistant Series.

A month later, IBM was giving away more free copies of Topview, this time to selected volume users. IBM had often given away demonstration disks (falling short of a complete program, but suggesting its capabilities), but this marked the first time Big Blue had parted with thousands of full-fledged copies, absolutely free.

One has to wonder how a tiny company like Quarterdeck could continue to survive in such a climate. Who but IBM could afford to give away tens of thousands of free copies of its software? On the other hand, it could be said that IBM couldn't afford *not* to give Topview away—considering the lukewarm reception it was getting. In June 1985, *InfoWorld* magazine concluded that Topview was "slow, memory-hungry and requires far too much technical knowledge." And even a free copy doesn't guarantee that anyone will use it.

Although Quarterdeck certainly couldn't afford to flood the market with free software, it had other ways of fighting back. First of all, it got good reviews. In September 1985, *InfoWorld* called

Desqview "a powerful, useful, clever windowing program." The reviewer even went so far as to say that Desqview "fulfills what Topview has promised." Quarterdeck's publicity firm couldn't have written it better.

A month later, Quarterdeck scored an important marketing coup. In October 1985, Quarterdeck announced that it had bundled Desqview onto the Rampage memory board of AST Research, Inc., the market leader with 40 percent of the board business. The combination was said to bypass the major technical limitations of both Topview and Windows.

It also gave Quarterdeck a big boost in sales. By that December, Desqview was hooked into four of AST's multifunction boards, "which makes us, by number of units shipped, the market leader," Myers claimed then.

Still, complicating the entire picture was the question of whether IBM might eventually abandon its own Topview operating environment in favor of supporting Microsoft's Windows. (Windows was announced in November 1983 but didn't ship until July 1985.) Microsoft did, after all, write MS-DOS, the operating system for the IBM PC, and then engineered Windows from there.

Instead, Windows too got a less than enthusiastic reception from the critics and joined the handful of operating environments waiting for people to realize that they couldn't live without them. In February 1986 *InfoWorld* rated Windows "poor" and said it required too much power.

Criticism notwithstanding, Microsoft had a distinct and undeniable edge: Analysts were predicting that future versions of MS–DOS would likely be based on Windows. Even with Desqview selling well with Rampage, hanging over it was the shadow of potential incompatibility with MS-DOS. The windowing battle was seen more and more to be between Windows and Topview, with the smaller entrants left to pick up the crumbs.

In any case, Myers professed not to be worried. "Our product works on today's machines," she said in early 1986. "People aren't going to get rid of their IBM PC XT or clones just because the prices on 80286-based computers dropped or because the first 80386-based machine has just come out."

Aside from the fierce competition among the few vendors of windowing software, there remained an even bigger challenge for all of them: how to win computer users. Even with Desq, Topview, and Windows on the market, corporate microcomputer managers reported that fewer than 1 percent of their users had expressed any interest in operating environments; most users were still working on the basics of computing.

By the end of 1986, however, more than 250,000 copies of Desq/Desqview were said to be in use, mostly by the corporate "power users." Myers remained confident that time would bring a surge in demand. "Given the choice, would you rather prepare a nine-course meal on a hot plate or four burners and an oven?" she asks.

Despite the formidable industry troubles of 1985 to 1986, Quarterdeck hung in there with a product that could only be considered a bridge to the future. Far more powerful computers—with extended memory and faster microprocessor chips—were just around the corner, and operating-environment software would be the first to maximize the new technology.

If the technology evolved as expected, it would play right into Quarterdeck's hand. Many computer users were envisioning being able to routinely run several programs at once, exchange data among programs and files instantaneously, and generally work the way office workers have always worked, whether they're secretaries or executives—namely, with interruptions.

It would take savvy, patience, and continued sales for Quarterdeck to see itself, and the industry, through to the next phase of office automation, but dedication is one thing the company has never lacked. "You have to have staying power, I think," Myers guessed early on. And she's got plenty.

Esther Dyson: Skipping a Beat

"I've made mistakes and corrected them several times," admits Esther Dyson. "I'd rather do that then try and bluff it out." In 1985 she made a highly visible misstep that took her away from her own newsletter, then she corrected it by returning six months later as if she had never gone.

In the last week of March 1985, Ziff-Davis Publishing Co. announced, with great fanfare, that it would begin publishing a daily electronic newspaper—accessible by personal computer—that summer. Dyson was named publisher and executive editor of what was to become the *Computer Industry Daily (CID).*

The idea of an electronic newspaper had long been bandied about by computer trade publishers, but no one had actually delivered the goods. In this case, the goods would be delivered both electronically and on paper, by MCI Mail. Priced at $1,500 a year for U.S. subscribers, *CID* would also be distributed in Japan, Western Europe, Asia, and Latin America.

At the announcement, Dyson told the press that there was too much information available about the computer industry, but that not enough of it was timely. "Our aim is to turn this mass of information into something more concise and more meaningful," she said.

Although Dyson had turned down the same offer from Ziff-Davis a year earlier, the more she thought about it, the more excited she got. Being on-line every day, heading a large editorial staff, and whipping the whole thing into shape began to sound even more interesting than what she was already doing. Within the year, she had decided that it was eminently more interesting. "I'm getting kind of bored writing about which retailer's going bankrupt and who announced a new PC," she admitted a month before the *CID* announcement.

CID would cover not only micros, but would try to interpret the entire computer industry, including hardware, software, distribution, marketing trends, and finance. The project seemed like a logical next step for someone whose stated goal was to make things understandable for people.

As part of the deal, Dyson was to sell her newsletter, *RELease 1.0,* to Ziff-Davis (for a rumored $1 million), while retaining ownership of EDventure Holdings, Inc. The plan was for *RELease 1.0* to cease publication when *CID* started up. Although she would still own the Personal Computer Forum, it was agreed that Ziff-Davis would manage it.

As far as insight, industry knowledge, and reportorial skills went, Dyson was as qualified to run *CID* as anyone possibly could be. But as the head of a 30-person operating entity, she had a lot to learn.

Well aware of her nonexistent managerial experience, Dyson looked at this new challenge the same way she had looked at her previous challenges. "I've always taken on jobs before I was qualified," she says. "It's much more fun that way." And she had grand plans for *CID*.

"I'd like to see it turn into *The Wall Street Journal,*" she said in 1985. "What *The Wall Street Journal* was in the thirties, I want *Computer Industry Daily* to be in the nineties—a national newspaper. The information industry will eventually no longer be a special interest, but integral to all business." One fact she may somehow have been blind to is that no one has ever had to pay $1,500 for a year's worth of *The Wall Street Journal.*

By July, Dyson was in the thick of it, managing a staff of 20 and expecting 10 more. The change was dramatic from her days as a loner, when she had a support staff of two. Although she had admitted back then to being "not a very good boss," she thought she was learning fast on the job. "Now that I'm doing it, I'm doing pretty well," she felt.

All efforts focused on a starting date of September 18. Full-page ads ran in trade magazines, and in August *CID* prototype issues went out to about 260 former *RELease 1.0* subscribers. Unfortunately, the reaction was not good.

"Part of the feedback we got was, 'Gee, we miss *RELease 1.0,*' " Dyson says. "So every time they said that, it was an arrow in *CID*'s back and a vote for the resurrection of *RELease 1.0.*"

Although the ads for *CID* had promised "the informed perspective and critical analysis you need," the publication actually sacrificed depth for breadth of coverage of the industry's many and varied segments.

It wasn't only the readers who didn't like what they saw. Neither Ziff-Davis, the staff, nor Dyson was pleased. "There was not enough insight and analysis," she admits, "and there's enough news in *The [Wall Street] Journal* and *The [New York] Times* to keep people going day to day."

A major problem for *CID* was staffing. "There is a difference between reporters and analysts," she told *Computer Currents* magazine. "We had some very good reporters, but not the analytical viewpoint. There just aren't a lot of people out there who know what's going on who are not already making $150,000 a year at a market research firm." Furthermore, electronic delivery proved expensive for Ziff-Davis, and readers considered even the introductory price of $995 too high.

But perhaps the most painful failing was in missing big stories because of deadline constraints. For a state-of-the-art newspaper, *CID* fell far short of the *Journal*'s and the *Times*'s coverage of the computer industry. Because of its delivery arrangement with MCI Mail, *CID* had a 4:30 P.M. EST deadline for the next day's issue—cutting California off at 1:30 in the afternoon. That proved to be a fatal flaw, since both the *Journal* and the *Times* closed in the early evening, allowing them to get the late-breaking West Coast stories with their usual efficiency.

The onslaught of arrows finally found their mark—right through the heart of *CID*. On the very morning in September when the first electronic issue was to have sizzled across the globe, the word went abroad instead that the whole project had been canceled. After an estimated $500,000 investment, *CID* seemed better off dead. "We decided to kill it before it was viable outside the womb," was Dyson's assessment hours after the news broke.

In the postmortem period, Dyson acknowledged that she had not been the right person for the hands-on management of the project—but neither was she meant to be. "There were probably only four people in the country capable of running the thing day to day," she told *Computer Currents*. As executive editor, she said, "I was hired to find that person and couldn't. What was needed was somebody who could run a daily newspaper, who understood technology broadly and could ask the right questions, as well as be at the desk five days a week and get the thing out," she explained. Admittedly, it was a hard bill to fill.

The final decision to abandon *CID* was made jointly by Dyson and Ziff-Davis's management. "I didn't come to them and say 'We want to close it down,' but it was not forced on me, or anything like that," Dyson says. "But I don't think I could have pushed them to keep it open, either. The point is, I see myself in this decision as part of management—not someone who had a shotgun put to her head and was told, 'Go close it down.' "

On a personal level, "Of course I felt sad," she acknowledges. "It was an emotionally wrenching thing. On the other hand, in some sense, it was a relief. I had known for several weeks it wasn't going to work, so it was a relief it was over."

Miscalculations in business may frequently be costly, but at least they usually occur in relative privacy. Esther Dyson, however, was denied the luxury of a low-profile mistake this time. For her first major setback, she had taken a spectacular fall on center stage during a performance viewed by the entire computer and publishing industries. It's not as if Dyson had never made any mistakes; it's just that before, she had had a smaller audience. She recalls a time at Oppenheimer, when she recommended Apple stock on a Monday, only to change her mind on Wednesday.

"I'm sure the salesmen were wondering, 'What's this dumb broad doing?' " she says, "but telling you about it now [which she did in 1984 in a crowded Park Avenue elevator], I'm not embarrassed at all. I felt the stock would be uncertain for quite a while longer and I was very happy about changing my mind, because once you make a choice, you have to stand behind it."

After her experience with *CID,* Dyson picked herself up and went on with the show, like the quick-witted and confident performer she is. She immediately resurrected *RELease 1.0* and, within two weeks, had put out an issue. Her laid-off *CID* staff was generously paid through December, thereby precluding overwhelming guilt feelings on management's part.

As fate would have it, Dyson still owned her newsletter and her PC Forum. "We never got around to signing anything," she explains. "It gave my accountant fits." That lapse in the particulars turned out to be the best part of the whole affair, because Dyson still had her most valuable possession—*RELease 1.0.*

"I treasure it more," she says. "Things are better because I'm more committed and excited. In a sense, the first time I owned it, I didn't even realize what I had, and now that I've grabbed it back from almost being owned by somebody else, I value it more."

Naturally, the Ziff-Davis fiasco caused *RELease 1.0* to lose some momentum, and quite a few subscribers. At the beginning of 1987, Dyson was still building her subscriber list back up to its previous level.

Philosophically the newsletter also changed somewhat. "It's become more intellectual, more interested in the products themselves and less interested in the business," Dyson says. "I've gotten older and wiser, so the content I think is better, and that's what some people I respect have told me.

"Other people have canceled because it no longer covers some of the more dealer-oriented things it used to or the Wall Street stuff," she adds. "But the people I respect still read it."

Ann Winblad: Money, Fame, and a New Start

Just as she was the first of these women to start her own company, Ann Winblad was the first to leave it. And she got out when the going was good. Back in September 1983, before the industry even dreamed of a slump, she and her three partners sold Open Systems to Uccel Corp. of Dallas for $15.5 million, giving them each $3.8 million in cash.

What was true of Ann Winblad as a child has certainly proved true in adulthood: She knows how to make money.

Only Winblad and cofounder Tim Dickerson stayed on at Open after the sale, he for six months and she for a year. Then late in 1984 she sold her house in Minneapolis, took her millions, and moved to San Francisco to be a consultant in the personal computer industry. She wanted to give back to the industry what she had learned from it as the head of a successful software company. By 1985 there were plenty of companies in Silicon Valley that could use her help, and Winblad had eight years of experience to draw on.

As the head of her own company, Winblad had good instincts to begin with. In the early days of the micro industry, there were no standards, many operating systems, and much confusion. Open Systems made a strategically wise move by continually adapting its entire line of accounting software packages to more and more operating systems and hardware architectures.

Open Systems software was designed to run on 8-bit, 16-bit, and 32-bit microcomputers based on a variety of microprocessor chips. Besides the IBM and compatibles, Open Systems software ran on every popular microcomputer around—more than 50 in all at one time—under many operating systems.

It would take the 1981 entrance of IBM, along with its legitimization of Microsoft Corp.'s MS-DOS operating system, to stabilize and narrow the focus of the industry as a whole. Because IBM created a de facto industry standard in the single-user-oriented MS-DOS, Open Systems found itself technologically way ahead of the game.

"I thought we were just doing a damn good job," says Open Systems cofounder Dan Webb. "I didn't realize we were doing the best job around." By 1981, Open had already been writing multiuser software for five years, so that its software was actually overdesigned for single-user operating systems. That's not to say it wasn't useful for single users. On the contrary, it was elegant, sophisticated, and powerful—and waiting for the future to happen.

By the mid-eighties the future finally caught up. Businesses increasingly wanted several people to be able to access one computer at the same time via separate terminals, so that one person could do word processing, for example, while another did accounting. This was a most efficient use of expensive computing resources.

While most vendors' existing application software was written to recognize only one user at a time, Open Systems's software, when used with a multiuser operating system, worked perfectly without modifications. "For the last three years we've been sitting on all the work we've done," Winblad said in 1984.

Profitable from its second year onward, Open Systems maintained its low Minnesota profile while climbing steadily up to the number three position among micro accounting software publishers, behind BPI, Inc., and Peachtree Software. Even then, BPI's software was less sophisticated and less expensive than Open's, and therefore not direct competition.

Successful as it was, even Open Systems thought it could have done some things better. "I was like any other small-business manager," Winblad recalls. "If maybe early on we'd removed ourselves more from the concerns of the day-to-day running of the business and (the key word is) *entrusted* that to other people, we could have leveraged our intelligence into better strategic decisions.

"I think we were very capable of running a much larger business and probably even a much more diversified business," Winblad says. "We didn't know that and we didn't really trust that, and we didn't have enough time to do that. I think we could have done bigger and better things," she says. "The more I'm out as a consultant and working with other companies, the more respect I have for my partners' capabilities and my own. I believe that really strongly."

The problem boiled down to insecurity, she feels. "It wasn't that we didn't trust other people in handling parts of the business . . . we didn't trust ourselves that we really understood thoroughly and could control the business in a changing, dynamic environment—but we really did."

Youth is no excuse, either, Winblad feels. "Everybody in this whole industry was so young," she says. "Some people were braver than others. But some people were more foolish than others, so I think we were very conservative: not very foolish, but not tremendously brave."

Nevertheless, the company did grow, and the founders had to adjust their functions accordingly. Instead of strictly technical work, as in the earliest days, the quartet had to make sure the machine they had built ran smoothly. Dan Webb, as chairman and president of the company, acted as "a moderator among the managers," he says. "I tried to keep people moving together in the same direction."

Tim Dickinson was the resident technical wizard and ran the company day to day. "He was the guy who watched the factory, so to speak," Winblad says. "He hated crowds but he really liked the business systems approach. So he'd look over the procedures and make sure everything was streamlined." Dickinson and Gary MacHalec switched off from time to time between handling the business legalities and overseeing production.

From 1978 on, Winblad acted as vice president of marketing, focusing on building the marketing, sales, and distribution capabilities of the company. "My job was to bring the company into focus as to where the markets were going, what we should be doing, what our key contacts should be," she explains.

Apparently she was the perfect person for the role. "People always liked Ann," Webb says. "People always saw her as the personality of the organization. She was the person who was out there doing the sales, doing the public speaking, being the public person.

"The fact that she's a woman—she really uses that to a tremendous advantage," Webb says, "because people expect her to be this little meek Goldilocks person. Her physical appearance is disarming, but she's a very intimidating person in terms of her business acumen. She's not easily buffaloed. She knows how to play hardball."

Even though Winblad may feel that Open Systems could have grown even further as a company, its sales had doubled every year since 1979, until by 1983 the firm brought in $7 million. The company had its products in more than 300,000 installations, big and small, and reviews of its software were unvaryingly excellent.

In fact, the company had grown far beyond the founders' original expectations. They had thought it would remain small and intimate, with little bureaucratic red tape and with management mostly by consensus. But after seven years, they were facing 100 employees every morning and a future that offered even more growth.

"No one in their right mind would run a company by an executive committee of four," Webb says. "It worked great until we had about 30 employees, but by the time there were 40, there wasn't enough focus of authority and responsibility."

Cofounders Dickinson, Webb, and MacHalec all were becoming increasingly uncomfortable. "They said to me, 'Hey, this isn't fun for us anymore. Is it fun for you?' " Winblad recalls. "It was more fun than I'd ever had, but I was concerned about their feelings."

Modern life being what it is, in mid-1983 the four trooped off to a psychologist to help them decide their future. The facts were clear. Two of the partners had no further interest in building the company. Webb and MacHalec wanted to get out—and soon. The two were "100 percent programmers," Winblad explains, so the business end of things was never as interesting to them as the technical side.

Tim Dickinson, less anxious to leave, was stressed out after seven years without a single vacation. Of the four founders, only

Winblad was still totally and enthusiastically committed to Open Systems. She wanted to stay and make it grow. Besides her love for business, what gave Winblad the drive to continue when the rest were dropping off?

One characteristic was her ability to roll with the punches. "I give ulcers instead of getting them," she says. "I work hard enough and I get tired, but I process stress. It doesn't stay around inside me. You can't fault yourself for errors or wallow in your mistakes." She also believes in taking long vacations. Month-long vacations, in fact, usually at the North Carolina beach house that she bought "when I was poor."

Just as the four founders' talents were individual and complementary, their personal needs and desires were diverse. As the partners examined their different attitudes toward their company seven years later, it became clear that drastic action would be necessary. The solution reached was acceptable to all.

The four agreed to sell Open Systems to a larger company. That way, Winblad and Dickinson could stay on after the sale and the others could walk away with their nest eggs. And the always-crucial element of timing was perfect: The appeal of micro tech was at its height in the summer of 1983, when Open was seeking a buyer.

Open Systems had no trouble finding an enthusiastic buyer in Uccel Corp. (formerly Wyly Corp.), a $150 million mainframe software company. The $15.5 million deal was clinched in September 1983. As expected, Webb and MacHalec bailed out, Webb got married soon after, and both men took some time off to decompress before moving on to other activities.

The acquisition process Open Systems went through is one of Winblad's proudest achievements. "I was responsible for negotiating with the potential acquirers," she explains, "and the acquisition agreement was probably one of the best anyone could get: an all-cash deal, no strings attached, a well-defined noncompete clause. It was a good deal and I felt it was a well-negotiated contract."

Along with that stands the fact that Open survived the acquisition. "It was able to [make the] transition into its next stage—being run by other people," she says. As executive vice president of Uccel's new subsidiary, Winblad earned a $70,000 salary and worked on company strategy, spending two to three days a week on the road.

In March 1984 Dickinson abruptly left Open Systems and made a dramatic leap from high tech to low tech. He moved to a cabin in Wisconsin with his wife and now spends most of his time enjoying nature—chopping wood, snowshoeing, and watching his beaver pond. He's also formally studying biology at the University of Minnesota. "It's such a change," Winblad marvels. "He's really detoxing. He was totally stressed out."

Meanwhile, before Winblad herself could leave Open Systems, she had to find a vice president of marketing and a financial officer for the newly acquired company. She set her deadline for Labor Day 1984 and, in the interim, became something of an industry superstar.

No longer was she just the founder of a low-profile, privately held company in Minnesota. Overnight she had become a self-made, 33-year-old multimillionaire, who happened also to be an attractive, single woman. What reporter could resist her story?

Not many, it seemed. In the months following the buyout, Winblad granted many interviews to the press—which found her much more interesting than the accounting software she had helped develop—and all the articles appeared in print at about the same time. In June 1984 she was written up in *InfoWorld* and *Fortune* magazines and graced the cover of *Money* magazine. August brought a two-page Q&A interview in *PC Week,* and in September there were short articles about her in *Cosmopolitan* and *Working Woman.* Not one magazine neglected to print her picture. She was also filmed for a PBS series called *Women in Management* that went on the air in March 1985.

"It was too much all at once," she says. Marriage proposals started pouring in, "interested" men sent her pictures of their kids, and strangers recognized her on airplanes. Some of the magazine articles contained enough information to track her down, and she had to get an unlisted telephone number.

In a media blitz even more intense than the one Portia Isaacson had engendered almost ten years earlier as the first woman to head NCC, Winblad had momentarily captured the national imagination, hungry with the yuppies' appetite for success stories. She had arrived.

Besides the loss of some privacy, the experience had other pitfalls. "I'm insulted when people are more interested in approaching me as this cute little blonde walking around with $3.8 million than as a person who worked hard and thinks hard," she told *The Minneapolis Star & Tribune* back home at the height of the attention.

It was in the midst of the ballyhoo that Winblad's Labor Day deadline arrived. She had set the date thinking, "By then, these new people better be here, they better be doing their jobs, and they better not need me." They were, they didn't, and she was free to leave.

"When I called Esther [Dyson] to tell her I was leaving the company, she said, 'Well, it's about time. You're like a divorced woman who just wouldn't get out of the house,' " Winblad recalls. "I said, 'Oh, thank you, Esther. That's a wonderful thing to say.' But it really was true. The psychological decision to sell your company means it's not your company anymore and you really should be moving it toward someone else."

Although one suspects there's a bit of longing when she speaks of the company she and her partners created out of thin air, Winblad claims she doesn't miss it. "Not unless I talk to the people back there," she says. "I do miss the day-to-day interactions with a couple of key people that I hired and who hung around with me."

Other than that, Open Systems is in the past for Winblad, and she definitely lives in the present, with a sharp eye toward the future. Although she is a millionaire, she doesn't flaunt her wealth, and she lives much as she always has. Her one concession was to buy a used 1982 Mercedes 380 sports car to replace her 1980 Volkswagen Rabbit.

"The money did change one thing," she admits. "People had heard I was running a company, privately held, so how credible was I, they wondered. The acquisition was the largest that year of a micro company, so people had to think, 'That company must be pretty good. Ann must have something going for her.' Then they could see we weren't just running an accounting business—we were in the computer industry, just like everyone else."

If there had been any question about that, Winblad's move to San Francisco, just north of Silicon Valley, proved that she was seriously committed to the personal computer industry.

6
Family and Career: Necessary Trade-Offs

One of the most compelling conflicts for the successful woman is the tug-of-war between her professional life and her personal life. There is always a trade-off when a woman with a family enters the business world.

There are also, of course, single women with full careers who have postponed or forgone the chance to have a family. They too are faced with choices that will affect the rest of their lives.

The ten women in this book dealt with diverse personal issues and found equally diverse solutions to them. But they all agree that there are no easy answers when it comes to juggling two rich but incompatible experiences.

"I can't say enough about how tough it is to do both," says Janelle Bedke. "It's not easy to maintain a relationship and devote so much time and energy to a business." Few women—or men—would disagree.

Among these ten women, all concur with Bedke's assessment, whether they're married or single. Of the seven who have married, six have been divorced. Of the six who divorced, three are remarried, one has maintained a single long-term relationship without the legalities, and two are only recently divorced.

Although their current situations vary, there is one thing common to all those who married: motherhood. And that's often where life has gotten very complicated.

Janelle Bedke: Finding a Way to Do Both

Janelle Bedke, for one, learned a lot about herself after the birth of her son. Bedke arrived at her first job at Hewlett-Packard in 1969 very young, very attractive, and one of the few female engineers in the place. Almost inevitably, a romance sprang up, and it wasn't long before Bedke found herself married to an HP hardware engineer.

"I always assumed I'd be married, but not at the expense of my career," she says. When she had a baby boy at the age of 21, however, problems set in. "I didn't realize how demanding children are," she explains. "I was very intense about it. I wanted everything to be perfect, and it isn't with kids."

Although she had always wanted children, once she actually had one she realized she would never be the Earth Mother her own mother had been. "It was not until about three months after I had Jeff that I began to realize that a career was very important to me and that I was going to have to find a way to do both," Bedke recalls. "That's when I made the decision to return to HP and begin to work on a part-time basis. I felt it was right for me to try to balance it—to work part-time and be at home part-time. Then, over time, I found I was spending more time at work and less time at home."

After a year of working part-time, Bedke made it full-time and found someone to take care of her son during the day. When her son was two, Bedke and her husband divorced and the child went to live with his father, who later remarried.

"[My husband] and I weren't looking for the same things in life," Bedke says. She discovered that he was more interested in "living within the rules and doing things according to the way things should be done, as opposed to wanting to kind of test the edges and take greater risks. I think a lot of him, and the divorce was amicable, but he just wasn't the right person for me."

Meanwhile, Bedke had become close to her immediate boss at HP, Ken Fox. After her divorce, Bedke and Fox decided to live together—and they've been together ever since. "It's really fascinating to see different personalities, what works and what doesn't work," she observes.

Although she and Fox obviously do "work," they have no immediate plans to make it legal, even though they are effectively married. "If we had a good reason to, we would," she says, "but we haven't found one yet. There are tax benefits to not being married and neither one of us is interested in having kids."

While Bedke may sound a bit hardheaded about her private life, in truth her decisions have not been without consequences. "In some ways I feel I failed as a mother," she admits. "I haven't overcome that yet, but I don't dwell on it." She takes comfort in the fact that her now-teenage son is "a very happy, well-adjusted child. If he weren't, I'd act on it and try to fix it."

As for her relationship with Fox, who left HP soon after Bedke did, much of its success lies in the fact that the two are equally ambitious and hard-working. As vice president of R&D for another very successful Silicon Valley software firm for five years, Fox was as happy as Bedke to put in 11- or 12-hour days during the week. In 1986 he joined a start-up company as general manager.

Neither one of them quite leaves the job at the office; Bedke often spends more time on paperwork after she gets home. "I fall asleep reading it," she says. Saturdays and Sundays, however, are reserved for each other. "We don't work weekends," she explains. "We both feel strongly about that."

Although the bulk of her time is eaten up by her work, Bedke has no regrets about her priorities. "I've given a lot to my career and business life and not put as much energy into my personal life," she acknowledges, "but I can't complain, it was my choice."

Her personal goal now is "to strike a good balance between my business life and personal life and to be a happy person," she says. "That sounds trite but I'm very serious about it. It's increasingly challenging to figure out how to have fun."

One minor dilemma Bedke faces is that nearly all her friends are in the computer industry. "A diverse set would be nice," she admits, "but how do you go about meeting them? I've never been one to start up conversations. Most of my friendships are very close and I've had them a long time."

Lorraine Mecca: Marriage, Motherhood, and Micro D

After her seven-year marriage to a man who didn't want a family, Lorraine Mecca took decisive action. Determined to have children and also wanting a nice little business, she married Geza Csige, got pregnant, and started Micro D to help her husband's computer-store business.

Because she had had to wait so long for what she really wanted in life, the unleashed Mecca plunged into everything at once, in a veritable frenzy of delight. She was six months into a difficult pregnancy when she started Micro D, never dreaming that it would take off like a shot.

By the time she realized that the business was a runaway success, Mecca was only a few weeks away from having her baby. Although the timing of the birth of Micro D contributed hugely to its success, the resulting workload put Mecca in a very tight spot. To have her baby, she spent only 12 hours in the hospital and was back at work (in an office at home) the next day.

That's when the inner conflict began. With her mother helping with the baby and Mecca forced to keep working, she felt cheated out of the luxury of being a full-time mother. Then her mother-in-law arrived from Hungary for four months, and Mecca could return to the office full-time. "Our offices were five minutes away, so as soon as the baby cried, I got in the car, drove home, and nursed her," Mecca explains. It was convenient but wrenching.

By the time her mother-in-law went back to Hungary, Mecca's husband had joined Micro D full-time, and he was happy to let Mecca stay home with their baby. But Mecca was in for a big surprise.

"I was torn [between the business and motherhood] until I had the opportunity to spend all day at home," she admits. "When my mother-in-law left I said, 'Okay, I wanted this baby, I'm gonna be a mom.' And I hated it. I couldn't stand it. It didn't mean I hated my daughter, but I hated being a full-time mom and housekeeper.

"I thought I would love it. That had been a goal for so long: to have a baby and be a mom. I'm one of eight kids, I had a supermom as a mom, and then when it was my turn to do it . . . I didn't like it," she says sheepishly.

"It takes a much more patient person to enjoy motherhood," Mecca feels. "The gains are so slow. You have them every day, but compared to the pace of business—I just don't have the patience." Once the reality of the situation set in, Mecca hired a Monday-through-Friday live-in housekeeper and went back to work full-time with Geza.

That turn of events made Micro D even more formidable than it already was. "Normally you have one individual working 18 hours a day," Mecca notes. "When two people are doing it, you double the impact."

Geza took over as the company's strategist while Mecca handled all the details of the business—and of his life. As she told *Fortune* magazine in June 1984, "I don't pay him; I give him an allowance. He doesn't need any money. He needs me and I keep him happy."

In her relationship with Geza, it is Mecca who is the gifted strategist. She has made herself indispensible to him, which is not surprising in light of the fact that she started Micro D to help boost his business.

"I'm still making life easy for him," Mecca said in late 1984. "I keep his gas tank full. He doesn't carry a wallet. I give him cash in $20 increments. I buy all his clothes; he never goes with me to buy them. I take care of him. My husband is brilliant. He can do tremendous things if I remove the obstacles."

The fact that all their Micro D stock was in Mecca's name never fazed Geza. "He's totally trusting," Mecca explains. "To have someone trust you that much is an incredible responsibility. You don't violate that kind of trust."

Although Geza obviously depends on Mecca for a lot, it's not at all one-sided. "I need him, too—desperately," she says. In a sense, at Micro D she felt she owed it to him to smooth the way, because he could have been using his talents in so many other ways. "He's capable of so much more than buying and selling," she said then. "I feel I'm really taking advantage of him."

But the advantages were, without a doubt, equally distributed. As Mecca herself put it in 1984, "My husband and I are a team, and the whole is greater than either part could be." Geza could essentially pick and choose his projects while Mecca ran the shop. "Geza feels most things don't deserve his attention," she acknowledged. "Most people don't have the luxury of saying, 'Let Mecca handle it.' "

Mecca certainly handled her share of company responsibilities, besides the usual CEO duties. For example, Geza disdained public functions. "Normally I do it alone," she said, "but I feel uncomfortable. I usually don't stay long. I do go out with small groups, maybe consultants. But I don't drink, so there's a little bit of strangeness there."

Geza's aversion to social events is an outgrowth of his emphatically casual style. "He won't wear a tie," Mecca explains. "He has ties and suits but he won't wear them. Geza would like to wear cotton cloth string pants and plaid flannel shirts and T-shirts to work every day. In [a formal color portrait in] the 1984 Annual Report, he's wearing cotton pants under that jacket," she laughs.

Some wives and business partners might have been dismayed by such stubbornness, but Mecca had more than enough polish to make up for Geza's rough edges. "One of the most fun things is that difference between my husband and myself," she laughs. "I love to dress up, so I'm the person who goes out and meets people. When it gets serious and they already have a good feel for the company, then we let them see Geza."

Whatever their differences, Csige and Mecca are a good team. "You always know what your own shortcomings are, that's really easy," Csige says, "and if you can just explain and verbalize that, then the other person has a real good chance of helping you and picking up the slack in those areas and supporting you.

"I have a much more 'go-get-'em, kill' attitude," he explains. "I feel my contribution to her was that I got her in a real brave attitude mode, where she really could go out and do things, and I think that gave her a lot of confidence; then she just took over.

"We were very supportive of each other in that she gave me the time to do what I was good at doing—specifically, what I enjoy doing," he adds, "and she was able to do what she enjoyed doing. I don't know whether it was by luck, or coincidence, or how, but that's how it worked out."

What does Mecca consider to be her greatest accomplishment in business? Not, as you might expect, making millions of dollars and being one of the few women to bring a company public. "Working with my husband and being married successfully" is her answer. "Not many people work with their husbands 24 hours a day."

What about the built-in tensions of total togetherness? "The problems are really much smaller than the rewards," she says. "The rewards are great. It's definitely made our relationship grow, and each of us has grown so much. I used to think all he was was a 'techie.' I realize now there's much, much more to him. More than anything else, I respect his business acumen and sense of market trends and gut feel of things."

But, even with this compelling dimension between them, family is more important to Mecca than anything else. She has said she would have given up Micro D in a minute if Geza had felt it was time to move the family to Hawaii or New Zealand—one of their goals. "Absolutely," she says. "I'm very much traditional in upbringing. My husband rules my home and women are supportive people. In the office," she smiles, "it's the opposite."

Her husband has given her her greatest strength. "I think of marriage as a kite scenario. Without a string, the kite doesn't fly. With a string, it can go almost anywhere. I've tried things I wouldn't have dared try—just knowing I've got someone on the other end of that string," she reveals.

It's not surprising, then, that her overall life goal is "to be the best wife and mother possible." She's not through with business, but her professional goals are separate and "very different" from her personal goals, she says.

In trying to be the best mother possible, however, Mecca has had serious attacks of conscience stemming from her dedication to Micro D. When both her children were still preschoolers, Mecca started taking Mondays and Wednesdays off, to ease herself out of the business gradually.

But she finds business "exciting, fun, and addictive," she says, and the arrangement lasted only about a month. Her kids pulled hard in the other direction, though. "Don't go," they'd tell her. "We want you here five days in a row, Mom. Why do you work? Dad makes money." Such logic was hard to resist, but Micro D won out as long as she was running it, in spite of her admission that "it breaks my heart when they say those things."

After she and Geza left Micro D in July 1985, they took some time off to consider what to do next. The children were overjoyed. "They're great," Mecca said, "except they're getting so possessive. Where they used to understand absolutely that I left for most of the day, now they want to go with me to take a shower.

"It's a little nerve-wracking, but I still have full-time help, so it's not impossible," she said. "They're definitely the best investment I ever made, and I can't believe they're really mine, but I still can't take a 24-hour conversation with a four-year-old."

After working hard to make her fortune, Mecca is now turning toward the humanistic elements in life. "My goals now are to develop personal relationships," she says. "I was looking through the people I dealt with, not at them. I know them in terms of how much money they made me.

"But relationships between people are the only important thing in life, and that's the goal for me now," she says. "Not many people really know me. I haven't allowed it to happen. I know many people, but they don't have any idea what I'd do in a given situation.

"I don't want to be totally predictable, but there are very few people, I feel, who when something wonderful happens to me, would understand the impact," she admits. "And there are very few people whose grief touches me. With very few exceptions, my friends are at a distance."

Now that Mecca's priorities are changing a bit, she's got a little patching up to do. Nevertheless, whatever the cost has been in personal terms, Mecca says the business has "absolutely been worth it. I'd do it again in an instant."

Lore Harp: Mutual Independence

For Lore Harp, going into business was a natural solution to her ennui. She had never quite fit in with her suburban housewife neighbors and was extraordinarily bored just staying home, even though, as she says, "I love my kids dearly."

When a *Harvard Business Review* interviewer asked her in 1982, "It didn't occur to you that you were an oddball, that something might be wrong with you?" Harp was quick with her response. "If you don't love scrubbing plates and making little knickknacks out of dough for the kids' Christmas trees?" she asked. "Not at all. It never crossed my mind."

Like Mecca, she needed a greater intellectual challenge than motherhood alone. Also pushing Harp out of the house was her admittedly unhappy marriage to Bob Harp, who later joined her at Vector Graphic but left the company after they divorced. "I was always very independent," Lore Harp says, "and that, I think, was one of the pitfalls of the marriage—that I was not the wife that totally depended on the husband for emotional, psychological, financial, and all the other needs. I was never Mrs. Robert So-and-So."

A lot has been written about how Vector Graphic fell apart in tandem with the Harps' marriage, but Lore Harp has never acknowledged a shred of truth in that theory. She will laughingly admit that the company may have earned its nickname as the industry's Peyton Place, however. Both she and cofounder Carole Ely shed their first husbands and remarried while running the firm.

The Harps divorced shortly after Vector went public in late 1981. By the following March, Bob Harp had left Vector "for personal reasons" and started a competing company. In July 1982 Lore Harp married one of the richest men in America, computer publishing tycoon Patrick J. McGovern, in a ceremony held in Switzerland.

For a woman who has declared, "I don't like to be dependent on anybody," it was an excellent choice. McGovern spends an enormous amount of time traveling all over the world to keep his far-flung publishing empire in order.

"It's not the kind of marriage where your husband comes home and fixes the kitchen sink if there's something wrong with it," Harp says. "I would never expect that of Pat or I would never expect him to mow the lawn. He's just not that kind of person, which is all part of your traditional marriage concept. I think we probably have a very contemporary marriage."

Because of their extensive travel schedules, Harp (who kept that name for her children's sakes) and McGovern are often apart. "Sometimes I don't see him for two weeks, but then we see each other for a week at a stretch," Harp says. "We have a calendar and we sit down and plot out where we're going to be and the time we're going to have together.

"We're not your normal 9-to-5 couple, but we talk to each other every day, regardless of where we are," she explains. Their mutual independence creates an essential understanding between them.

"That's the only reason Pat could even have thought of ever getting married again," Harp explains, "because he had to be married to somebody who was not going to always be needing him there, even though at times I do get a little impatient." And, even though she says they have a "super" relationship, she sometimes wonders whether she and her husband are quite married enough. "Well, the thing is, so many things go through your mind," she admits. "You think, well, should you really be home and spend more time together or have this open, meet-in-different-places type of relationship?"

But, without a doubt, such an open marriage has strong benefits for partners who are similarly entrepreneurial. Harp has plenty of time to devote to her own business ventures, and she has the full support of her husband. "We have a great deal of respect for each other and we're really committed to the relationship," she says.

Harp, who has moved over to a low-tech business enterprise, feels that her work is an integral part of her life. "Business and personal goals—I think they're one and the same," she says, "because business takes so much of your personal life that you really can't separate it out.

"If I had a different personal goal, I'd say, 'Well, I'll retire and stay home, or live on a boat, or go meditate in Nepal' or something like this," she says. "I've no intention of doing that, so I think my business and personal goals are very interrelated. I look at business with a great degree of emotional and other satisfaction and fun. I don't look at it as drudgery."

Portia Isaacson: "A Little of Something That's a Lot"

Portia Isaacson seems to have been reincarnated several times over without ever having to die. She's had five marriages and five divorces. She's had several careers in academia and in business. For years, she admits, ambition blinded her to everything but her work, and consequently she lost everything but her work. Besides that, she usually married for all the wrong reasons.

Isaacson's first two marriages—both of which she rushed into very young—produced three sons but were otherwise regrettable, she feels. Her emotional neediness pushed her headlong into both of them. Neither was based on common goals or understanding and both were short-lived.

Her third husband, Jimmy Isaacson, was the first one that really "counted," in her view. "The men that I've had very successful relationships with—even if they do sometimes change—I've become involved with, always, through my profession," Isaacson explains. "And, in fact, that part of the relationship remained a very important part of it throughout."

She and Jimmy had "a wonderful eight years together," Portia Isaacson says. "I have nothing negative to say about it before, during, or after it." The only bad thing about that marriage, in fact, was that it ended—largely because of her overwhelming ambition.

That personal failure was undoubtedly the central tragedy of Portia Isaacson's life. Because she was totally unprepared for the divorce, she quickly leaped into another ill-fated marriage. David Wilson was Isaacson's best friend, but he took a serious chance when he became her fourth husband. It wasn't long before that marriage, based largely on Isaacson's raw emotional need, went the way of her first three. Fortunately, she and Wilson remained steadfast friends, and he is still extremely close to her and her children.

Isaacson may have been needy from the start, but what is it about her that has attracted so many husbands? She has her own theory. "I am as driven to have a close personal relationship as I am, I think, anything else," she explains. "So if I don't have one, I'm actively looking. I don't know that that's all positive, by the way. It probably stems from insecurity of some type—of just wanting to have that relationship."

Still, many people who are "actively looking" fail to find that close relationship even once, let alone five times. "Maybe I'm more devious than most," she laughs. "I really don't know. Maybe I'm lucky."

In her fifth marriage, to Egil Juliussen, Isaacson put into practice her costliest lesson. "My marriage is the single most important thing to me, period," she said of it. It was the first time in her life that people had taken precedence over her career, and perhaps only because she had achieved much of what she had set out to do.

While the two were married and were running Future Computing, they were a perfect blend of guts (Isaacson) and follow-through (Juliussen). "Egil is really Future Computing's strength," she said then. "My Ph.D. is in computer science and I thoroughly understand the technology and I also know the retail channels extremely well.

"But Egil's background includes eight years at TI, where he was their top computer strategic planner and did market forecasting at the corporate level. His expertise is what Future Computing does: make market forecasts, talk about how markets grow, analyze company strategies," she says. "He brought to our company the quality and leadership to produce the kind of data we produce."

It was when Isaacson's attention turned away from the personal computer industry—after ten years—that her relationship with Juliussen crumbled. "Our relationship was primarily work-related," Isaacson explains, "and as I decided to leave the computer industry, basically, and have new interests and so on, we just really didn't have much to share any longer."

After six years of marriage, they separated early in 1986 and were divorced by the end of the year. They had "the world's friendliest divorce," she says, and they're still partners in three new companies, although her involvement is minimal.

Just as she has weathered numerous crises in her search for her own personal happiness, Isaacson has faced many challenges as a mother. She has sacrificed, certainly, but her sacrifices were somewhat double-edged. "I did not really get to enjoy my children when they were young," she says. "Things were really bad, we didn't eat very well, so enjoying my kids was almost impossible."

But even when the financial worries abated, Isaacson was too busy with her career to be as close to them as she might have been. "I knew I was sacrificing them to my own ambitions," she admits. "It wasn't like I didn't know it. I consciously decided to. And my rationale all those years—and I still think it's a valid one—was that unless I am what I can be, I have nothing to give them.

"If I give them a little of something that's a lot, through achieving and going with what I feel I have to do," she feels, "that is better than giving them a lot of something that is unhappy, dissatisfied, didn't go for it, and so on." That doesn't mean she felt good about it while it was happening. "For years I felt guilty because of all this, as all women do, but I learned to deal with that. I don't feel guilty now."

Isaacson doesn't have to feel guilty, because her three sons, now in their twenties, have turned out beautifully. "I keep my fingers crossed," she says. "I think, 'My God, I must have been really lucky.' "

Their teenage years were trying, as teenage years frequently are, but with the added pressure of a local epidemic of youthful nihilism. In her sons' early teen years, the family lived in Plano, Texas, which made headlines with 18 teenage suicides in six months.

"It has to do with the mobility of the family," Isaacson feels. "Plano is one of those awful communities you've heard about: It's a new community, everybody's new, they don't have friends, they've been in school together only six months, and the peer pressure is extraordinarily high.

"My kids all succumbed to that in one way or another," she says. "It had very different manifestations in all three." Isaacson acted quickly to head off potential disaster. "When I saw them start having troubles, I didn't screw around with them. I'm very action-oriented.

"When it looked like they were going to go off the deep end into drugs or drop out of school or whatever, I'd start working with them on, 'Let's do something really different.' Uniformly they'd come up with the idea that they had to change their peer environment totally. I just worked on it aggressively to put some excitement in their lives. Thank goodness I could afford it." Two sons ended up in private schools in the United States and the third in a boarding school in Europe.

"I had to borrow the money for tuition," she says, "but I believed in it so strongly and it turned out I was so right. It's been slow, but now all three are virtually model young men. They're just fabulous. Not perfect, but close. I take them out to dinner and I'm just proud as punch.

"They've had an interesting life of their own following me around," she says, "and they've come out very comfortable with change and risk, and they're wanting a little adventure in their lives."

Her oldest son, in particular, is following his mother's example. "Allen is just a little capitalist," she says. "I really like him. He's economically motivated. He lives and breathes computers. It's all he does, it's his whole life." In fact, after Allen Isaacson got his degree in computer science, he took a job in one of Portia's new companies.

Ironically, her only regret is that her kids don't remember their early years of poverty, from which she protected them so well. "In later life, I came to understand that it would have been very good for them to have been consciously through it with me," she says. "But you don't think that way in the beginning."

Instead they recall a seemingly endless supply of money. "I manage them like a business and I have for several years," Isaacson reveals. "I'm their authority figure, and that's derived from the fact that I'm the source of all funding. They have a weekly allowance, I pay all their bills, and if they do well in school, they get lavish vacations."

Isaacson is committed to paying for their educations, but after that, they're on their own. "It can be the ultimate, it can include grad school and it can be with style," she says. "In fact, they'll have trouble getting a job that pays them as well as I fund them, but they have to perform, I have to approve the curriculum, and when the education's done, that's basically it." Except for a generous trust fund—tappable only when they reach 40. "I don't want to take away their motivation," she laughs.

Besides affording such freedom of choice, Isaacson's monetary success has given her a satisfaction that goes deeper than her wallet. Because the world of computers and high tech is so far removed from her humble beginnings, none of her many accomplishments mean a thing to the people of Stratford, Oklahoma, or even to her own parents. They simply don't understand what she has done.

"What does a Ph.D. mean to them?" she asks. "Even if I went back and took them by the shoulders and read my resume to them, so what?" For years, that was a source of frustration to Isaacson, who still harbored resentment toward the town that had never seemed to appreciate her.

"I had gotten to a place where I was fine, but when I would go back there, all those old feelings came overwhelmingly back over me," she says. "I would emotionally go back in time. I would get the anger back, I'd shrink if I saw somebody I didn't want to see.

"I never knew quite how to prove that I was successful," she says. "Somehow I had this desire for them to say, 'Yup, she made it, in spite of all that, she made it. Yeah, we were wrong.' " Still, they could see no reason to say that.

After the sale of Future Computing to McGraw-Hill, however, the glowing publicity did the trick. "I've found that money talks," she says. "Now there is a tangible that they understand, so it's like closure for me now. It's really a very good feeling because it makes all of any negative feelings [toward the town] totally disappear."

Jacqueline Morby: Remarkable Stability

In sharp contrast to the hardship and personal turmoil of Portia Isaacson's life is the enviable stability of Jacqueline Morby's experience. She has been married to Jeffrey Morby for more than 25 years, and they're still happy.

"It's amazing," she marvels. "We've been married since we got out of college, but we don't feel like we've been married that long." What's their secret? "It's no secret," she says. "It's luck and everything else. But the basic reason is we have a lot in common. For example, we both love sports, travel, reading, movies, and the theatre."

Others wonder how Morby executes her balancing act between job and family so gracefully. "Our people spend 60 percent of their time on the road," TA Managing Partner Kevin Landry told *Venture* magazine in July 1986. "I don't know how Jacqui does it. It's tough on all of us who are married."

But to her it's not an issue. When asked whether the constant travel bothers her, she quickly replies, "Oh no, it's fun. If I stick around too long, I feel like I'm not getting anything done."

Still, success comes at a price, and—as with all these women—time has been her major sacrifice. "I don't have time to do the things I love to do," she acknowledges. "I love to cook and entertain. It's hard to plan ahead to do it with my schedule."

When she is home, she's with her family. "On weekends, we spend time with the kids, go to movies, and just be together," she says. "We see less of our friends than we used to."

Unlike some whose very identities are wrapped up in their careers, Morby doesn't rely so much on TA Associates for her sense of self. That may be partly because she spent several years quite contentedly as a homemaker before entering the business world.

"I have quite a full life," she notes. "My two children are very important to me, and they're very active. My husband has a very complicated career, and he's also very active. Plus we're very busy together." TA is extremely important to her, there's no doubt, but it isn't everything.

In fact, when she decided that venture capital would be the "something worthwhile" for which she was searching back in 1975, she had a rather amazed husband on her hands. Jeffrey Morby, a highly successful businessman—now vice-chairman of American Express Bank—was surprised to learn his wife would be joining him in the business world after years as a housewife. Surprised, but not displeased.

"He was absolutely elated and excited about my career," she recalls, "but he couldn't believe I was going into business. He thought, 'How boring.' But I chose a different avenue than he did and he's found it great fun. Through me he knows all the small companies."

Naturally, there were changes at home, but they didn't happen overnight. "All my traveling was a gradual transition," Jacqui notes. "At first, it was just a couple of days here and there. Because I was gone, he suddenly had to worry about the kids' homework, dinner; he had to pay attention to things.

Although her success in business has added a whole new dimension to her marriage, Jacqui says she and her husband aren't noticeably closer than they were before. "It's about the same," she says. "We're not further apart, either. We've always been very close, but probably [my success] was a surprise to him—and to me. Who knows what one can really do?"

Ann Piestrup: Fighting Traditional Expectations

Like Bedke and Mecca, Piestrup had fond images of being a kind of Earth Mother: staying home, baking bread, and keeping house. But her husband's heart attack during Ann's pregnancy changed all chances of that. With a baby on the way, Ann felt enormous pressure to become financially independent, and her ideas about education led her into the world of software.

With the thought that she might end up as her family's sole wage earner, it was almost inevitable that she would take the dramatic risks she did to start The Learning Company. "I sacrificed a calm peaceful life, but that's not what I really wanted," she says. "I probably wouldn't have stayed home and done that, anyway."

Mel Piestrup, who eventually recovered his health and later started his own company, was immeasurably helpful at home while Ann spent the necessary long hours building The Learning Company. In many ways, in fact, the company was a family affair. When Ann appeared on *The Phil Donahue Show* (for the second time) in the spring of 1984, her husband and daughter went with her.

Most of the audience at first argued mightily against the idea of children playing with computers at home. "I want my daughter to sit at the kitchen table and play with crayons like she always has," Piestrup recalls someone in the audience saying.

When Donahue interjected, "Let's hear from Sarah Piestrup," up popped the then-six-year-old Sarah in blue jumper, red blouse, and white tights, Piestrup recalls. "She looked darling, and everyone just went, 'Oooh.' I turned from the evil computer-wizard lady into a mommy who was genuinely concerned about her child, and how her child would meet the future."

Sarah, in fact, has been testing TLC software since she was two. Her mother's sincere efforts to please her own daughter eventually backfired, however—for a while, anyway. "I wanted my daughter to have surprises, to discover things experimentally," Piestrup has said. "I wanted her computer experience to resemble sandbox play."

At times, however, Sarah's computer experience more closely resembled staying after school. For example, Piestrup recalls, "I was in *Fortune* magazine with her and the photo shoot was about five hours, so she never wanted to touch Bumble Games [software] again. On *The Phil Donahue Show,* she did Juggles' Rainbow and Juggles' House and it became kind of a 'thing' and she decided she didn't like computers.

"It was just kind of overdone," Piestrup admits, "because I tested so many things with her." Another problem arose when Piestrup became an official IBM Personal Computer tester at home. "I had to be sure a certain number of children played with the computer every day, so I had a little schedule and I had all these children coming to use the IBM.

"And they were coming, not to see my daughter, but to see me and the IBM," she says. "So it got to be kind of a sore point, that they weren't coming over to play with her, but to see her mother."

At school, when Sarah freely announced that she didn't like computers, the irony was lost on no one. "It was like a joke in the school—'Ann Piestrup's daughter doesn't like computers'—and I think she got some attention for hating them," Ann says. Sarah has since changed her mind and renewed her interest in computing.

Besides the resentment from her daughter, Piestrup sensed a growing resistance in her husband. Even though they had both earned Ph.D.'s, Ann suspects that her husband on one level expected her to be a traditional wife.

"We were raised in the fifties," she explains. His outward support—and it was outstanding—apparently masked his inner expectations. "Underneath he resented how tired I was and the long hours I spent working," Ann says.

Money also became an issue between them. "We lived comfortably, but we never had that much money," she explains. Even though she was the founder and CEO of a successful software company, Ann Piestrup purposely gave herself a low salary compared with most heads of Silicon Valley companies.

"At one time I had maybe a million dollars' worth of stock, but it was never publicly traded," she explains, "and this is what happens. You have to dress and look a certain way, and yet the company's cash flow might not be so great, so you don't pay yourself particularly well.

"This is a tension on a lot of people, where it's expected that you're rich and you're really not," she says. "I had a nice salary, but it was not that great. I really went without for the first four years of the company, just to make it go." But continually sacrificing time and money to the company caused more and more problems at home.

By the end of 1984, Ann and Mel Piestrup had separated—largely, she feels, because of the pressures from The Learning Company. "It's part of what happens to people in Silicon Valley," she said shortly after the separation. "He attributes our difficulties a lot to the intensity of the entrepreneurial nature."

Being on her own after 12 years of marriage made her ouster from The Learning Company, only a few months later, that much more painful. "I thought, 'Oh my God, I've lost my husband and my company,' " she recalls. At the same time, Ann Piestrup managed to gain something from the experience. "I've worked out my own identity by separating," she said a few months after the split. "It's a difficult time for me, and yet I feel more contented than I have in my whole life."

Ann and Mel Piestrup divorced in 1986, and she went back to using her maiden name, Ann McCormick. "I feel a tremendous new beginning. I feel some sadness still about not being married," she acknowledged at the time, but at home she had discovered a new-found peace. "My child and I get along a lot better because there's no anger in the house."

On the professional front, she was freed from her deep sense of responsibility toward her company. "I had carried so much in my heart for The Learning Company—almost more than I could stand," she says. "I feel an emotional freedom not to have the burden of 30 people, payroll, venture capitalists, a marketing department, a sales department, and an R&D department."

After a normal period of mourning for her losses, Ann Piestrup continues her odyssey into the future of technology. She has made her mark and solidified her reputation; now she can pick and choose her own projects. After leaving TLC, she quickly got involved in other educational projects at the leading edge of technology. "It's very, very exciting and more creative," she says. "I'm much more in my element again."

Joyce Wrenn: Family Her Top Priority

For Joyce Wrenn, family has always been the top priority. Nevertheless she eventually found herself wielding plenty of clout for one of the most powerful companies in the world.

Like Mecca, Wrenn entered the business arena with the idea of helping her husband launch his own career. But unlike Mecca, Wrenn had to sacrifice her own advanced studies to do it. Did she resent the fact that she was the one to halt her education? "In some ways," she acknowledges, "but as it turned out, I was so challenged at work, and got into management, that I was able to establish a career for myself while he was in school. I'm not sure I would have had that ability otherwise.

"I was a very independent person," she notes, "but there were *so* many social pressures on women—to raise families right away and join the Junior League and do all kinds of other things. I did feel some resentment about having to cut back on my master's program."

By the time Wrenn had financed her husband's advanced degrees, she was one of the few women in management at IBM, and from there she moved steadily upward. "The jobs I had at IBM were always in an advanced area, so I really had a chance always to learn," she says, "and at the time we were really ahead of the universities.

"So, in that respect, the education I would have gotten in math would have looked good behind my name, but it would have been more academic than practical," she says. "I don't think it hurt me professionally. I can't say, 'I am Dr. Wrenn,' as my ex-husband can say, but I have had a *really* challenging and fun career, and maybe [my limited education] blocked a few opportunities, but so be it."

Wrenn delayed motherhood until age 31, by which time her career was in full blossom. That strategy—almost the norm in the 1980s—was still quite unusual in 1967.

"There's been an ongoing challenge all the time," she explains, "in that I chose to be a little different from the rest of the group. One has to achieve the right kind of balance, and I would listen to people—but I had to do what I wanted, even though people often asked, 'Why aren't you having kids?' or 'Why do you have this career?' I had to have enough conviction in what I was doing to be able to continue."

Thanks partly to her very supportive parents and husband, Wrenn persevered against the tide. She also kept her priorities straight. "When my daughter was quite young, I turned down some moves and promotions, and I'm not sorry," she says. "Life is a series of trade-offs, and I can honestly say I'm comfortable with the choices I made. I was always able to find challenging work that was fun, so it all balanced out."

Her move into microcomputers was, in fact, partly for personal reasons. Wrenn loved living in California and thoroughly enjoyed her job in the General Products Division, but at the same time she had become enamored of the personal computer and intrigued by the idea that IBM could produce one. Ironically, her decision to move to Boca Raton, Florida, was made easier by unfortunate circumstances.

"I was newly divorced [after 25 years of marriage] and, even though my ex-husband and I are very good friends and it was a friendly divorce, it's still a wrenching experience," she says. "I guess it's just typical that, where you had friends as a couple, you begin to form new friendships as a single person.

"Also, I had a daughter who had just started high school," she explains. "So I concluded that if I were going to move, that would be the time to do it, before she got further along in high school. And the job was *so* attractive. So for all those reasons, I decided to go."

Of course, the move itself was a wrenching experience for both Wrenn and her daughter, who essentially left their old lives behind. But, again, there were no regrets. Wrenn and her daughter moved to Boca in January 1982 and spent a rewarding 3½ years there, long enough for her daughter to finish high school and for Wrenn to see the Personal Computer through its overwhelming first phase of success.

During her first year in Boca, Wrenn met Gus Gregory, who owned a real estate business there. "I wasn't terribly anxious to remarry," she recalls, "but then I met Gus. We dated for a couple of years and got to know each other really well, and I thought, 'He is so super, and he's willing to put up with all the things I want to do.' "

They married in February 1985 and went on a month-long honeymoon to South America. "I almost never take that much time off," she explains, "but he wanted to as well, so we thought, 'Heck, why not?' "

Not long before Wrenn left on her honeymoon, she was solicited by Bank of America in San Francisco with what seemed like a very attractive job offer. Wanting to eventually return to California but not seeing the opportunity to do so through IBM, Wrenn decided to take the job.

Never mind that her new husband owned a business in Florida. "Gus is very supportive of what I'm doing," she said after a few months at Bank of America. "He told me, 'If it looks like a good opportunity for you, go for it.' He knew when he married me that I probably wouldn't spend the rest of my career in Boca." He was considering establishing part of his business in California, but Wrenn left BankAmerica before he had set anything up.

The career move was in sync with her personal life in at least one respect: "My daughter was graduating from high school that June," Wrenn says, "so it was a good break point for me, to consider a move to another location—as long as my husband was willing." Her daughter, Brie, chose a college in California, two hours' drive from San Francisco.

After only a year, however, financial troubles at BankAmerica sent Wrenn looking for another job. She found one in Dallas, midway between her husband in Florida and her daughter in California. Nevertheless she and her husband manage to spend most of every week together, and her daughter visits often.

Joyce Wrenn's daughter finds herself in a world very different from the one the young Joyce faced. Joyce had to pave her own independent way 20 years ago, but in the meantime the world has come around to her way of thinking. "Brie doesn't know exactly what she wants to do," Wrenn says, "but she assumes she will have a career."

Like Joyce, her daughter "is her own person and independent," Wrenn says. Unlike her mother, Brie Wrenn "has absolutely no interest in computers." An outstanding student, as her mother was, Brie also is in a position to draw on the wisdom of someone who has made the long journey. "I've tried to give her the benefit of what I've gained," Wrenn says.

Therese Myers: Lost Time

Terry Myers' stated personal goal in life is to "get married and have kids . . . quickly." Her total dedication to Quarterdeck Office Systems has paid off in business success, but robbed her of crucial years of personal time.

"You miss opportunities to meet somebody," she says, "but the choices that were there weren't more attractive than the work." Whoever the choices were, they would have had to be awfully patient to put up with the kind of schedule that Myers kept. "We were here every other night until 2:00 A.M. six days a week for ten months," she says. "No one who worked all those hours was married. We were all single. None of us could have had families then, in terms of hours. I had no personal life and would just see friends occasionally."

When Myers did manage to spend time with her friends, they were a very diverse group. Unlike many people in the insular computer industry, Myers can claim: "None of my friends are in this business. All my friends are my friends. It's more interesting that way."

Quarterdeck cofounder Gary Pope put off marriage also, until late 1986. "I think after you go through a struggle and end up where you at least have some security in the business end, then you can deal with the other," Myers says. "But I am concerned about it." Intensely private about her personal life, Myers will only acknowledge that she is "closer" to her goal than before.

Having paid such a potentially high price for success, does Myers regret it? "No," she says. "To feel comfortable as a person, the last two years have been very valuable."

Esther Dyson: Work and Play Intertwined

Esther Dyson counts among her friends almost no one totally outside the computer industry. One result of this is that there is sometimes a very fine line to tread in her dealings with people. "I like to flatter myself that I have a lot of genuine friends as well as sources," she says, "but I don't have illusions that everyone just loves me for my wit and charm."

Unlike Bedke, Mecca, and Piestrup, Dyson never had visions of baking cookies for a brood of kids; in fact, she feels that she got a good enough dose of it while she was growing up. "I had four younger half-sisters and a brother," she explains, "and, although my [step]mother would argue, I helped bring them up." Still single, she claims not to miss having a family of her own. "I don't have a great deal of interest in bringing up babies, since I've gone through that."

That doesn't mean she's sworn off domesticity altogether. "I do hope to get married at some point, and when I do, it will probably be to someone divorced with two teenagers," she predicts. One thing is certain: She's in no rush. "I may not be happily married and adjusted, but I'm very happy doing what I'm doing."

The bond between her personal and professional lives has extended even into her most intimate relationships. "I'm one of the few people to have my sex life in *Business Week,* along with

Pia Zadora," she says. *Business Week* disclosed to the reading public that Dyson had had an affair with Bill Ziff, cofounder of Ziff-Davis Publishing Co.

Dyson has no qualms about discussing it. "The fact of the matter is it was a fairly significant thing in my life," she says. "It was a very furious but rather brief [one-year] relationship—and had a lot less to do with all the business things than anybody will ever believe.

"I certainly joined Ziff-Davis because I was seeing Bill, and it seemed the simplest way to handle things," she acknowledges. "But, once I was there, I didn't talk to him about the business. He didn't want me to. And that was fine with me, but I'm sure that wasn't what people thought."

Twenty years her senior, powerful, witty, and intelligent, Ziff seemed a good match for the precocious Dyson. It was the first time she had felt so committed to anyone.

"I've been picky," she says. "I've never been close to getting married before, although I've had relationships with people who I think are totally wonderful and we've remained good friends, but there's been nobody I was remotely interested in spending the rest of my life with.

"I've always said I'd be happy to have a personal life if you could offer me one that was really exciting," she says. "Then along came one and I was really excited. My challenge was to have a personal life and a career at the same time, which I guess is the challenge that faces modern women."

In the end, it was a challenge that could not be met, she felt, without sacrificing her whole identity. Unfortunately, Ziff and Dyson were equally strong-willed people who couldn't bring themselves to change their lives completely for the other. Their relationship dissolved around the time of the demise of the *Computer Industry Daily.*

Nevertheless Dyson does not regret the experience. "Even though the relationship with him didn't work out, I think it made me a little more human," she says. "For example, he's a fairly big proponent of taking vacations and having a personal life, and he made me realize some of the value of that." Before Ziff, Dyson was notorious for going years without a vacation.

Still, she has always managed to slip some pleasures into the business. What she's doing has brought her closer to her immediate family. "I left home at 16, so I haven't seen much of my [half-] sisters for a long time," she explains. Her heavy travel schedule now allows her to meet up with them in any number of cities, and she sometimes invites a sister along to her industry events.

"I get treated very well," she says. "To share it with someone is a lot of fun. My sisters are not really interested in computers, and business is a foreign world to them. But they're smart, alert, interested people, and computers are part of modern life. I try to show them that businesspeople are not all ogres."

Ann Winblad: Indifferent to Marriage

"I'm indifferent to the idea of marriage," says Ann Winblad. "I'm always on airplanes and distracted. At some point in a relationship, either you commit or you don't." So far she hasn't, even though she started Open Systems with her then-boyfriend Dan Webb after they returned from a romantic motorcycle trip to Europe.

"It [turned into] a professional relationship," she says. "It was difficult to keep it a personal relationship, partly because I was more focused on the business than he was." Proof of that allegation lies in the fact that, since leaving Open Systems, Webb has willfully turned away from business, except tangentially, to focus more on his personal life. He has since married and had a son.

"I'm not worried about being single," Winblad says. "Maybe I'll feel it later. I don't have three kids at home, I've never been married, but these were conscious decisions.

"It takes a tremendous amount of time and effort to run your own business, especially in such a competitive industry," she explains. "In a personal relationship under those conditions, the other person has to be very understanding, because my attention span is limited and we both end up spending a lot of time alone."

Many women in their thirties suddenly start to hear the ticking of their biological clocks, but Winblad is not one of them. "I don't think about it," she says. "I'm not saying, 'Gosh, I'd better hurry up.' I may regret it when I'm 50 and say, 'Why didn't I get married and have three kids?' Anyway, it's not out of the picture."

She has a "very, very close relationship" with a highly successful contemporary in the business, but remains circumspect beyond that fact. "There are so many people watching what I'm doing, and there's only so much of me to go around," she says. "I don't want to give my personal stuff to reporters. Once you start, it's gone."

She will acknowledge that, although the relationship is "wonderful," both parties are somewhat puzzled by it. "We're both slightly confused about what it means," she says. And for her, there's just a hint of another uncertainty. "Maybe I don't know how to go from a relationship to settling down," she theorizes. "On the other hand, if I didn't work, maybe I'd create my environment—like creating a business."

In some ways, she feels, it's easier for a man to put business before a family. "In terms of myself," she says, "if I had a child, it would seem so coldhearted to give birth and then drop him somewhere. A woman has to figure out what to do with kids. It's her responsibility.

"There are cultural expectations of women," she adds. "No one asks how much time a man spends with his kids, but they always ask women. Responsibility keeps getting heaped on women. People keep telling you you should feel bad about your decisions, so they must be constantly reevaluated."

Despite her extraordinary success at a young age, her innate competitive drive and her millions of dollars, Winblad says her family is the most important thing to her. In a way it's a problematic attachment, because she has less and less in common with them.

"I have a hard time now sitting around and spending a lot of time with my sisters and parents," she says. "They're on one channel, they've got one program going, they don't skip around. I'm very happy to be with them, but you can't go back. In this industry, people are so wired, energetic, and willing to explore the different things they're thinking about."

As for her family's reaction to her success, Winblad explains that she gets no special treatment. "My parents are so proud of every one of us," she says. "If anyone asks my father about 'Ann's millions,' he'll say, 'All my children are worth millions to me.' "

Although she admits it "sounds so trite," Winblad joins many others in expressing her ultimate personal goal as, "I'd like to stay a happy person." Trite it may be, but not insincere. For the adventurous Ann Winblad, "the feeling of exploring" would satisfy her wish.

Epilogue: The Future

"I'm a ruined person. I'm not virginal anymore," says Ann Winblad, with far more pride than regret. Her assessment springs from the richness of her experience. "I've run my own company, created my own circumstances. I don't know if I can really work for anyone else again."

Such a reaction is almost inevitable after a person has completed such a long and exhausting journey as these women have. The feeling of being at a point of no return is far from unique and not altogether distressing. After a great success, one stands expectantly on the threshold of the future, even while recognizing that some options are no longer available.

Those Who Left

Ann Winblad's sudden release from the responsibilities of running a 125-person company was an unaccustomed delight after her long period of intense commitment. "I feel I'm the luckiest person in the world. I have the ability to focus now more than ever because I've eliminated so much distraction. I've freed up another 50 percent of my mind," she said shortly after leaving Open Systems. "It's the first time I've stood still in ten years to evaluate the capabilities I have and don't have."

With a $3.8 million nest egg from the sale of her company, Winblad could afford to take as long as necessary to assess her situation. The change in circumstance was so dramatic, however, that at first she found the limitless vista a bit dizzying. "I was really panicked for a while, about four months," she admits.

Even after she calmed down somewhat, she still felt nervous about her open-ended existence. "It's tempting to pick a large corporate structure and go in and make it work, but that'd be such a cop-out, like saying, 'I can't handle freedom,' " she said a few months after moving to California. "I have to stop myself from leaping in and doing something just for the sake of doing it.

"I don't want to screw up during this time. It's a weird time because I have no responsibilities. There are absolutely no rules right now." Ironically, Winblad felt that her independence carried its own obligations.

"It's a hard thing to use freedom to make a contribution," she found, "but I owe it to myself and to everyone I've worked with. I could have just disappeared and written a column for the Farmington [Minnesota] newspaper. But I want to open up my mind and I want to help the industry." True to her determination, Winblad used her latitude to study the rest of the industry closely and see where she might best make a contribution.

Her examination of the promising area of artificial intelligence (AI) turned up a disappointing lack of progress. "I was really prepared to dig in," she says, "but I was able to learn it all in two months. I'd like to get into AI, but there's nothing to get into yet. There's not a real market for it."

With nothing overwhelmingly compelling to claim her attention and energy, Winblad scaled back her work time from the 65 hours she had given to Open Systems every week to 40 hours of rather miscellaneous advising. She also enthusiastically took up some leisure pursuits, such as tennis, racketball, and horseback riding, as well as a little traveling.

By 1987 Winblad had carved out a new niche for herself as a "very, very busy consultant," working on four or five major strategic projects a year for companies in such areas as AI, financial services, and factory automation. "It's a very good experience for me," she says, "and the companies I've worked with have improved, so it gives me a strong sense of satisfaction."

For those who were intimately involved in the birth of the microcomputer industry, however, there sometimes comes a nagging suspicion that it was a once-in-a-lifetime thrill. "Maybe the best times are past, you always think," Winblad admits, "but then a year goes by and it's really exciting."

With plenty to look back on, Winblad looks ahead to even more. Ultimately she would love to run another company of her own. "But I don't believe you just say, 'Okay, I want to run a company now,' and all of a sudden one materializes, or you just create one to have a company," she says. "I think too many entrepreneurs do that. They think, 'Well, I did this once, I can do it again.' But timing is such a critical element and of course product as well."

When the right situation does come up, however, she plans to do things a little differently. "The actual day-to-day running of a business is not that hard to do, but you have to spend a given amount of time and energy on it," she explains. "I'd like to create a business situation—maybe I failed at it the last time around—where there's a healthier balance for myself between paying attention to day-to-day and strategic thinking."

One of the best things about her experience at Open Systems is a gratifying sense of fulfillment. "I've learned so much," Winblad says. "I don't have to prove myself to anyone. I'm very happy with myself. And I've gotten used to the fact that people have a lot of respect for my capabilities."

Such sentiments are shared by virtually all these entrepreneurial women. *Ann Piestrup,* now vice president and in-house visionary at start-up VPL (Visual Programming Languages) Research, Inc., in Redwood City, California, is similarly aware of the value of her efforts on behalf of The Learning Company.

"Because I went for it, I was always right at the edge of what I knew about," Piestrup explains. "If an Assembly language programmer wanted a $10,000 microprocessor-analyzer, how was I to judge? Or trying to determine the merits of an IBM contract—I could barely follow it, let alone evaluate it. I was up against that every single day for so long that I learned a tremendous amount.

"I've done 300 interviews, so I know how to handle myself because I've been prompted by Regis McKenna for years on end," she says, recalling the heyday of The Learning Company. "I'd have seven interviews a day, say, in New York with the editor-in-chief of *Time* magazine and someone from *The Wall Street Journal* and several others. The Regis people would advise me ahead of time what to emphasize. Then they'd be there to guide each interview, and they'd critique me for 20 minutes afterward, seven times in one day," she remembers. "It was very grueling because I was really trying to do well. So I had enormous training, way beyond what most people would get. And now if I go to CES [the annual Consumer Electronics Show]—boy, do I know how to handle myself!"

Not only does Piestrup have more ammunition personally, but her name alone carries a strong charge. "People idealize me even more than I deserve," she says. "Doors open for me that just wouldn't be open to other people; I walk right in and it's like people are presold. And here I am at a new little company that I really believe in, and I have the reputation of having done something exceedingly fine. It's just wonderful."

It was very hard for Piestrup to walk away from her first company. In the time between leaving The Learning Company and officially joining VPL, she went through a couple of "fallow" months when she admits she simply couldn't muster the energy or enthusiasm for much more than tending her home and garden.

But her reputation held her in better stead than she expected. "A lot of things I thought would be lost—like, 'Oh, my gosh, I've lost my company,' " she acknowledges. "But I'm finding that all kinds of people are calling and wanting to work here. There must be 20 people just waiting until we can hire them."

Although Piestrup faced some economic uncertainty immediately after her departure from The Learning Company, in 1986 she found a buyer for all her TLC stock. The sale brought in a tidy sum that eliminates yet another possible source of anxiety.

VPL Research, incorporated in 1985 by Jaron Lanier (who was 24 at the time), has produced a highly versatile programming language said to allow ordinary people to write their own software or alter existing programs. If VPL's product lives up to its developers' promises, it could open up a whole new world of experience to even the most phobic of computer novices.

The company is developing software for the whole spectrum of computers, from complex supercomputers to home personal computers—which is where Piestrup fits in. She is in charge of the consumer and education division and, as such, continues to fulfill her dream of "shaping the future of education through technology." Toward that end, VPL targets such imaginative goals as letting children use their entire bodies to interact with computers.

One project Piestrup has been thinking about for years, and is finally working to implement, is a "School of the Future." Although such a school could take a variety of forms, it would undoubtedly allow children to use computers and telecommunications freely. "It would be a beautiful environment where kids would learn to use the computer as a tool and have an enormously good time," Piestrup envisions.

"For example, they could bring in their science projects, and the Apple Macintosh computer would become a scientist's notebook. And along the way, they would learn to type and do word processing and do science drawings, and maybe create a tutorial to explain the science project."

There's no doubt that running a company is extraordinarily hard work. Freed from the administrative worries she faced as the head of her own company, Piestrup now can let her mind and vision soar where they may. "I'm much more in my element now than when everything turned into venture capital and marketing and dressing for board meetings and all that," she says. "I'm very happy."

Although Piestrup is committed to VPL, she admits she just doesn't feel the same about it as she did about The Learning Company. "It's very hard to do a second [company] with the same intensity," she says. "I just can't be up for it. I'm very interested in VPL and really like the people, but this isn't mine in the same way."

For that very reason, things are a lot easier on her. "I'm not going at this as hard as I did The Learning Company, but maybe more smartly," she says. "I don't work the hours I did at TLC but I know so much more that I can do things quicker. A few phone calls gets things done."

Piestrup also has more time for herself and her family. "I remember during one interview at The Learning Company, somebody asked me if there was anything I regretted, because I was having such a good time and it looked so completely enviable," she recalls. "I said I had gone that day to a ballet recital of my daughter's and I had thought, 'My daughter's been taking ballet lessons and I've never gone to one.' And what a delight it was to see my beautiful little daughter moving like that. But there wasn't enough time for things like that. And now there is."

For *Lorraine Mecca,* leaving Micro D brought on a long-term depression. Even though she and her husband had always planned to leave the company after five years, their departure left an unexpectedly huge gap in their lives. "I went through a pretty severe withdrawal," Mecca says. "I think Geza and I both did.

"Micro D was so much a part of who I was and what I was—and, although I'm the same person, having that mirror reflecting was hard to do without," she explains. Only after nearly a year and a half did Mecca feel healed, even though she still "definitely" missed running Micro D.

During that time, Mecca investigated several possible areas for future projects and indulged her love of writing by starting an autobiography, focusing on the history of Micro D. That effort remains on the back burner, however. "There was just no way I wanted to say some of the things that kept coming out on the typewriter," she laughs.

She may stick to the "safer" area of fiction in the end. "I also want to write a sexy computer novel," she declares. "It would be a lot of fun to do, even if I never showed it to anyone but my husband."

Discussions with various television people about her idea for a "Technology Minute" series, with Mecca as the announcer, convinced her that wasn't for her, either. "I was told if I wanted to do that, I had to commit myself to becoming a celebrity," Mecca says.

"I don't want to try to become a celebrity—no way," she says. "If I become a celebrity as a result of something I'm doing, that's fine, but I don't want what I'm doing to be just being a celebrity. I'm too old to become a beauty queen." Although some might argue with her on that point, Mecca says she has dropped the television idea completely.

More realistic, she feels, is the possibility of starting a business in the realm of care for the elderly at some undetermined point in the future. Mecca currently sits on the board of a new company, Alzheimer's Research, Inc., in South Carolina.

"I have an interest in it because I'm part of the baby boom generation," she says. "We're going to be the largest numbers of old people ever. I think one of the best opportunities in terms of business is things that relate to old people: making their lives longer or more productive or less uncomfortable. I think it's where the next 50 years of business opportunity exist."

Still, after Micro D, Mecca felt no compulsion to do anything in particular. "I'm not driven," she said. "There's nothing looming out there that I can't rest without doing. On the other hand, starting Micro D was an overpowering thing that I had to do."

So satisfied was she with her success at Micro D that she felt almost guilty at her good fortune. "Things have been so wonderful for so long, it's hard to believe," she said. "Even if something [bad] happens, it's okay, I'm ready for it. It's only fair."

But the worst that happened was the malaise Mecca felt at being cut free from her old moorings. And in spite of her discomfort, she had the rare opportunity to spend uninterrupted time with her family, alternating between homes in Dallas and Hawaii. "My kids get better every day, they're just so neat," she says.

After 16 months away from Micro D, after having sold all her stock in the company, and after considering various alternatives as her next step, Mecca made some new commitments. "I think I'm recovered enough that I'm ready to get going again," she said at the end of 1986.

By that time, she and her husband, Geza Csige, had formed a new company, CsiMec, a charter fishing operation based in Hawaii. Yes, it's a radical departure from computers, Mecca admits, "except that it's going to be highly computerized."

That's where her Micro D experience will prove invaluable. "I've learned so much," she says. "One of the things we're going to do is put every customer we've seen in a database, and they'll get monthly newsletters, so we'll be going for rebooking of the same people."

At the operations end, CsiMec planned to computerize its boat scheduling as well as the usual record-keeping tasks. "There's a whole lot of computerization that no one here is doing that we're already setting up," Mecca said a few weeks before they officially opened CsiMec's portals. Eventually Mecca and Csige plan to expand the operation geographically as well as branch out into other recreational areas.

How does charter fishing compare with the micro industry? Understandably, it's a bit slower. "One of the most enjoyable things about the micro business was that, because it was moving so fast and we caught the tidal wave right in the beginning, the learning experience was so great that it was impossible to be at all bored," Csige explains.

"We were just caught up 24 hours a day in new learning experiences, things that were new and always changing," he recalls. "So we never reflected on our experience, because we were always learning new things. This business is an application of everything we learned in the past, and now we have the time to apply it."

Still, Csige insists they aren't bored. "I think the thing that's very strange and hard to overcome is that there seems to be an inertia, like you're dragging something," Csige says, "as opposed to, 'I'm hanging onto a rocket and it's shaking and I'm gonna fall off.' Here you're saying, 'Why isn't this thing moving faster?' "

But industries as explosive as the micro industry don't pop up every day. "There's nothing I can think of right off the bat that's going to equal the experience of that," Csige acknowledges. "You get to participate in something like that perhaps once in your lifetime, and I just thank God we were fortunate enough to be at the right age, the right place at the right time, doing the right things. It just seems like Lady Luck was there all the way."

Mecca doesn't necessarily need another huge success to be happy, but a high-quality product is paramount to her. "This sounds silly," she says, "but my goal now is to do the best I can with what I'm going to do. It doesn't have to be big and multi-billion-dollar, but it's got to be the best at what it is. We're going to have the best charter operation over here." And, without being definite, Mecca doesn't discount the possibility of another foray into the world of high tech.

That is in marked contrast to the complete turnaround experienced by *Portia Isaacson,* who claims to have forsaken the computer industry entirely.

"I've become extremely interested in metaphysics and, in particular, astrology," she explained in late 1986. "I don't know exactly what I'm going to do with it, but right now I'm just studying all the time."

Studying is, after all, her natural inclination. "I still have academic approaches to things," she said in 1984, when Future Computing was still in full swing. "I can get in a corner for a year and study the hell out of something and be as happy as a lark—and not even care if anybody else ever benefits from it.

"I just have a curiosity of wanting to know and understand. That's really where Future Computing came from," she explains. "I couldn't stand not thoroughly understanding everything there was to know about the personal computer industry. It turned out that was a good way to build a business, but most of the other subjects I've ever been curious about weren't."

Whether or not metaphysics can be made profitable, Isaacson has nevertheless formed a company around it, called the University of Life, which she says "will undoubtedly someday be a publishing company and run workshops and seminars having to do with living." If that seems a bit open-ended, consider Isaacson's undeniable premise that "everyone is a student in the University of Life."

Anyway, she laughingly admits, "I've always wanted my own university." For someone who has spent almost equal portions of her life in academia and in business, that may not be such an odd ambition.

Although Isaacson is no longer intimately involved in the personal computer industry, and in fact doesn't bother to follow it, she and ex-husband Egil Juliussen are still partners in three technology-oriented companies they set up after leaving Future Computing.

Intellisys, Inc., is devoted to the promotion of the computerized, electronic Home of the Future, in a deluxe edition of which Isaacson lives. Isaacson, Inc., now dormant, handled computer-industry mergers and acquisitions and for a time published a newsletter.

"What I found was that the company had to be me," Isaacson says, "and I was not willing to put the time into it that it needed, so the company still exists, but we're not taking new clients and we discontinued the newsletter."

InfoTrek, Inc., owned by Juliussen, publishes the *Computer Industry Almanac,* listing major companies, associations, trade shows, market statistics, and product information. Isaacson is on the board of directors of InfoTrek, although she isn't really active in any of the three enterprises. "I just go in every now and then and check on things," she says.

As part of their divorce settlement, Juliussen received Storeboard, Inc., at one time the heart and soul of Future Computing, later bought by McGraw-Hill. Storeboard is the vehicle through which as many as 1,000 retail computer stores reported their sales figures to Future Computing at its height. No longer a part of Future Computing or McGraw-Hill, Storeboard still publishes its statistics for the same clients as Future Computing did.

Isaacson's only direct involvement in the micro industry is her seat on the board of directors of Microsoft Corp. But Isaacson is nothing if not unpredictable. She may be on an astral plane in 1987, but there's always 1988.

"I'm leaving Isaacson, Inc., in existence," she explains, "because it has all the licenses and everything required to be a securities dealer, and I might want to do something with it one day if I brought the right person into it."

But whatever is in the future of Portia Isaacson, it probably isn't the role of entrepreneur extraordinaire. "I'm fascinated by the entrepreneurial spirit," she says, "but not because I want to be one again. I don't think I ever do. I seriously doubt whether I'll ever build another large business, because I've never done anything twice in my life to start with."

One thing is certain. She wouldn't even consider retiring. "I have more of my career left than I've already spent," she says. "Odds are I'll probably live into my eighties—my family is very long-lived and very active—and I'd never do nothing. That's not even possible."

However minimal her involvement may be in the personal computer industry, Isaacson holds strong ideas about the future of the technology. "Today, because it's strictly business, it's lost some of the excitement," she acknowledges, "but I think if you jump out 100 years, I really think the personal computer will be regarded as the necessary first step in personal robotics.

"Personal robotics is very important; I believe all the way-out stuff. You could say I believe we're wasting our time looking for intelligent life in space because we will have built it here on earth before we find it anywhere else.

"I think the symbiotic relationship between man and another form of intelligence—which will be the machine, which will have its ultimate implementation in the personal robot—is where this is going," she predicts. "And almost everything you've ever read about what a robot can be will actually happen."

Futuristic projections aside, there's one thing that Isaacson really wants to see happen—soon. "I've been known for a lot of things in my life, I've been tagged with a lot of labels," she noted while still at Future Computing. "In recent years it's been kind of 'personal computer industry guru analyst,' or maybe even 'computer industry guru analyst,' and that's a nice role but I'm tired of it.

"I don't mind being known as that because it's accurate," she concedes. "Now, though, I want to be credited with having built a business and I want to be recognized because of my business's performance. And, by the way, this is something women aren't really supposed to be able to do—it's okay if it's a man. So over the next few years, I'd like people to look at Portia and say, 'Boy! She built a business and she did it from zero, from the ground up. She built a very profitable, well-run, well-respected corporation.' "

And she did. Even though Future Computing dwindled in size and clout after the McGraw-Hill acquisition, Isaacson will always have built it from scratch, and will remain known for having done so. Does she mourn the diminishing of her creation? "I'm detached from it," she says. "Besides, the whole industry is a shadow of what it was.

"I don't blame McGraw-Hill at all," she insists. "Had I owned the company myself at the time the industry took a dive, I might have been able to turn the company quickly enough into another type of business, to make it survive at the size that it was, but frankly I doubt it. I think McGraw-Hill's done just fine with

Future Computing. It was a difficult business problem and—that's the way it goes."

As *Lore Harp* is quick to point out regarding her former company, "Vector Graphic is a thing of the past, and I'm on to the future." Impatient with questions that probe the preamble to her present life, Harp understandably saves her enthusiasm for her latest enterprise, an imaginative new product that she hopes will change the personal habits of women everywhere.

"From all indications I've had, it could be the next Kleenex," Harp said during the start-up phase of her new company, Aplex Corp. in San Mateo, California. "It" is LeFunelle, a disposable, dissolvable paper funnel that allows women to urinate while standing up.

"Just think of all the times you've been on airplanes or in stadiums or any other public place and how filthy the bathrooms have been," she says. Her own informal survey of 1,000 women she interviewed while traveling turned up an "enormous concern with unhygienic conditions," she reports.

Most women, she found, have already given up sitting on public toilets, in favor of squatting awkwardly over them. With LeFunelle, women can have the same freedom from contact as men have, without becoming contortionists.

"We're not saying there's a real health risk from toilet seats, but it's an unpleasant experience," she told *Venture* magazine in July 1986. "You don't have to explain the problem to any woman."

Changing basic human behavior is never easy, of course, but easy isn't what interests Harp. Besides, as she told *Venture,* "If it were easy, a lot of people would have done it." She cites the introduction, in 1936, of the revolutionary Tampax tampon, which the clergy at first condemned as unvirtuous and the medical establishment considered unsafe. Despite their protestations, and despite necessary changes in female behavior, tampons became the norm.

By the end of 1986, a month after Aplex had started offering its product, the firm was shipping about 100 boxes a day, each box containing 20 funnels. Press coverage was picking up and Harp had done several television and radio interviews. Aplex was also negotiating with "two companies in Japan, a major broker for the military, and a company in Chicago," Harp noted.

Sales projections, in the best of all possible worlds, predict $2 million in sales for 1987, $7 million in 1988, and $40 million by 1989. "If things continue the way they are and recognition is as good as it appears to be developing," Harp said in late 1986, "those figures will be very achievable."

Those figures would also depend on the success of Aplex's planned second product, a LeFunelle dispenser for public rest rooms. Other (as yet unannounced) hygiene and cosmetic products are also in the works.

Her latest effort follows a disappointing three-year foray into venture capitalism, managing the fund she set up in 1982 with husband Patrick McGovern. "I really felt it was going to give me all the psychic rewards I was looking for," she says. "But there was always that nagging feeling in the end, that one hasn't come to closure.

"You make an investment and the companies will do well, but then a company gets sold and all you get is a check in the mail," she observes. "But you had nothing to do with it, in essence. The only thing you did was you contributed thoughts and support and money, but you didn't really have a lot to do with most of the other strategies.

"After I'd done Vector—building a company from totally nothing to fairly good size with an international distribution network, having gone through raising venture capital, having gone through taking the company public and all that sort of thing—I felt I could make a great contribution to other young companies that wanted to start in business," she explains. The reality was quite different. "Most entrepreneurs don't want all the help I thought I could bring," she found.

While she's back in a product-based enterprise, one might ask whether Lore Harp plans to some day get back into high tech as well. "I never like to predict what I'm going to do," she laughs. "I'm having fun with what I'm doing, but I don't know if I will always stay in this field. I may sort of merge technology back in. But, really, I hate to be so precise about what I might or might not do, or will or will not do."

Imprecision about one's future plans has its good points. For one thing, it leaves open the possibility of radical change. Or, as in *Joyce Wrenn's* case, two radical changes.

When she left IBM Corp. after 24 years, Wrenn expected a rather long second career in the banking industry with her new employer, Bank of America. Unfortunately, her arrival in May 1985 coincided uncomfortably well with the bank's reporting of huge losses—totalling $337 million for that year.

That was not quite what she had had in mind when she accepted the chance to work closely with systems genius Max Hopper. Especially disappointing was Hopper's decision to return to his former employer, American Airlines, just six months after Wrenn had joined him at the bank.

Still, she stuck it out at the bank for another year until she felt comfortable leaving her new staff behind. Since she had promised Hopper her "first nickel" if she ever decided to leave the bank, she called him in 1986 at American Airlines, besides looking around at other opportunities.

In the end, it seemed most attractive to continue their professional association, so in November 1986 Wrenn moved to Dallas and joined yet another industry. Her position, "manager of data and application services" at American, isn't that different from what she did at the bank. The difference lies in the environment.

The American Airlines computer systems division has a reputation for being innovative and risk-taking, something Wrenn finds stimulating. "The environment I find here reminds me of the atmosphere we were in in Boca Raton [at the IBM Entry Systems Division]," she says. "There's an awful lot going on, people are working very, very hard, there's a good spirit of teamwork and a good spirit of, 'Yes, we have one more thing to do and somehow we'll manage to fit it in and do it well.' "

The fact that she has made two major job changes in as many years doesn't bother Wrenn in the least. "I thrive on challenge," she says, "and after having come through the Bank of America, it's even easier. You learn what things to do, how to approach things, and I thrive on the change. It's exciting to me. I look at people who've been in the same place for 20 years and I say, 'Oh, how boring,' but whatever is right for them."

Will Wrenn spend the rest of her career at American Airlines? "In view of the events of the last few years, I hesitate to predict what might happen in my life," she laughs. "I look back and five years ago, when I was in California, little did I know I'd go to Florida, meet and marry a wonderful fellow from there, go to the bank, leave the bank, go to American—but my intent would be I would like to [stay at American]."

At the same time, Wrenn is acutely aware of the spirit of consolidation in U.S. industry. "It's really hard to say whether the complexion of things will be the same two years from now as it is now," she says, "so I tend to be very flexible and hold onto the values that are important to me, and let the other things change and not get uptight about them. That's the only way I know how to proceed."

Assuming that Wrenn does reach retirement at American Airlines, she hopes to go back to Santa Cruz—"one of my favorite places in the world"—and pick up her education where she left off back in the 1960s. "I had started on a master's degree when my first husband was getting his, and then I had to stop it because we put him through school for his master's and his Ph.D.," she says. "But I'd probably go back for a Ph.D., just for the hell of it, because I enjoy learning."

She would like to do some consulting at the same time, and thinks she could offer her fellow students some insights into the real world. "I could probably impart some of my experiences, especially as a woman in this industry, and just the practical experience of managing in this industry."

But Wrenn doesn't ever plan to slow down. "I figure that would keep me pretty well occupied in my sixties and I plan to live well into my nineties, so then I'll have 30 more years to *really* play," she says. "I can't ever see myself not working at something. The question is what I might do later in life. I have a lot of hobbies, a lot of things I'd like to pursue, but whether I turn them into something that's producing income, I don't know."

Those Who Stayed

Only four of these ten women are still involved with the enterprises that made them famous, and they claim to have no intentions of moving on in the foreseeable future.

After being reunited with her almost-lost *RELease 1.0, Esther Dyson* continues contentedly, even gratefully, writing and producing her well-respected newsletter. With ever more sophisticated technology on the micro scene, Dyson believes that her newsletter is becoming accordingly more intellectual.

Back in her glassy Park Avenue offices, she once again is down to a small staff and her own writing. Dyson sees herself continuing with her newsletter "for as far ahead as I can see," she says, "which is years—not decades and not months."

And although she has never been big on career planning ("If you plan your life too carefully, you've got to plan a good funeral"), there are a few things she can envision doing, down the road. One is "probably something to do with venture capital," which is the path her predecessor Ben Rosen took with spectacular success. Like Rosen's path, too, is her impulse to go on the boards of a number of companies and help them along, "when I'm no longer an impartial observer."

Another possibility is to write a book "of some sort or other," she says, "very, very far in the future." Not sure whether it would be fiction or nonfiction, she settles on a combination of both. "A roman à clef, maybe," she suggests. "There are too many delightful things in the industry that I can't write about that I'd like to write about someday."

But she does not, in any way, see her current life as simply a stepping-stone to the future. "I really like what I do," she says. "I'm not working now to do something else. I'm trying to do a good job right now. I'd rather be a little more flexible, see what happens. God knows I didn't even know this kind of job existed a few years ago, so I couldn't have had plans for it.

"If you do what you're doing," she adds, "you keep on getting better and you don't get bored. That's sort of my goal, never to be bored. I'm a lot smarter and better and wiser this year than I was last year, and I hope next year I'll be able to say the same thing again."

Also very much still in the microcomputer industry is *Therese Myers,* resolutely charting new waters with Quarterdeck's well-received Desqview software. With only 15 employees by mid-1987, Quarterdeck in size alone is like a dinghy compared to the Microsoft and IBM yachts. But in terms of guts, the tiny company is a sassy speedboat, ready to rev up a spray and leave the giants bobbing in its wake.

"They've stuck it out a lot longer than a lot of people would have thought," says the astute Dyson. "They have good products and they don't get too grandiose, and as long as you keep your expenses below your revenues and you produce decent products and find some sort of a market, you can last, which is what they seem to be doing."

But can Quarterdeck keep it up, in light of the fierce competition? "I think they probably will," Dyson says. "They've pretty much made it over the hump. They're certainly not anywhere where they can rest, but they've proved they can stick around."

One reason for Quarterdeck's success is its excellent instincts for making seemingly prescient strategic moves. When Compaq Computer Corp. introduced the Deskpro 386 in 1986, a powerful new, mainframe-like microcomputer, it was expected to revolutionize the way people use micros. The only problem was a serious lack of applications software written specifically for the advanced 80386 chip the machine was based on.

While several manufacturers were still scrambling to develop software that would take full advantage of the machine's capabilities, in October 1986 Quarterdeck shipped the first windowing environment for the computer that took advantage of its extended memory and added power. "It's going to set the trend for the rest of the software industry," said one beta tester regarding Desqview Version 1.3. In early 1987, *InfoWorld*'s readers chose Desqview 1.3 as the "Best New Idea of 1986."

For a small outfit like Quarterdeck, of course, there are always outside forces to contend with, but Myers is convinced that her company is in a position to respond well to whatever may happen. "We've never been in such a good spot," she said in late 1986. "People are starting to use us because there's nothing else out there that you can really use. And we now know we can compete with future versions of DOS, and we know we can compete on the 386 level. It's not as much of a concern."

Quarterdeck's increased confidence is highly gratifying after the years of struggle against seemingly insurmountable odds. "It's been quite interesting because we were really competing against power, and that power was Microsoft—but we were actually competing against vaporware [industry jargon for a preannounced but nonexistent product]," Myers says. "We've been fighting myths for so long.

"And we were competing against cultism because everybody sort of joined up and was part of this cult," she says. "It's very satisfying that we're getting the visibility that we are now. I'd say the odds [against us] have gone from 100 to 1 down to something reasonable."

What does Myers see in Quarterdeck's future in the next few years? "Gary [Pope] and I laugh about this," she says, "but, having gone through what we've done, we think it's not unlikely that Desqview will be the standard operating environment, despite what everybody says right now. It's anybody's game," she acknowledges, "but we have over 250,000 users right now, so whatever you say, we have a pretty loyal base."

Will Quarterdeck become another high-tech megacompany? "I don't know if we want to," Myers says. "We want to offer products and we want to be a size that we can control and develop and sustain products. I don't know if there's a need to be a big company."

As to whether Quarterdeck might ever go public, that too is unpredictable. "It really depends on the opportunities and what it takes to take advantage of it," Myers says. "We are competing with *such* formidable people, but we've been very successful at doing alliances, which leaves us independent. As you become more successful, you have more opportunities you can take, but you have to have some way of funding some of these things. So I don't know the answer. It's not out of the question, but you wouldn't want to jump there just for the sake of doing it."

For Quarterdeck, undoubtedly, continued success hinges on some unknowns. "Clearly it's the case that we have some opportunities in the next two years that could make us a major company," she says, "or maybe they wouldn't, depending on how we take advantage of them."

Still, Myers wouldn't have it any other way. She does not wish she had sold her company to any of its four suitors in 1983 or again in 1985, when Microsoft itself made an offer at year-end. "I still feel we did the right thing because we were the only ones who had the vision," Myers says, her competitive spirit wonderfully intact.

Also in the maelstrom of competition is *Janelle Bedke,* whose Software Publishing Corp. did some fast footwork in 1985 and 1986 in order to catch up with its own audience. "They're going in the right direction but unfortunately they should have done it sooner," Dyson assesses.

"People often misunderstand why they [themselves] are successful," Dyson observes. "I think Software Publishing thought they were successful because of the particular products they had. Actually they were successful because their [first] products suited the market at the time, but they didn't notice the market changing, and now they've noticed it."

The evolving market, along with changes in SPC's operations between 1985 and 1986, caused a drop in 1986 sales to below 1984 levels. From 1985 sales of $37 million, SPC went down to $23 million in 1986. "Yes, it was a decline," Bedke acknowledged. "We think we understand why; we don't expect those types of declines to continue. Quite the reverse: We now have a more solid base that's growing in a healthy way.

"The thing that gives us a lot of encouragement for the future," she said at the end of 1986, "is that our IBM and compatibles business has been growing steadily and continues to be fueled by the new products that we've been announcing. We feel, as we look to the future, that our business base is a lot more controllable and stronger, contrasted with 1985." Dyson agrees. "I think they have a fairly strong base to build on and some really improved products."

Bedke goes even further, with her long-held belief that Software Publishing, now the fourth-largest public company that publishes micro software, will someday be right at the top. "I certainly have not given up on my goal of eventually becoming the number one personal computer software company," she says. "We still believe in our product strategy and our people and our ability to execute, and we think that we understand the business better than some of our competitors.

"We feel that some of our competitors were lucky enough to have a one-time hit, and at some point the one-time hit goes away," she adds. "Plus, it's still a very young industry, and with new technologies coming on board, there's a lot of room for jockeying for position."

What has changed is her estimate of when she might reach her goal. Whereas Bedke used to see the end of the eighties as the probable time frame for it to happen, she has extended her deadline a few years. "I'm going to say in the next ten years," she said in 1986.

"It's funny when you have to start thinking in those terms," she says. "I think we're so used to this industry, where things happen within a couple of weeks. But I think things are beginning to stabilize to some extent, and your time frames have to be a little bit further out to be realistic. Things are just not going to happen overnight anymore."

But, as Bedke has always said, "We're in it for the long run. We want to be here 20 years from now. Not many companies think in those terms."

In August 1987—to "maximize both our strengths," Bedke explained—she was named president of the company and former president Fred Gibbons remained chairman. As chairman, Gibbons would focus on long-range strategic planning while Bedke's role expanded to include all functional areas of the company.

By the end of 1986, venture capital funding was practically nonexistent for the micro software industry, which made the surviving players happy enough. As Software Publishing president Fred Gibbons told a trade group, the decline in venture capital money flowing into the software industry was good in that it removed much of the hype and excitement that used to drive products.

Jacqueline Morby is long past making microcomputer industry investments, but she is still deeply committed to venture capital. Her micro investments, in fact, represented only a fraction of her total investments. "I have always done all types of investing," she says.

What is her ultimate goal? The same as any venture capitalist's: "To be one of those people that's invested behind one of the great companies," she says. "Everyone dreams of having a DEC [Digital Equipment Corp.] or an Apple. Some of [my investments] have the possibility."

Satisfied as she appears to be with her career, does Morby ever think about starting her own company? "One always does," she admits. "But it doesn't make a lot of sense because, as a partner, I own part of TA Associates. It's a big, prosperous organization and I like all the people a lot. It's a great place to be."

Oh, and one more thing. "We're very powerful."

Notes

Prologue: Ten Women with Power

Page

12 Lore Harp: "I was very firm in negotiating . . .": Eliza G. C. Collins, "The Entrepreneur Sees Herself as Manager," *Harvard Business Review,* July-August 1982, pp. 140–150. Reprinted with permission. Copyright © 1982 by the President and Fellows of Harvard College; all rights reserved.

21 Jacqueline Morby: "In the beginning . . .": Jeffrey L. Seglin, "Can Old Boys Change?" *Venture,* July 1986, p. 66. Reprinted by special permission. © 1986 Venture Magazine, Inc., 521 Fifth Ave., New York, N.Y. 10175–0028.

21 Jacqueline Morby: "I sometimes find out . . .": "Women: The New Venture Capitalists," *Business Week,* Nov. 2, 1981, p. 100. Reprinted by special permission. © 1981 by McGraw-Hill, Inc.

21 Lore Harp: "I feel that most women . . .": Eliza G. C. Collins, "The Entrepreneur Sees Herself as Manager," *Harvard Business Review,* July-August 1982, pp. 140–150. Reprinted with permission. Copyright © 1982 by the President and Fellows of Harvard College; all rights reserved.

21 Lore Harp: "If women want to . . .": Ibid.

22 Lore Harp: "I'm not a feminist . . .": Michael S. Malone, *The New York Times,* July 10, 1983. Copyright © 1983 by the New York Times Company. Reprinted by permission.

Chapter 1: The Stirrings of Ambition

Page

77 Hans Bethe: Kenneth Brower, *The Starship and the Canoe* (Holt, Rinehart & Winston, 1978), p. 21.

Chapter 2: The Birth of an Industry

Page

103 Lore Harp: "We had more marketing appeal . . .": Susan Benner, "Next Stop Wall Street," *Inc.* cover story, March 1981. Reprinted with permission, *Inc.* magazine. Copyright © 1981 by Inc. Publishing Corporation, Boston, MA.

104 Lore Harp: "It was a question . . .": Eliza G. C. Collins, "The Entrepreneur Sees Herself as Manager," *Harvard Business Review,* July-August 1982, pp. 140–150. Reprinted with permission. Copyright © 1982 by the President and Fellows of Harvard College; all rights reserved.

104 Lore Harp: "Most of our competitors . . .": Ibid.

105 Lore Harp: "One of the things I can do . . .": Ibid.

115 Warren Robinett: Michael Doyle, "Taking the ABCs On-Line," *The Palo Alto Weekly,* March 13, 1985. Reprinted with permission.

116 Rocky's Boots: Erik Sandberg-Diment, "Game Focusing on Basics Promises to Become Another Software Classic," *The New York Times,* July 19, 1983. Copyright © 1983 by the New York Times Company. Reprinted by permission.

Chapter 3: The Micro Boom

Page

139 Philip Estridge: "How the PC Project Changed the Way IBM Thinks," *Business Week* cover story, Oct. 3, 1983, p. 86. Reprinted by special permission. © 1981 by McGraw-Hill, Inc.

146 Mitch Kapor: Erik Larson, "Companies Aided by IBM's Success Fear Growing Dependence on Firm," *The Wall Street Journal,* Dec. 12, 1983, p. 29. Reprinted by permission. © Dow Jones & Company, Inc., 1983. All Rights Reserved.

149 Terry Myers: "I hate machines . . .": "A Friendly Frontier for Female Pioneers," *Fortune,* June 25, 1984, p. 81.

154 Desq: John Lombardi, "Desq: A Complex Integrating Package from Quarterdeck Office Systems," *InfoWorld,* July 30, 1984, p. 47.

Chapter 4: Winds of Change

Page

175 ". . . skidded dramatically . . .": Michael W. Miller, "Personal Computer Industry Ends 1985 with Sales Spurt After Worst Year

Ever," *The Wall Street Journal,* Jan. 10, 1986. Reprinted by permission. © Dow Jones & Company, Inc., 1986. All Rights Reserved.

175 "Last year saw an explosion . . .": Charles Stein, "The Slowdown That Won't Go Away," *The Boston Globe,* Sept. 17, 1985, p. 43. Reprinted courtesy of *The Boston Globe.*

176 Gideon Gartner: Steven Burke, "Saturation Blamed for Slump," *InfoWorld,* Aug. 12, 1985, p. 37.

180 Teri Perl: Michael Doyle, "Taking the ABCs On-Line," *The Palo Alto Weekly,* March 13, 1985. Reprinted with permission.

Chapter 5: Still in the Game

Page

205 Fred Gibbons: J. Keith Butters, "Software Publishing Corporation (A)," Case 9-285-034, Boston: Harvard Business School, 1984, pp. 25–26.

209 Headline: "Software Publishing Lashed by Setbacks," *The Wall Street Journal,* Jan. 27, 1986, p. 6. Reprinted by permission. © Dow Jones & Company, Inc., 1986. All Rights Reserved.

211 TopView: Richard Duffy, " 'TopView' Debut Stirs Little Interest Among Major Software Vendors," *PC Week,* Feb. 19, 1985, p. 1. Copyright © 1985 Ziff Communications Co.

212 Desqview: Marc Stern, "Desqview Clarifies Windowing System," *InfoWorld,* Sept. 9, 1985, p. 39.

216 Esther Dyson: "There is a difference . . .": Wendy Woods & Stan Politi, "Esther Dyson, Reigning Queen of High Tech," *Computer Currents* cover story, Jan. 14–27, 1986, p. 48.

217 Esther Dyson: "There were probably only four people . . .": Ibid., p. 48.

225 Ann Winblad: "I'm insulted when . . .": Steve Gross, "Firm's Rapid Growth Ends Partnership," *The Minneapolis Star & Tribune,* Oct 1, 1984, p. 1M.

Chapter 6: Family and Career: Necessary Trade-Offs

Page

230 Lorraine Mecca: "I don't pay him . . .": "A Friendly Frontier for Female Pioneers," *Fortune,* June 25, 1984, p. 80.

234 Lore Harp: "If you don't love scrubbing plates . . .?": Eliza G. C. Collins, "The Entrepreneur Sees Herself as Manager," *Harvard Business Review,* July-August 1982, pp. 140–150. Reprinted with permission. Copyright © 1982 by the President and Fellows of Harvard College; all rights reserved.

241 Kevin Landry: Jeffrey L. Seglin, "Can Old Boys Change?" *Venture,* July 1986, p. 66. Reprinted by special permission. © 1986 Venture Magazine, Inc., 521 Fifth Ave., New York, N.Y. 10175–0028.

Epilogue: The Future

Page

265 Lore Harp: ". . . enormous concern . . .": Daniel Cohen, "Lore Harp Is Back on Her Feet," *Venture,* July 1986, p. 42. Reprinted by special permission. © 1986 Venture Magazine, Inc., 521 Fifth Ave., New York, N.Y. 10175–0028.

265 Lore Harp: "We're not saying . . .": Ibid., p. 42.

265 Lore Harp: "If it were easy, . . .": Ibid., p. 44.

Index